Northern Winework

Growing Grapes and Making Wine in Cold Climates

ISBN 0-9709784-0-5

Printed in the United States of America by Eau Claire Printing Company, Inc.

Published and distributed by Northern Winework, Inc.
9040 152nd Street North
Hugo, MN 55038
U.S.A.

17090 116th Street North
Stillwater, MN 55082
U.S.A.

Contents

Acknowledgements

We would like to acknowledge the following contributors for their dedication and enthusiasm for this project. Thanks to Paula Marti for her early review of the manuscript and great ideas about how to present this material. We give our thanks to Katie Parke-Reimer and Barbara Parke for doing an outstanding job of editing the manuscript. Mark Hart deserves our thanks for using his creative flair and hard work in laying out our book. Thanks also to Jim House of Eau Claire Printing, Inc., for his generous technical and production support, and ongoing encouragement of the project. We grossly underestimated the amount of work needed from him to make the book print-ready. Jim has guided us through all of this with patience and good nature.

Thanks are due to our Baltic friends, Michael Gundersen and Peter Lorenzen in Copenhagen, Meeri Saario in Helsinki, Jaan Kivistik, Harri Poom, and Peter Viikholm in Estonia, Andris Dishlers, Gvido Dobelis, and Andrash Fazekash in Latvia, and Romuald Loiko in Belarus, for making us aware that viticulture existed in that part of the world and for providing a tremendous amount of information for this book that had never before reached the West. Special thanks also to Tom's oldest Baltic horticulture friend, Lennarth Jonsson from Sweden, who, during Soviet times helped us establish some connections to that part of the world and laid the groundwork for all the information-sharing and kinship that has transpired since. Our friends in Quebec have been generous in both sharing their information and their wine—Many thanks to, Mario Cliché, Roland Harnois, Alain and Mariette Breault, and Etienne Heroux and Monique Morin. Thanks also to Dr. Wang Li Xue in China for translating and sharing her research results on grapegrowing in Inner Mongolia. Finally, we both are indebted to Minnesota-Wisconsin grape breeder, Elmer Swenson. Without Elmer's fifty years of pioneering grape breeding work, we simply wouldn't have that much to write about.

Each of us has some special acknowledgements to make. First and foremost, Tom would like to thank Bob for saying "yes" four years ago when asked if he would write the winemaking portion of this book.

Acknowledgements

Tom would like to recognize Bob and friends Gordon Rouse and Wilbur Thomas for their many years of creative, open-minded experimentation with grape varieties and winemaking techniques, and for sharing their insights with him. Tom is indebted to these three guys for thoughtfully evaluating well over one hundred experimental wines from our research program over the past five years, the results of which are reflected in many chapters of this book. Finally, Tom wants to thank Peter Hemstad for many years of enthusiastic discussions about grape varieties and grape breeding, and for inspiring his curiosity about northern viticulture around the world.

If Tom were not such an agreeable fellow, Bob, not imagining the difficulty of writing part of a book, would be less thankful for luring him into the perilous waters of authorship. Since Tom's vision of what the book could be has become a reality, the struggle has been worthwhile, so Bob is, in fact, thankful. He is grateful to Tom for arranging our information-sharing adventure to the Baltic countries, sponsored by the U. S. Department of Agriculture and the Minnesota Grape Growers Association, a project that contributed greatly to what we have subsequently written.

Bob became a dedicated winemaker, with the help of the Purple Foot Wine Club, a group of zealots who will talk endlessly about the finer points of wine chemistry and wine evaluation as though nothing else matters. Special thanks to Mike Barrett, who helped Bob get beyond the basics, and begin to understand the chemistry underlying winemaking. Joe Palla also deserves credit for being an exemplary winemaker who is willing to share his secrets. Likewise, Gordon Rouse, with his balance of technical knowledge and tasting judgement has been a great influence.

Philippe Coquard and Robin Partch, who are two of the best commercial winemakers we know, patiently answered Bob's many questions about their experience with hybrid grapes. Dr. Andrew Reynolds of Brock University, and Dr. Phillip Portoghese of the University of Minnesota were especially helpful in unraveling the mysteries of organic chemistry to an often-puzzled winemaker.

Bob also needs to acknowledge Linda Zick, Darrel Rosander, and Felix Norman, who showed him by example why winemakers need to broaden their knowledge of winemaking styles and be able to judge wine analytically.

Now, we return to Elmer Swenson, a kind and generous man whose influence will be felt for many decades to come. We dedicate this book to him.

Foreword

If we lived in California we would be growing and making wine from Zinfandel and Chardonnay grapes rather than writing a book about new hybrid grape varieties with names like Frontenac, Troubador, and Prairie Star. We don't live in California though. We live in Minnesota where wine grape growing has been considered improbable enough to challenge breeders, growers, and winemakers to develop new varieties and methods to produce better quality wines. Twenty years ago few believed it could be done. Twenty years from now we expect to see it being done regularly. Right now growers in our area are eager to plant wine grapes where they have not been grown before.

We have been influenced heavily by our local growing and winemaking experience. Both of us have small vineyards on the northern edge of the Minneapolis-St. Paul metropolitan area, which many would say is well beyond the sensible range for growing wine grapes. Winter temperatures of -31 °F (-35 °C) are an annual occurrence here and temperatures of -40 °F (-40 °C) occur at least one year out of every ten. Where we live matters because the cold winters make it an ideal test area for many new grape varieties. Many grape breeders live and work in our area, including Peter Hemstad, David Macgregor, Herb Fritzke, and the world-renowned Elmer Swenson. So ironically, Minnesota is a hotbed of northern viticulture research and development activity.

Why do we not recommend growing *Vitis vinifera*? Some growers have pushed the boundaries of vinifera grape growing into very northern climates, including into Minnesota. With special care, some of these vinifera vines can survive the winter and produce a good crop. In an outstanding growing season, with good heat accumulation and a sufficiently long frost-free season for ripening, these vines can produce wines comparable in quality to those produced from similar varieties in California, Oregon, France, or Germany. But in typical growing seasons, vinifera wines in Minnesota and like climates are simply not up to the par established by more classic wine growing regions. The quality does not justify the extra effort and risk involved in growing them.

Consequently, we have looked for ways to optimize the harvest and wine quality of hybrid grape varieties that tend to succeed in climates where the classic *Vitis vinifera* varieties fail. Most, if not all of the hybrid grape varieties grown in the north have had their potential for wine quality enhanced by vinifera genes. Asian and North American native grape species have contributed genes to these hybrids that allow them to withstand cool, short seasons or cold winters, or extreme disease pressure.

In the grape growing section of this book we focus on topics of special importance to growers on the northern fringes of viticulture such as cold hardiness, site selection, variety selection, winter protection, training systems, and techniques to aid proper ripening. Our goal is to help you make the most out of your climate by making wise variety and site selection decisions and by applying the cultural techniques necessary for good fruit quality. You will not find chapters here on grapevine propagation, planting, and weed control because these subjects are already covered in our recommended texts. What you will find in this book is a significant amount of not previously presented new material.

Our winemaking section concentrates on how to make high quality wines from the hybrid varieties available in the north and ripened within the constraints of cool temperatures and short growing seasons. The challenge here is that many hybrid grape varieties that are outstanding in the northern vineyard are quite capable of producing flawed wines. The winemaking chapters describe ways to avoid or counter the flaws characteristic of these varieties.

The foundations of this book have been a long time developing. Tom has been reading about and working with plants since he was nine years old. He has planted two vineyards in Minnesota and has been breeding grapes for six years. He also has traveled widely around the northern fringes of the grape growing world learning all he can about grape culture problems, solutions, and prospects. Bob did not start making wine at nine years old, but he has been trying to push the limits of standard winemaking for the last ten years, usually by blending together different wines to compensate for the aromatic or flavor shortcomings of unblended ones. Bob's interest in winemaking caused him to plant his own vineyard. What he knew about growing things before then came from learning from his wife's gardening experience and observations while gathering wild edible plants and fruit.

In some ways our lack of knowledge in each other's specialty has helped us write this book. Tom learned what kinds of vinification problems in northern grape varieties could and could not be solved by winemaking techniques. Bob learned how sensitive vines are to proper growing and pruning methods and how it ultimately affects wine quality. We both learned that we must explain details of our specialty in terms that could be readily understood by people not immersed in the subject.

The ideas we present in this book come from our direct experience in grape growing and winemaking, from research papers, correspondence with experts around the world, and visits to vineyards and wineries in ten U.S. states and eight countries. We have synthesized the existing research literature and related it to grape growing and winemaking problems specific to extreme northern regions. We have supplemented it where necessary with our personal observations and experiences, or those of our colleagues. The product, we believe, is a practical book that tells what to do and explains why it works.

We are still in a pioneering stage of development with new northern grape varieties and winemaking techniques for them. Working with the best new hybrid grapes is still a work in progress. In another twenty years we will be able to provide definite recommendations on growing and making wine from many of those new varieties. We could have waited those twenty years to write this book. However, serious amateur and small commercial grape growers and winemakers need information now. Therefore, what you will be reading in the following chapters is the best information we can put together at the present time. We are confident that most of what we have to say is drawn from enough experience that it will hold up over time, but we look forward to gaining enough new information to publish a revised edition.

Chapter 1

Cold Climate Grapes and Wines: People and Places

This book captures the knowledge and experiences of the many northern grape growers and winemakers we have met during our travels. These are people who have "pushed the envelope" of viticulture. They have succeeded in growing grapes and making wine in regions more northerly than could ever be imagined. These are folks who know what –40 °F (–40 °C) feels like, who know how long it takes for one meter of frost in the soil to disappear in the spring, who have seen the temperature dip to 0 °F (-18 °C) in April, who have experienced frost on Swedish Midsummer Holiday. These people have found new and creative ways to go about the business of grape growing and winemaking in climates that far exceed the traditional boundaries of grape growing described in most textbooks or imagined by traditional winegrowers in North America and Europe.

So, who exactly are these cold climate adventurers of the viticulture world and where can we find them?

Wisconsin grape breeder, Elmer Swenson and Meeri Saario, Finnish viticulturist and researcher.

Peter Hemstad, University of Minnesota grape project leader.

Minnesota

Minnesota has a history of grape growing dating back to 1870. Minnesota (ten year low of −40 °F) has a growers association of 500 members, 50 acres (20 hectares) of vines under cultivation, and five commercial wineries. Internationally recognized, Elmer Swenson, has been breeding cold tolerant grape varieties since 1943. His varieties have made possible the fledgling commercial wine industry in Minnesota. A state-funded grape research program has been in place at the University of Minnesota for 15 years. The grape breeding work of project leader and Minnesota native, Peter Hemstad, promises significant future growth of the grape and wine industry as it releases new cold tolerant wine grape varieties.

Quebec

Quebec, Canada is the most successful example of grape growing for wine production in a cold winter region. The Province of Quebec, Canada has 215 acres (87 hectares) of grapevines (315,000 vines) under cultivation and 36 commercial wineries. Vine plantings are increasing at a rate of 100,000 vines per year. This is in a region with a ten year low temperature of −38 °F (−39 °C). The first grape variety developed specifically for Quebec conditions, Vandal-Cliche, was released for commercial production in 1997, and will foster continued growth in this cold climate region where the French tradition of winemaking and grape growing live on.

Mario Cliché, grape breeder and Alain Breault, vine nurseryman, leaders in the new Quebec wine industry.

Wisconsin

Count Agoston Haraszthy is best known as the founder of Buena Vista Winery and the modern day California wine industry. But on his way to California from his native Hungary, he first attempted commercial grape production and winemaking at Prairie du Sac, Wisconsin. The count failed and moved on to fame and fortune in the Napa Valley. A hundred years later, Bob Wollersheim purchased the old Haraszthy site in Wisconsin and started what has become the most successful commercial winery in the midwestern United States. Wollersheim and his winemaker, Burgundy native, Philippe Coquard, have become well-known throughout the U.S. for their remarkable red wines produced from the French-American hybrid grape variety Marechal Foch. In 1997, Coquard was named the Blockbuster Winemaker of the Year, an honor given annually to the American winemaker who has the greatest number of first place awards in major American wine competitions.

Latvia

Quebec, Minnesota, and Wisconsin are the more familiar examples of winemaking in the far north. Now for the first of many obscure examples, consider the case of Latvia (Latitude 57 °N; ten year low of –38 °F or –39 °C), which lies between the Baltic Sea and the former Soviet republic of Belarus. Dating back to the Seventeenth Century and the times of Jacob, Duke of Curland, grapes were cultivated in Latvia. This tradition of grape growing and winemaking in Latvia faded over the centuries due to wars and occupations, but it did not die. By 1939, a grape growing revival was underway. Two kilometers of vineyard terraces near the village of Sabile were rebuilt and three thousand vines were planted.

Wollersheim Winery's award-winning winemaker, Philippe Coquard.

Latvian grape breeder, Pauls Sukatnieks, and his protégé, Andrash Fazekash (circa 1965).

World War II brought German and, later, Soviet occupation to Latvia. The fledgling grape growing industry was destroyed. However, some irrepressible spirits persisted. Throughout the Soviet years, Pauls Sukatnieks quietly worked on a collective farm, breeding new grape varieties that would ripen during the short Latvian season and withstand the unpredictable Arctic blasts that disrupt their otherwise moderate winter climate. Gvido Dobelis experimented with Sukatnieks's varieties and with winemaking at his summer home outside Riga. His books and magazine articles kindled enthusiasm for grapegrowing among Latvians. In the current post-Soviet era, the terraces on "Wine Hill" near Sabile are being re-planted with Sukatnieks's varieties Zilga, Agra, Veldze, and Sukribe. A new variety trial is underway at the Dobele Experiment Station. As the president of the Latvian Grapegrowers Association Gvido Dobelis continues to popularize grape growing in Latvia. The legacy of grape breeding left by Sukatnieks is being carried on by his protégé, Andrash Fazekash, a Latvian farmer with a genius for both poetry and plant breeding.

Jaan Kivistik (right), cool climate grape growing expert and promoter, along with his wife Vaike, and Bob Parke in Rapina, Estonia.

Danish wine industry leader, Michael Gundersen.

Estonia

At 60° Latitude, Estonia is the most northern of the Baltic countries. It is a most unlikely place to find a vineyard, but here you find grape growing at its creative best. Jaan Kivistik, a pomology instructor at the Rapina Agricultural College, started collecting grape varieties from around the Soviet Union, Europe, and North America during Soviet times. His persistence in seeking out and testing super-early ripening and winter hardy varieties, such as Varajane Sinine and Jubilinaja Novgoroda, has made viticulture possible in this region of extremely cool summers and cold winters. Kivistik's student, Harri Poom, works at grape breeding near the town of Vandra. Poom looks forward to the day in which one of the grape selections from his breeding program is grown commercially in Estonia. Six wineries have appeared since Soviet times. Their total production is over 200,000 gallons (740,000 liters). The entire production is currently fruit wine, but it is only a matter of time before the first commercial Estonian grape wine appears on the market.

Denmark

It is a little known fact that the Danes now have excellent Danish wines to go with their fine Danish cheeses and lox! Until ten years ago, grape growing was unheard of in Denmark. Thanks to grape growing pioneers Jens Michael Gundersen and Peter Lorenzen, Denmark is now an official European Union appellation or grape growing region. Their grape growers association has grown to 250 members. Gundersen and Lorenzen scoured Europe for grape varieties that ripen in the cold, wet climate of Denmark. Their efforts were rewarded. Rondo from Germany, Reform from Hungary, and Castel 19.637 from France form the basis of the new Danish wine industry.

Sweden

The Skane coast of Sweden is famous for its apple production and also offers a relatively hospitible environment for super-early ripening grapes, so it is not a surprise that amateur grape growing thrives in southern Sweden. Kimmo Rumpunen, working at the Swedish University of Agricultural Science in Balsgard, has made this recent growth of grapegrowing in Sweden possible by meeting the demand for plants of select early-ripening grape varieties. Each year, Rumpunen micropropagates and sells 25,000 grapevines to commercial nurseries in Sweden, where they are purchased by Swedish gardeners and planted out in home vineyards.

Inner Mongolia

The city of Huhhot is best known as a staging area for tours of the Gobi Desert. It is the gateway to nomad country. Inner Mongolia is a region of severe cold in the winter, with no snow cover. The deep cold in the soil here would seem to make grape culture impossible. Yet, Inner Mongolia has a well-developed commercial grape culture, with more than 2000 acres of vines under cultivation. Dr. Wang Li Xue, working at the Inner Mongolia University of Agriculture in Huhhot, has spent many years perfecting techniques for deep ditch cultivation (planting vines below ground level to combat the killing effects of deep frost). More recently, Dr. Wang has developed varieties that survive these winters without protection. Her research and teaching have fostered the growth of viticulture far into northeastern China, almost to the Amur River, to such unlikely areas as Qiqihar, Jilin, and Harbin.

Cold climate grape propagator extraodinaire, Kimmo Rumpunen, Balsgard, Sweden.

Russia, Ukraine, and Belarus

The post-Soviet era has made us aware of significant viticultural activities in many regions of the former Soviet Union. Five thousand acres (2,000 hectares) of grapes, mostly the variety, Alpha, are grown in the Primorskii region of Siberia (Latitude 45°). State-sponsored grape breeding programs, have produced numerous varieties, selected for cold hardiness. These programs are in place at Michurinsk (Latitude 52° 60'), Moscow (Latitude 55° 45'), Orenberg, (Latitude 51° 55'), and Novocherkask in Russia (Latitude 47° 20'), and Minsk, Belarus (Latitude 53° 67'). A new commercial grape production venture, Agrofirma im. V.I.Lenina, recently started near Minsk on a former collective farm, with 60 acres (25 hectares) planted in new Belarusian grape varieties. We are only beginning to understand what has been accomplished during the last 50 years in these countries and what they have to offer to cold climate viticulture and winemaking.

The Far North

Lastly, we must recognize all the amateur growers and winemakers who are growing grapes and making wine simply for their own consumption and pleasure, in areas that can only be described as the far frontiers of viticulture. From the membership rolls of the Minnesota Grape Growers Association, we know that these small-scale growers are hard at work growing grapes, producing, and drinking their own wine in the following locations:

Belarussian grape researcher, Dr. Romuald Loiko in his greenhouse in Samochvalovitchy, Belarus.

Whitehorse, Yukon (latitude 60° 05')
Brandon, Manitoba (latitude 49° 55')
St. John's, New Brunswick (latitude 45°)
Aberdeen, South Dakota (latitude 45° 10')
Fargo, North Dakota (latitude 46° 55')
Duluth, Minnesota (latitude 46° 50')
Hallstahammar, Sweden (latitude 59° 38')
Vitebsk, Belarus (latitude 55° 20')
Vilnius, Lithuania (latitude 54° 80')
Helsinki, Finland (latitude 60° 05')
Laerdal, Norway (latitude 61° 20')

This book is dedicated to these small-scale growers and wine producers who persist at the difficult task of growing grapes and making wines in cold climates.

Chapter 2

The Vine and Winter Cold

How Vines Acclimate To Cold

It's mid-December. Winter is at hand. The ground is frozen, the days are short, and the snow is beginning to pile up. Skis or snowshoes have become the best means of transportation in the vineyard! The vines hang dormant and apparently lifeless on the trellis. A few odd clusters remain on the vines, coated with ice from a late November sleet storm. Dormant? Yes. Lifeless? Hardly. Vital physiological changes, that will prepare the vines for the extreme cold of mid-winter, are still ongoing. The vines are continuing the physiological process of cold acclimation that began back in the warm summer days of August, as the fruit began to color and ripen.

Early Season Acclimation

The first phase of the vine's acclimation process begins shortly after veraison. The flow of photosynthates shifts from supporting shoot growth to supporting ripening and sugar storage. Instead of fueling new shoot growth, carbohydrate flow concentrates in the fruit clusters, the roots and the woody portions of the vine. Shoot growth slows, then stops.

The vine also undergoes changes to reduce the water content of its tissues. Under the freezing cold conditions of winter, less water means higher concentrations of natural antifreezes in the tissues and, potentially, less ice formation in the tight spaces between and within cells. Leaf stomata remain open widely to increase transpiration during this early acclimation period. Also, suberin and callose, substances which impede the flow of water from the roots to the trunk and canes, are deposited in the vascular tissues of the vines, at first slowing, but eventually ceasing the flow of water through the vine. Periderm forms, turning the canes from green to brown.

This process of hardening off is stimulated by both the decreasing day length and the decreasing temperatures of late summer and early fall. In

August, vines sense the decreasing day length and begin cold acclimation well ahead of fall frosts. Some Manitoba *Vitis riparia* vines growing at the Minnesota Horticulture Research Center in Chanhassen, Minnesota are so adept at this that they are completely hardened off and have dropped their foliage by early September! These remarkable *riparias* aside, most vines also sense the decrease in temperature that occurs through September and October, which further stimulates acclimation. By mid-October, the buds and canes of the most winter hardy vines are already prepared to tolerate temperatures around 0 °F (-15 °C to –18 °C).

Deep Cold Acclimation

The differences between varieties in cold hardiness that we observe in our northern vineyards are largely due to variability in two freeze protection mechanisms. Grape species and varieties vary widely in their ability to attain deep levels of "supercooling" and produce natural cryoprotectant substances.

Deep Supercooling

When daily temperatures remain below freezing, the vines begin a second phase of cold acclimation through which they achieve their maximum level of midwinter cold tolerance. Researchers believe that at least two processes are involved in deep cold acclimation. One process that occurs during this time is supercooling of water within the cells of vine. As the temperature drops gradually, water moves from inside the cells to the spaces in between. There, in this intercellular space, the water can freeze without harming the vine. As the cells lose water, the concentration of solutes (salts and proteins) inside them naturally increases, and the well-known freezing point depression phenomenon occurs within the cell. The temperature at which water freezes inside the cell drops and the water remains in liquid form despite extremely low temperatures.

Cryoprotectants: Natural Antifreeze for the Vine

More recent discoveries indicate that a second natural mechanism exists for protecting the vine against severe winter cold. With the onset of cool fall temperatures, carbohydrate metabolism in the vine shifts from production of disaccharides (sucrose) to that of monosaccharides (fructose and glucose) plus a less commonly known sugar called raffinose. The peak of raffinose production in the dormant vine occurs at midwinter, precisely when the vine is at its maximum level of cold acclimation. It appears that raffinose in water solution acts as a cryoprotectant or natural antifreeze inside the cell. It lowers the freezing point of the cellular water and prevents it from freezing at all but extreme temperatures. The exceedingly hardy North American grape variety Valiant, for example, is extremely productive of raffinose during acclimation. Chardonnay and Riesling, in contrast, are not.

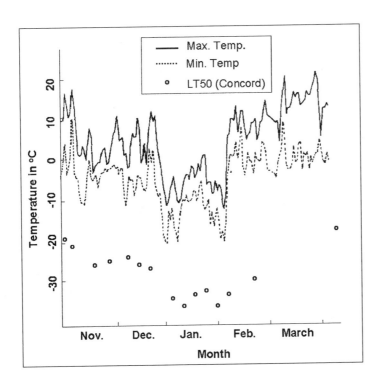

Figure 2-1. Level of vine acclimation tracks changes in winter temperatures (Proebsting, 1982).

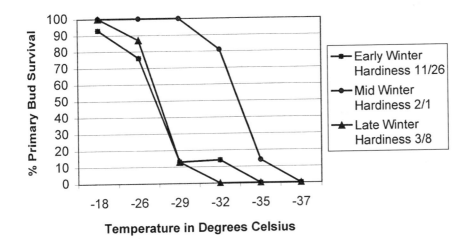

Figure 2-2. Vine cold hardiness peaks in mid winter. It is less in early winter and in late winter (from freeze chamber tests with the variety Sipaska by Plocher and Rouse, 1998).

Deep Cold Acclimation and Temperature

This phase of deep cold acclimation occurs steadily but very slowly over a period of many weeks, tracking the gradual decreases in daily temperatures. Figure 2-1, reported from actual field data, shows how vine cold acclimation follows the winter temperatures. Notice how during the prolonged cold spell from mid-December to mid-January vine acclimation (shown as LT50) continues to increase. Figure 2-2 shows how the hardiness level for a typical grape variety varies considerably over the course of the winter, reaching its peak in midwinter. Early winter and late winter hardiness levels are lower than at mid winter.

Species Differences in Cold Acclimation

Different *Vitis* species vary dramatically in the extent to which they can acclimate to severe cold. This is illustrated in Figure 2-3. Herein lies the potential for genetic improvement of vine cold hardiness. Hardy hybrid grape varieties have been produced by crossing extremely cold hardy species, such as *Vitis riparia*, with species of lesser hardiness, such as *Vitis vinifera*.

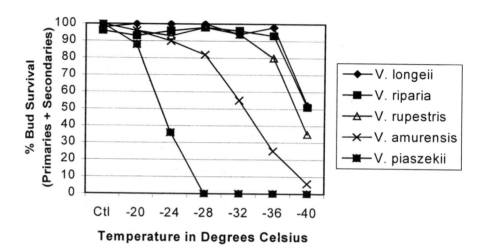

Figure 2-3. Winter hardiness (bud survival) varies between different Vitis species. (from Hemstad's freeze chamber data, 1990).

How Winter Injury Occurs

Unfortunately, there are limits to protection by supercooling and biochemical protectants. Vines can acclimate only so far. At some extreme temperature, even the supercooled water inside the cell freezes. At the moment of ice formation, a burst of heat energy is released as water changes state from liquid to ice. Captured on infrared film in Figure 2-4 on Color Plate 1 (found at the end of this chapter), this moment of bud death is spectacular!

At extreme temperatures, cryoprotectant substances in solution also eventually reach their freezing point. Ice forms inside the cells of vine tissues causing an expansion in cellular volume of 8 to 9%. The cell walls stretch, but eventually burst from the forced expansion and irreversible winter injury occurs.

Winter injury also occurs when vines fail to regulate water flow up through the trunk and canes during the winter. Recall that vines respond to shortening day length in the late summer by depositing suberin and callose in the fluid-transporting sieve tubes in the phloem layer of the trunk and canes. *Vitis riparia* and *Vitis labrusca* vines are quite adept at this tactic for blocking upward water movement during the winter. Some *Vitis vinifera* varieties, such as Gewurztraminer and Merlot, are not. Vines such as Gewurztraminer are susceptible to a sudden flow of water through the trunk and canes during winter warm spells. When the temperature drops sharply, this water is trapped in the phloem cells, freezes, and causes trunk and cane injury.

If the cells that burst from freezing happen to be those involved in fluid transport in the vine, the phloem tissue sieve tubes, additional injury may occur due to local dehydration effects. Cracks may form in the dead phloem tissue and spread outward through the phellum or exterior layer of the canes and trunk. This provides an open pathway for sap to run out in springtime, causing dehydration around the area of injury. Figure 2-5 in Color Plate 1 shows a microphotograph of cracked phloem and phellum tissue that breaks through to the outside surface of the trunk. Figure 2-6 in Color Plate 1 shows the telltale sign of sap leaking out of the trunk through such a crack early in the spring.

The Problem of Fluctuating Temperatures

Beware the mid-November cold snap! Sudden subzero cold spells in early winter may damage a vine that is still on the down slope (see November in Figure 2-1) of this slow acclimation phase and not yet prepared to withstand a severe cold challenge. This is particularly problematic during seasons when the second phase of cold acclimation starts late or progresses slowly due to unusually mild late autumn temperatures or excessive rainfall throughout the early autumn.

Beware the January thaw! Sudden warm spells above 32 °F (0 °C) in mid-winter can cause the vine to deacclimate, and actually reverse progress toward deep acclimation. Acclimation to deep levels of protection takes place over a period of many weeks. In contrast, deacclimation caused by warm spells occurs in a matter of days. Early and mid-winter warm spells can quickly reverse the gains in cold tolerance made by the slow process of acclimation and render the vine susceptible to a sudden drop in temperature.

The extent and rate at which vines deacclimate during warm spells depends upon their state of endodormancy. All vines go through a period of time during which they refuse to deacclimate above a certain point in response to warmth. Endodormancy can be viewed as another natural protective mechanism for the vine, one that prevents it from deacclimating completely and budding out prematurely during late winter warm spells. To see for yourself, try to get a grape cutting to root and bud out at indoor temperatures in November. It absolutely refuses to break bud.

Some grape species and varieties, however, are more sensitive to these midwinter thaws than others. *Vitis amurensis* and its hybrids, such as Michurinetz, often have good early winter hardiness but are very prone to rapid deacclimation and injury during mid and late winter warm spells. *Vitis amurensis* is very well adapted to the Siberian climate in which the first thaw signals spring. Transplanted to a climate that has mid winter and late winter thaws (such as Minnesota, Quebec, and the Baltics), the *Vitis amurensis* vine confuses nature's signals. It misinterprets the temperature rise during a January warm spell with that of spring. The vine begins to deacclimate prematurely. *Vitis vinifera* vines are quite different, having evolved in climates that have fluctuating mid and late winter temperatures. They tend to remain well acclimated despite winter warm spells and deacclimate at a time appropriate to the climate. Interspecific hybrids can fall anywhere between these two extremes.

Recognizing and Assessing Winter Injury

Every spring, prior to pruning, you should assess winter injury. The extent of vine injury determines how the vines must be managed during the spring and summer. As Chapter 6 will describe, plans and formulas for dormant pruning, green pruning, suckering, and nitrogen fertilization all must be modified if vines are severely injured. Therefore, it is of the utmost importance that growers learn to recognize the symptoms of winter injury on vines.

The first good opportunity for assessing winter injury is in late winter or early spring after all threat of severe cold has passed. Cane samples should be collected from dormant vines, with the variety and location of the vines carefully labeled, packaged in a plastic bag, and taken indoors for examination. Cane samples should always be collected from the lower or middle portions of the cane, rather than the tips, which tend to be more susceptible to injury. Samples should be collected from the same location on all vines (low, mid, high on the trellis). The material should be placed in a refrigerator for about a week to allow it to gradually warm up. The dead tissue will begin to oxidize during this time. Just before you plan to examine the buds, expose the material to room temperature for about 24 hours. The next day, the samples can be analyzed.

Cane Injury
Using a sharp razor blade, first slice away the periderm or bark from the cane sample. Then slice into the cane about 1/16-1/8 inch deep so the cambium layer is exposed. Figure 2-7 in Color Plate 1 shows that this layer is bright green in live and healthy vine tissue. It is grayish-green to gray to light brown in damaged or dead tissue.

Bud Injury
Similarly, the buds on the cane sample can be examined. Beginning at the outer tip of the bud, slice off a thin cross-section and examine the remaining portion of the bud under a hand lens. What you will see from this first section is largely the primary bud. Continue the examination by slicing additional cross-sections. About halfway through the sectioning, the secondary bud will appear. Finally, as you slice a last cross-section near the base of the bud, the tertiary bud should be visible. Figure 2-8 in Color Plate 1 shows three buds sectioned in this manner. The primary, secondary, and tertiary buds are all indicated on the pictures. Live buds are bright green. Damaged or dead buds are typically grayish or brown in color.

Be sure to discriminate between the three bud primordia types in your assessment. Secondary buds are typically more cold tolerant than primary buds. Therefore, a single bud can have a dead primary bud primordium within it but have live secondary and live tertiary primordia. Others will have dead primaries and secondaries but a live tertiary. This is important in that a live secondary bud will grow and produce fruit, albeit with 30 to 50% of the productivity of primaries. Tertiary buds will produce little fruit but can be a source of new growing shoots in a vine ravaged by winter injury. Your pruning must account for the crop and the vegetative growth that secondary and tertiary buds will produce (See discussion in Chapter 6 on retraining winter injured vines).

Later in the spring, after the vines have started to bud out, you can assess winter injury to buds by looking carefully at the angle at which the growing shoot has emerged. Figure 2-9 in Color Plate 1 illustrates that shoots growing from primary buds always point at an angle toward the tip of the cane while secondaries grow straight up. The figure also shows some good examples of normal, healthy bud break and shoot growth.

Trunk Injury
You can make shallow slices into the trunk of a vine if you suspect that it has suffered winter injury. Scrape through the several layers of bark and examine the underlying tissue. Live trunk tissue will be light green to cream-white in color. Dead tissue will be brown. Also, look for cracks and splits in the wood, and droplets of sap flowing out. Figure 2-10 in Color Plate 1 shows just what this cracking looks like in an injured trunk.

Recall that trunk injury usually involves the disruption and death of tissues responsible for the flow of water and nutrients from the roots. A vine with severe trunk injury may actually push buds in the spring. However, the transport of water and nutrients from the roots to the emerging shoots will be faulty. As soon as carbohydrate reserves in the canes are exhausted, the shoots will begin to wilt and die or grow in a stunted manner.

Another clue that the vine has suffered severe cane or trunk injury is the lack of sap flow from pruning wounds. As temperatures warm in the spring, the sap will begin to flow in healthy vines. Globs of sticky sap will begin to emerge at all the cut ends of canes on the vine. If you do not observe sap flow at the normal time (or at all), there is likely severe injury to that trunk or cane. Careful observations of sap flow are extremely important because vines can have live buds on severely injured canes.

How do you determine what is "normal" sap flow and shoot growth? A few standard reference vines come in handy for comparison purposes. Vines of super-hardy varieties such as Beta or Valiant should grow normally every spring regardless of the winter cold. Comparing the spring sap flow and growth of more tender varieties to that of these hardy benchmark vines will help you assess normal shoot growth observed on the more tender varieties.

Measuring the Winter Cold

Do you know how cold it got in your vineyard last winter? Unfortunately, many growers don't. This makes it difficult to interpret winter injury on your vines and make any informed decisions about what to plant in the future. Can you rely on radio or TV weather reports for good temperature data? Absolutely not. Winter temperatures measured at municipal airports are typically 5 °F to 10 °F (2.7 °C to 5.5 °C) warmer than temperatures in outlying areas. If your vineyard is even slightly outside the city heat shield it will experience colder temperatures than the city. Can you just look at the thermometer next to the back door of your house and know how cold it is in the vineyard? Not really. The heat given off by your house can have great effects on those readings. Since the lowest temperature of the day typically occurs in the wee hours of the morning, you may want to invest in a thermometer that will record the low temperature for the day. We use the Taylor Mini-Max thermometer which is inexpensive and can be found in most garden supply catalogues. You should place the thermometer in you vineyard about four feet (1.2 m) above the ground and facing north or east, so it is not warmed by midday sun. Do not point it toward the south. Although it is not essential, you might want to enclose the thermometer in a small three-sided white shelter to keep it free of snow.

Other signs, too, can help assess the effects of the winter cold. For example, other grape varieties of well-known hardiness can be used as a standard reference. A vine of wild riparia or a Beta or Valiant vine in the vineyard can provide a high end benchmark for hardiness. You will know that if these are damaged, then the most severe winter conditions possible in your area have prevailed. Damage on other varieties can be interpreted accordingly. A common variety such as Foch provides a good benchmark in the low to middle hardiness range. You would expect to see little damage on "hardy" varieties under conditions in which Foch suffers damage. The condition of other perennials also can be used as a guide to the severity of the winter. For example, in the area north of Minneapolis and St. Paul, Regent Apple trees suffer significant injury in an extreme winter.

References

Forsline, P. Winter cold acclimation and deacclimation. *Eastern Grape Grower and Winery News.* April-May,16-19, 1984.

Hamman, R.A., Dami, I.E., Walsh, T.M., and Stushnoff, C. Seasonal carbohydrate changes and cold hardiness of Chardonnay and Rieslng grapevines. *American Journal of Enology and Viticulture.* 47-1, 31-36, 1996.

Hemstad, Peter. Freeze chamber comparison of bud hardiness in Asian and North American *Vitis* species. Unpublished data. University of Minnesota Horticulture Research Center, Chanhassen, MN. 1990.

Howell, G.S. Cultural manipulation of vine cold hardiness. . In: *Proceedings of the International Symposium on Cool Climate Viticulture and Enology.* R.E. Smart, R.J. Thornton, S.B. Rodriguez, and J.E. Young (Eds.). New Zealand Society for Viticulture and Oenology. Auckland, New Zealand. 98-102, 1988.

Paroschy, J. *Water regulation and freeze injury in grapevines.* Doctoral Thesis. Guelph University, 1978.

Paroschy, J. Low temperature injury symptoms in Canadian grapevines. *Vinifera Wine Growers Journal.* Spring, 17-28, 1982.

Paroschy, J.H., Meirering, R.L., Peterson, R.L., Hostetter, G., and Neff, A. Mechanical winter injury in grapevine trunks. *American Journal of Enology and Viticulture.* 31-3, 227-232, 1980.

Pierquet, P., Stushnoff, C., and Burke, M.J., Low temperature exotherms in stem and bud tissues of Vitis riparia Michx. *Journal of the American Society for Horticultural Science.* 102-1, 54-55, 1977.

Plocher, T. and Rouse, G. Cold Tolerance of New Minnesota Grape Selections Compared to Northern *Vitis riparia:* Implications for Grape Breeding. 1999 *Annual Report of the Minnesota Grape Growers Association.* March, 2000.

Pogosyan, K.S. Effect of freezing rate on survival of grape tissues. *Soviet Plant Physiology.* 18-1, 145-150, 1971.

Pogosyan, K.S. Biological principles of grape cultivation in high-stemmed training systems under the continental climate conditions of southern USSR. In: *Proceedings of the International Symposium on Cool Climate Enology and Viticulture,* 217-226, 1984.

Pogosyan, K.S. Effect of freezing rate on survival of grape tissues. *Soviet Plant Physiology.* 18-1, 145-150, 1971.

Proebsting, E.L., Amedullah, M., and Brummond, V.P. Seasonal changes in low temperature resistance of grape buds. *American Journal of Enology and Viticulture.* 31-4, 329-336, 1980.

Seyedbagheri, M.M. and Fallahi, E. Physiological and environmental factors and horticultural practices influencing cold hardiness of grapevines: a review. *Journal of Small Fruit and Viticulture.* 2-4, 3-38, 1994.

Stushnoff, C., Remmele Jr., R.L., Essensee, V., and McNeil, M. Low temperature induced biochemical mechanisms: implications for cold acclimation and de-acclimation. *NATO Advanced Research Workshop on Interacting Stresses on Plants in a Changing Climate.* Wye, UK, 13-19 Sept., 1992, 647-657. NATO ASI Series 1: Global Environmental Change. Vol 16, Springer-Verlag, 1992.

Color Plate 1

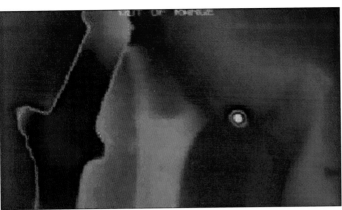

Energy release from sudden ice formation at the moment of bud death. Captured by infrared phography. (Courtesy of Kim S. Jones, Guelph University)

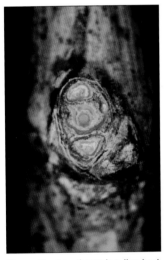

Cross Section through a live bud (Courtesy of Rick Hamman, 1996)

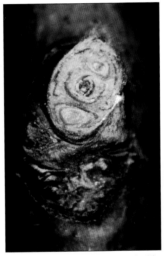

Cross Section through a bud with a dead primary primordium, but live secondary and tertiary primordia. (Courtesy of Bruce Bordelon, 1995)

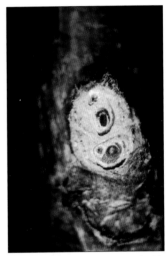

Cross Section through a bud with dead primary, secondary, and tertiary primordia. (Courtesy of Bruce Bordelon, 1995)

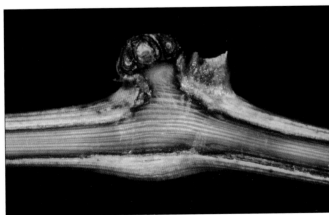

Horizontal section through a cane showing live green phloem and cambium tissue. (Courtesy of Rick Hamman, 1996)

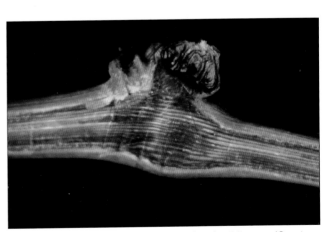

Horizontal section through a cane showing dead tissue. (Courtesy of Rick Hamman, 1996)

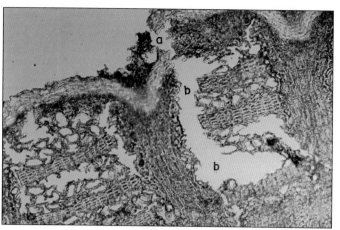

Photomicrograph of cracked phloem and phellum due to freeze injury of trunk. (Courtesy of Dr. John Paroschy, Chateau des Charmes, 1982)

Normal shoots from a primary bud (left) and secondary bud (growing straight up). (Courtesy of Dr. Helen Fisher, HRIO, Vineland, Ontario, Canada)

Sap leaking from winter injured portion of trunk in early springtime. (Courtesy of Dr. John Paroschy, Chateau des Charmes, 1982)

Normal primary bud. (Courtesy of Dr. Helen Fisher, HRIO, Vineland, Ontario, Canada)

Splitting due to winter injury and dehydration in the trunk of Gewurztztraminer vine. (Courtesy of Dr. John Paroschy, Chateau des Charmes, 1982)

Dead primary bud, with live secondary bud (straight up) and live tertiary bud pushing. (Courtesy of Dr. Helen Fisher, HRIO, Vineland, Ontario, Canada)

Chapter 3

Grape Varieties

Sixteen thousand grape varieties are listed in the International Vitis Inventory maintained at the Federal Research Institute for Grape Breeding at Geilweilerhof in Germany. Yes, 16,000! This does not even include many of the varieties grown in the more obscure parts of the grape growing world such as Minnesota, the Baltics, Belarus, and adjacent regions of Russia. There is truly a wealth of grape material from which northern grape growers can choose. In this chapter we will sort through this genetic wealth as best we can. We have focused on varieties for which, at a minimum, we have reliable data about hardiness and ripening period. For some varieties we also have data on spring frost susceptibility and suitability for wine. We will define these four factors: hardiness, ripening period, spring frost susceptibility, and wine suitability. We will categorize varieties on these four factors. Detailed descriptions, including photographs, of thirty northern wine grape varieties are included in Appendix A.

Is it Hardy?

Very few varieties of grapevine are truly hardy. The varieties Valiant, Sipaska, Suelter, Alpha, and Beta and a few newer selections could be called hardy because they have survived many years of trial under a wide range of stressful winter conditions. Most other grape varieties show intermediate levels of winter hardiness. The severity of winter temperature that they can withstand will vary from early to mid to late winter during the same year. Also, their hardiness will vary from year to year. In addition, different parts of the vine, roots, trunk, canes and buds can show different levels of hardiness in the same cold environment.

Variations Over a Single Winter
Vitis amurensis and its hybrids are a good example of how winter hardiness can vary over the same winter. These varieties, such as Severnyi, Michurinetz, and Rondo, typically show good early winter hardiness, but are prone to deacclimation during mid-winter and late-winter warm spells. Stating that Michurinetz has good winter hardiness is not

accurate. A more accurate statement is that Michurinetz has good early winter hardiness but is susceptible to injury during mid and late winter thaws. Grown in parts of Siberia, where midwinter thaws do not occur, Michurinetz may be perfectly hardy. However, in Minnesota, where a January thaw is an annual event, Michurinetz may need winter protection. In this case, the conditions under which Michurinetz is hardy, rather than susceptible to injury, is a crucial qualifier to Minnesota growers.

Variations From Season to Season

Winter hardiness will be affected by a host of weather conditions throughout the growing season and subsequent winter. Excessive rain in the late summer and autumn will delay hardening of shoots. An early killing frost that defoliates the vine before the shoots are ripened will impair the ability of the vine to harden off. Mild temperatures that persist into the late autumn will slow the progress of the cold-dependent second phase of vine winter acclimation. Under these circumstances, an early severe cold snap can cause significant injury to the vines. Given the range of possible weather conditions in the North, it is not surprising that the same variety will show some variation in hardiness from year to year. How a variety performs across this range of fall and winter conditions over a number of years will determine what hardiness claims can be made.

Variations in Hardiness of Various Vine Parts

During open winters when there is little or no snow cover the roots of the vine are exposed to extreme deep cold and become susceptible to injury. For example, Minnesota growers have experienced years in which the variety St. Croix has survived midwinter temperatures of –30 °F (-34.5 °C) with no injury. However, in years of –30 °F (-34.5 °C) with no snow cover, the St. Croix vines have been severely injured, primarily due to root injury. The above-ground parts of the variety Kay Gray have shown extraordinary winter hardiness, often down to –40 °F (–40 °C). However, in open winters, they have suffered root injury at temperatures considerably less than this.

Hardiness Ratings

In Table 3-1, we have grouped grape varieties into three categories of winter hardiness. The first group contains those elite varieties that have repeatedly shown good survival under rural Minnesota conditions, even at temperatures as cold as –40 °F (–40 °C). Assuming a sufficiently long season to mature their wood and good vine health with no disease damage, these are close to absolutely reliable for a vineyard that experiences lows down to –40 °F (–40 °C).

Many varieties are of intermediate levels of hardiness and appear in the second category. Under good conditions for hardening off in the fall and with some snow cover for root protection, the varieties in this category usually can tolerate midwinter lows of -31 °F (–35 °C) . A few, such as Zilga, Prairie Star, Louise Swenson, Frontenac, and Vandal-Cliche, are actually somewhat hardier than this, having shown significant bud survival at temperatures below -31 °F (–35 °C).

Finally, many excellent wine grape varieties for northern viticulture fall into the category of tender vines. These require some sort of winter protection such as snow, soil, straw, foam panels, or spruce branches in order to survive winter temperatures much colder than –15 °F (-26 °C). In Chapter 4 we discuss winter protection methods for these tender varieties.

Hardy to –40 °F (–40 °C)		Hardy to –31 °F (–35 °C)		Tender	
Reds	**Whites**	**Reds**	**Whites**	**Reds**	**Whites**
Sipaska (II)	ES 10-18-30 (II)	Varajane Sinine(I)	S-675 (I)	Rondo (II)	Jubileinaja Novgoroda(I)
D.M. 8521-5 (III)		Hasansky Sladki (I)	E.S. 6-16-30 (II)	Castel 19.637(II)	Sukribe (I)
Troubador (III)		Zilga (II)	Kay Gray (II)	Joffre (III)	Veldze (I)
		E.S. 5-4-16 (III)	E.S. 5-3-89 (III)	Millot (III)	Reform (II)
		Sabrevois (III)	LaCrescent (III)	Foch (III)	Bianca (III)
		St. Croix (III)	Louise Swenson (III)		Ravat 6 (III)
		Frontenac (IV)	Prairie Star (III)		Seyval (III)
			St. Pepin (III)		LaCrosse (IV)
			Vandal-Cliché (III)		
			Swenson White (IV)		

I=Ultraearly II=Early III=Midseason IV=Late

Table 3-1. Hardiness ratings and periods of ripening (I-IV) for selected grape varieties.

Will it Ripen Fruit in My Climate?

Books and nursery catalogs are full of claims about grape varieties that ripen early. These claims are mostly without substance. In truth, time of ripening can be described accurately only in terms of the amount of heat and the number of frost-free days required to produce fruit with chemistry useful for winemaking. The levels of sugar and acid that denote ripeness will vary between varieties. For example, at a sugar content of 19 °Brix, Seyval and Frontenac will usually lack full development of their varietal flavor. Seyval will taste citric and Frontenac herbaceous. They would not be considered fully ripe by a winemaker. In contrast, other varieties such as Rondo, Millot, Joffre, and Castel 19.637 make quite acceptable wine with characteristic flavors, at 19 °Brix. Still other varieties, such as Kay Gray and Vandal-Cliche, must be harvested at lower brix and before full ripeness to avoid an undesirable flavor in the fully matured fruit.

Table 3-1 shows the typical period of ripening for each grape variety: ultraearly (I); early (II); midseason (III); late season (IV). Within each category, ripening will be earlier or later depending upon the exact requirements of each variety for heat. The ripening data can also be affected by cultural practices such as cluster thinning and leaf removal.

Ultraearly

Grapes that ripen ultraearly are those that require only 600-800 DDC base 10 °C (1980-1440 DDF base 50 °F) and 110-135 frost free days to mature fruit suitable for winemaking. These varieties will ripen even in the Baltics. Not surprisingly, all of them are of Baltic or Russian origin.

Early

Early varieties require more heat, on the order of 800-1000 DDC base 10 °C (1440-1800 DDF base 50 °F) and 135-150 days to mature. These varieties mature well in Denmark, Nova Scotia, and eastern Quebec, where good wines have been made from them.

Midseason

These varieties need 1000-1250 DDC base 10 °C (1800-2250 DDF base 50 °F) of heat. In Minnesota and New York, typically they are harvested for wine in early or mid-September, several weeks before the first frost.

Late season

Varieties labeled as late in Table 4-1 need more than 1250 DDC base 10 °C (2250 DDF base 50 °F)) to fully ripen for winemaking, often substantially more. Sometimes they are grown in cooler areas and made into wine when less than fully ripe. However, they develop their full varietal flavor and character only with a good amount of heat and a relatively long growing season. For example, Seyval rarely reaches full flavor maturity in southern Minnesota. However, in Madison, Wisconsin, with slightly more heat and longer growing season, it ripens reliably and produces wines with good body and a rich, almost Chardonnay-like nose.

Is it Susceptible to Spring Frost injury?

Table 3-2 compares some northern grape varieties and selections in terms of onset and rate of growth. In our collection of some 200 varieties, the onset of bud growth occurs over a period of ten days to two weeks. Some varieties begin to break bud two weeks before others. Moreover, the rate of growth following bud break differs between varieties. For example, Sipaska and Foch are two of the earliest varieties to break bud in the spring. Once the bud scales have cracked, however, Sipaska quickly proceeds through bud swell and burst, and shoots appear. In contrast, Foch opens its buds and pushes out shoots rather slowly, taking up to a week longer than Sipaska.

You can use this variability in onset and rate of growth to your advantage in combating spring frosts. A grower with a site susceptible to late spring frosts should plant varieties that either begin growth late or push out shoots slowly, following budbreak.

Does it Set Fruit Under Cool and Wet Conditions?

Many of the countries in the most northern region of grape growing experience cold and wet conditions during the period preceding bloom and during the bloom period. Temperatures below 55 °F (12.7 °C) can prevent pollen tube growth and development in most grape species and varieties. However, a few interspecific hybrids have shown an unusual ability to grow and set fruit under even the most adverse conditions. We observed this first-hand in the Baltics in 1998 where growers had just experienced a terrible pollination season for grapes. The varieties that had pollinated well that year really stood out. We found that the most reliable varieties for fruit set in cool wet climates are Rondo, Reform, Zilga, Sukribe, Varajane Sinine, Hasansky Sladky, and Jubileinaja Novgoroda.

Is it Good for Wine?

Sure, it's hardy, but is it good for wine? In all honesty, very few of the varieties shown in Table 1 are sufficient to produce single variety wines. But, as we will tell you in the second half of this book, northern winemaking is often not about producing varietal wines. Usually, it requires blending two or more varieties to achieve a complete and balanced product. Some varieties are rather neutral in flavor and may lack certain other traits such as good color or tannins. These varieties are plain or out of balance by themselves but may be usable in large portions as a base wine for blending. Other varieties may have one or two outstanding traits. They may have color, tannin, or aroma that can contribute to the blend. The point is that a well-planned northern vineyard should include a number of grape varieties, some to serve as a blending base and others for their special characteristics. Tables 3-3 and 3-4 will give you an idea of how some of these varieties

Variety	Onset of Growth	Rate of Growth
Vitis riparia	Very Early	Fast
Sipaska	Very Early	Fast
Hasansky Sl.	Very Early	Fast
Zilga	Very Early	Fast
Varajane Sin.	Very Early	Fast
Rondo	Early	Ave-Fast
Frontenac	Early	Average
LaCrescent	Early	Average
Kay Gray	Early	Average
D.M8521-1	Early	Average
E.S. 10-18-30	Early	Average
Troubador	Early	Average
Foch	Early	Slow
Louise Sw.	Mid	Fast
Prairie Star	Mid	Average
Seyval	Mid	Average
E.S. 6-16-30	Mid	Slow
E.S. 5-3-89	Late	Average
S-675	Late	Average
Ravat 6	Late	Average
E.S. 5-4-16	Late	Average

Table 3-2. Variation in onset and rate of growth of some northern grape varieties and selections.

Color	Tannin	Base Wines	Fruitiness
Castel 19.637	Castel 19.637	Castel 19.637	Foch
D.M. 8521-1	D.M. 8521-1	E.S. 5-4-16	Frontenac
Frontenac	Troubador	Foch	Hasansky Sladky
Rondo		Frontenac	Joffre
Sabrevois		Millot	Sabrevois
Troubador		Rondo	Varajane Sinine
		St. Croix	
		Troubador	

Table 3-3. Wine blending characteristics of some red wine varieties.

Neutral Base	Aroma	Body and Alcohol
E.S. 6-16-30	E.S. 5-3-89	Bianca
Kay Gray	Jubileinaya Novgoroda	E.S. 10-18-30
LaCrosse	LaCrescent	LaCrosse
Louise Swenson	St. Pepin	LaCrescent
Prairie Star	Swenson White	Prairie Star
Reform		Ravat 6
Seyval		
Sukribe		
Vandal-Cliché		

Table 3-4. Wine blending characteristics of some red wine varieties.

have been used in our own winemaking here in Minnesota. These are illustrative, but not exhaustive, of the many possibilities.

References

Ampelografiia SSSR.   Redaktsionnaia Kollegiia.   A.M. Frolov-Bagreev, Moskva,. 6 Volumes, 1946-56. (In Russian)

Vinpressen. Foreningen af Danske Vinavlere (translated: *The Wine Press*, The quarterly journal of the Danish Wine Growers Association). Peter Lorenzen, Benny Gensbol, Knud Kruse (Eds.). Copenhagen, Denmark. Volumes 5-9, 1997-2000.

Annual Report of the Danish Wine Growers Association. Peter Lorenzen, Editor. Copenhagen, Denmark. 1997-1999.

Dobelis, G. *Vinogas.* (transl. *Grapes*). Darzkopja Biblioteka, Riga. 1989. (in Latvian)

Dobelis, G. *Vinogas Latvija* (transl. *Latvian Grapes*). Druka, Jelgava, 1994. (in Latvian).

Horticulture Society of the Latvian Republic. . LLK vinogu razas izstades numurs, *Arzkopibas Un Biskopibas Zurnals.* Volume 10, Number IV, 1939. (special issue of the Latvian Horticulture Journal devoted to the Grape Show of 1939; in Latvian).

Kivistik, J. What grape to select?, *Maakodu* (transl. *Country Home*, the popular journal of the Estonian Ministry of Agriculture). Tallinn, May,1993. (translated into English by Harry Teder).

Kivistik, J. and Kivistik, U. *Viinamarjad koduaiast.* (transl. *Home Grapegrowing*). Valgus, Tallinn, 1996. (in Estonian)

Kivistik, J. Tagasivaade viinamarjasuvele (transl. "Looking back on last summer's grape harvest"), *AED.* 19, 15 January, 1996. (in Estonian)

Loiko, R. E. Grapegrowing in Belarus. *Notes From the North* (Journal of the Minnesota Grapegrowers Association). Volume 22, Number 4, 6-7, 1996..

Loiko, R.E. and But-Gusaim, A. *Sorta Vinograda v Belorussii* (transl. *Grape Varieties for Belarus*). Belarusian Research Institute for Fruit Growing. Samochvalovitchy, Belarus. 1998. (In Russian)

Annual Report of the Minnesota Grape Growers Association. Mark Hart (Ed.) Minneapolis, Minnesota. 1980-1998.

Plocher, T. Kay Gray and her daughters. *Annual Report of the Minnesota Grape Growers Association.* 25-28, 1998.

Plocher, T. and Parke, R. *Exploration of Disease-resistant, Cold-tolerant Grape Selections in the Baltics and Belarus.* Final Report for Grant # 59-3148-8-016, U.S. Department of Agriculture Foreign Agriculture Service, *International Cooperation and Development, Research and Scientific Exchanges Division. Room 3230, South Building Washington, D.C. 20250-1091. November, 1998.*

Plocher, T. and Rouse, G. Cold tolerance *of new Minnesota grape selections compared to Northern Vitis* riparia: implications for grape breeding. In: Proceedings of the 50th Anniversary Conference of the Belarusian Research Institute for *Fruit Growing, Pinsk, Belarus.* August, 1998. Also reprinted in Annual Report of the Minnesota Grape Growers Association, 29-31, 1998.

Sukatnieks, *P. Vinogu skirnes audz*esanai briva daba (transl. "About grape varieties that can be cultivated in the open"). *Horticulture Journal of Lat*via. 3-8, 1962.

Sukatnieks, P. Vinogu skirnes brivai dabai (transl. "Grape varieties suitable for *open growing"). Horticulture* Journal of Latvia. 6-7, 1967.

*Sukatnieks, P. Jaunakais vink*opiba (transl. "Newest grape varieties"). Horticulture Journal of Latvia. 1969.

Sukatnieks, P. Dvietes vinogas (transl. "Grapevines developed in the Dvietes region"). Horticulture Journal of Latvia. 3-6, 1981.

Vandal, J. O. La Culture de la Vigne au Quebec. University of Laval, Quebec, 1986.

Chapter 4

Fostering Vine Winter Survival

There is scarcely a more joyful task than pruning and tying grapevines on a warm sunny April day. The smell of cool, damp soil, dry grass, and a breeze with a hint of honey is heady stuff. But the joy of the day quickly disappears if one consistently finds dead buds, canes, trunks, and, most deflating of all, completely dead vines. What can be done to increase the survival of tender and marginal varieties during the worst of winters?

This chapter reviews some grape growing practices that will increase the survival of your grapevines in regions with very cold winters. These include some obvious techniques such as winter protection and grafting to super hardy rootstocks, as well as some basic vineyard management practices such as the use of ground covers, drain tiling and deep tillage for deep root growth, and good disease control. Training and pruning practices that help ripen the fruit on your vines will also help mature the wood and foster the vines' ability to survive winter cold. Training for sun exposure and balanced pruning are the subject of Chapter 6.

Protecting Tender Grape Varieties

It is November in Minnesota, Quebec, Belarus, Estonia, Latvia, and Russia. The weather is miserable: cold, wet, and windy. Working in the vineyard is the last thing you want to do. Yet, for many northern growers, this is the time to prepare your vines for the winter. In many northern regions, desirable varieties can be grown only with winter protection. We do not recommend that people grow tender grape varieties. In some areas, though, there may not be another option.

Once the vines are well-dormant, they must be cut down from trellis, pinned to the ground, and covered with soil or mulch. Most people think that this can be done only on a small scale. The Dietrich-Jooss Vineyard in Quebec, Canada cultivates 11.5 acres (4.6 hectares) and 17,000 vines, all of which are protected with soil every winter. Agrofirma im. V.I.Lenina in Belarus grows fifty acres of tender grape varieties and protects them all every winter. Inner Mongolia grows 1750 acres (708 hectares) of vines. All the vines are protected against the winter cold. While this is not the optimal approach for northern grape growing, winter protection of tender vines can be made more feasible if one pays special attention to vine training (see Chapter 6) and proper techniques for vine winter protection.

How Much Soil?

To be effective in cold climates such as Minnesota and Belarus, the vine needs to be covered with at least 8 in. (20 cm) of soil. In areas with little snow cover, at least 20-24 in. (50-60 cm) of soil covering will be needed. Make sure the mound of soil is spread fairly wide out into the row, around 30 in. (75 cm) to each side of the vine. This will protect shallow roots that project out into the row. Figure 4-1 shows this.

Figure 4-1. Covering and uncovering vines with soil. (Courtesy of Charles Knox).

Deep Growing

In the winter, Inner Mongolia is cold and extremely dry. Open winters are the norm and frost penetrates more than a meter into the ground. Soil temperatures get extremely cold. Experience in Inner Mongolia suggests that, without snow cover, simply piling a mound of soil over a vine is not sufficient protection, particularly for the vine's shallow roots. Temperatures can reach –15 °F to –20 °F (–26 °C to –29 °C) at the base of a 12 in. (30 cm) mound of soil, cold enough to completely kill *Vitis vinifera* vines, severely injure hybrids, and damage roots on most varieties. The Mongolians solve this problem by trenching. Vines are planted in permanent troughs or trenches at least 12 in. (30 cm) deep. The winter temperature at this depth rarely drops below 0 to –5 °F (-18 °C to –21 °C). This trench is filled in with a permanent cover of dirt, a little each year over the next four to five years until it reaches to ground level. The main root system of these vines is very deep, with the roots starting 12 in. (30 cm) below ground level. They are virtually immune to winter injury. Some shallower roots develop over the years and are more susceptible to cold, but without much affect on the vine. A 12 in. (30 cm) mound of soil placed on top of this provides protection for canes and trunk.

Burying Vines in Trenches

Pioneer Minnesota grape grower David Bailly had a slightly different notion of trenching and winter protection. Like the Mongolians, he observed that the soil at ground level, even under a 12 in. (30 cm) mound of dirt, is much colder in midwinter than the soil below ground level. Bailly concluded that piling a mound of dirt on top of a vine was not adequate. Rather, his experience showed that the trunk and canes of the vine are better protected when they first are laid down into a trench and then covered with soil. A 6 in. (15 cm) deep trench is cut along the row, rather close to the vines, using a hydraulic grape hoe. The vines then are bundled and laid down in the trench to be covered with soil.

Technology for Burying Vines

Victor Dietrich in Quebec invented a special plow, shown in the photograph below, for burying vines. The device is just a bit smaller than a country snowplow. It pulls from a three-point hitch and heaps up to two feet of soil on low head-trained vines. Two passes are made down each row. The first pass does the deep furrowing and hilling up. On the second pass, a "smoothing wing" is extended from each outer tip of the main plow. When extended, these wings flatten the hill a bit and broaden the width of coverage around the vine out into the row center. If the hilling is too sheer, it leaves the vine head and roots too exposed to severe cold creeping in from the sides or row centers. The wings on Victor Dietrich's device create a broader mound that better protects against this problem.

Figure 4-2. Technology for covering vines with soil: the Dietrich plow (left) and the Guertin soil remover (below).

In the spring, removing the ridge of soil under the trellis is a problem. After the bulk of the soil is pulled away with a plow or hydraulic hoe, a narrow pile of dirt still remains directly under the trellis, around the vines. Most vineyards simply remove it by hand, a tedious chore. But the Guertin's of Quebec, have invented a clever mechanical solution to this problem. They have fitted an old garden tractor with a hydraulic "foot" that can be activated by the driver as he slowly drives along the row. When activated, the foot flies out and kicks over the ridge of dirt. The seat of this tractor also has been modified, so that the driver can sit sideways, facing the vines. Figure 4-2 shows the Guertin's device.

Other Methods for Winter Protection

What if you have a relatively small number of vines to cover? You have many options.

Straw

Straw is a good protective material until it gets wet, whereupon it loses all its loft and ability to trap insulating air. If you chose to protect your vines with straw, apply it as late as possible in the fall. Avoid rain.

a.

Cornstalks

For those who have them in large quantities, shredded cornstalks work great for winter protection. Because they are water resistant, they maintain their loft better than straw in the rain.

b.

c.

Figure 4-3. Alternative materials for winter protection: a) Straw mulch, b) Cornstalks, c) Foamboard, d) Geotextile.

Foamboard

Minnesota grower Herb Fritzke invented a clever way to use standard foil-backed one inch construction foamboard to protect vines. Cut a single 4 ft. x 8 ft.(122 cm x 244 cm) piece of foam board in half lengthwise. This gives you two 2 ft. x 8 ft. (61 cm x 244 cm) pieces. Then slice each of these pieces down the middle again but without cutting all the way through the board or the aluminum backing. Fold the two sides to form an upside down "V". Reinforce along the cut with glue or duct tape if necessary. This "V"-shaped tent is placed over the vine and pinned to the ground as Figure 4-3c illustrates. When it is –31 °F (–35 °C) outside, the temperature inside the tent will be between 0 and –10 °F (-18 to –23 °C), sufficiently warm for everything but *vinifera* to survive. Also, the shiny aluminum backing reflects the sun and tends to maintain a constant cool temperature for the vine inside even during midwinter warm spells. This method works even when there is no snow cover. The tents are re-usable for many seasons.

Geotextile

Gilles Benoit of Vignoble Despins in Quebec has been successful in covering his tender low head trained vines with Arbotex™ geotextile. The 5 ft. (1.6 m) spool of protective fabric is simply rolled out down the row

d.

of vines in the fall. Soil is thrown up over the edges of the fabric to hold it firmly in place or it is pinned down with wire hoops. In the spring it is easily rolled up. Arbotex provides around 13 °F (7 °C) of temperature protection compared to ambient air temperature at mid winter. The initial cost of geotextile is significant, but is offset very quickly with a reduction in the labor cost of spreading and removing soil or mulch. This technique is still experimental, but is well worth trying.

Snow Fence

Every fall, the northernmost vineyard in Ontario, located at Lake Temiscamingue, installs snow fence down the middle of each vineyard row. This causes the snow to drift over the vines. If you can count on good snowfall, this is a pretty efficient alternative to protection by soil.

The Risks of Winter Protection

Death due to winter cold is obviously final so other risks seem relatively less important. Nonetheless, we will mention these risks so that you can minimize them.

Open Winters and Root Injury

If it doesn't snow, the soil covering your vines will freeze deeply, sometimes to a temperature that will kill the roots. If a dry winter is forecasted, you might consider covering your vines with mulch on top of the soil covering. In climates that are routinely very cold and very dry (e.g. the Canadian prairies) always use both soil and mulch.

Rotting Under Wet Spring Conditions

If vines are left to lie in the mud in springtime, the buds will tend to rot. Vines need to be exhumed and placed on the trellis at just the right time.

Trunk Injury and Crown Gall

Twisting and bending vines to force them flat on the ground can cause injuries. These injuries become sites for Crown Gall and the rapid demise of the trunk. Be gentle!

Springtime Cold Injury

In the early spring on cold nights, the temperature on the ground can be colder than the air. Vines lying on the ground with buds beginning to push can be damaged on such nights. Again, get them up on the trellis early.

Rodents

Mice are always delighted to see a nice grapevine under the winter snow. They will be even more pleased if there is a nice cozy layer of straw in which to nest! If the mouse population in your vineyard is not kept under control, your vines will suffer as they lie protected from cold but not from hungry mice under the snow.

Grafting to Enhance Winter Hardiness

For some time, northern grape growers have speculated that better wood ripening and winter hardiness could be induced in varieties of marginal hardiness by grafting those varieties on superhardy rootstocks. At the very least, debilitation of the vine due to root injury following open or snowless winters is virtually eliminated.

By superhardy, we do not mean Couderc 3309, the common standard of rootstock hardiness around the conventional grape growing world. Couderc 3309 has shown severe injury in Minnesota at temperatures of only –25 °F (-32 °C). If you live in Quebec or Minnesota, you do not want Couderc 3309 or other common commercial rootstocks under your vines. So what can you use for a super hardy rootstock? Elmer Swenson's selection E.S. 15-53 is an excellent choice. Minnesota 1095 is another one that may be released by the University of Minnesota as a named rootstock in the near future.

E.S. 15-53 is an open-pollinated seedling of MN 78. We have used E.S. 15-53 as a rootstock for literally dozens of grape selections for many years. Grafts on E.S.15-53 have consistently callussed and rooted well and have shown excellent scion compatibility with interspecific hybrid varieties. It is vigorous and imparts vigor and increased productivity to the scion variety. It is early maturing and extremely winter hardy. E.S. 15-53 also has been used as a rootstock for the variety St. Pepin in the ongoing rootstock trial at the University of Minnesota. Their results with E.S. 15-53 have been similar to ours. E.S. 15-53 is an excellent rootstock for low vigor selections such as E.S. 5-3-89, E.S. 10-18-30, and D.M. 8521-1. Also, it can slightly improve the hardiness of marginal varieties such as LaCrosse, St. Pepin, and St. Croix.

Ground Covers for Insulation

Ground Cover Moderates Temperature

Ground cover or sod between the rows of vines has a significant moderating effect on soil temperature. Data recorded at the University of Minnesota in St. Paul during the open winter of 1981 showed that on bare ground, frost had penetrated 20 in. (52 cm) deep by mid-December. Frost was present only 9 in. (22 cm) deep in sod-covered ground. By March, the soil temperature at 4 in. (10 cm) deep in bare ground had risen to 38 °F (3 °C). The sod-covered soil was still frozen at 32 °F (0 °C). The sod covering served to slow freezing in the fall and early winter and to delay thawing in the spring. Both are very desirable effects for the northern vineyard.

Perennial Cover Between Rows

In all but the driest regions of the north, where water availability is not a major issue in vine growth, we recommend growing a permanent sod between the rows of vines. Kentucky Bluegrass produces a nice vineyard sod. But you might also consider using a mix of grasses and forbs for your permanent vineyard ground cover. A mixture of bluegrass and Dutch white clover, yarrow, large and small plantains, and small burnet will provide a fine ground cover. This mix also will fix a variety of soil nutrients including nitrogen, potassium, and calcium. When this ground cover is mowed and mulched with a rotary mower, the clippings are blown around the vines. They decompose and slowly release their accumulated nutrients to your vines.

Annual Cover Within Rows
Clean-cultivate a strip of ground 3 ft. (1 m) wide directly under the trellis. In the late summer, sow a thick crop of annual ryegrass or oats in this bare strip. These grains will grow up to about 6 to 8 in. (15-20 cm) before being killed by frost. The roots and debris they leave behind will insulate the soil around the vines.

Removing Barriers to Root Growth

Vines with a large, highly branched root system can store an adequate supply of carbohydrates and amino acids to support the vine over the winter and by spring still have sufficient reserves remaining to support new growth. Under good soil conditions, the vine's roots will extend two meters or more down into the soil. Larger and deeper roots also mean better access to subsoil nutrients, access to subsoil moisture during droughty conditions, and less susceptibility to extreme winter temperatures. A high water table combined with poor drainage or physical barriers such as a shallow hardpan will restrict root growth to the shallow layer of soil in the vineyard. The vine will grow poorly and be vulnerable to winter injury and the debilitating effects of drought.

Figure 4-4. Area of dead and poorly growing vines in an otherwise healthy vineyard, due to a strip of poorly-drained soil. (Photo courtesy of Dr. Helen Fisher, Horticulture Research Institute of Ontario)

Dealing With a High Water Table
Many vineyard sites that are otherwise suitable or even attractive have soils that are classified as "imperfectly or poorly drained". Soils with high silt and clay content tend to suffer from poor internal drainage. During periods of heavy rainfall or snowmelt, the water table may even extend up to the surface of these soils. Vines have some tolerance for standing water during dormancy. But even during dormancy the flooded root tissues eventually begin to rot. At warmer temperatures, during periods of active

vine growth, flooding causes root and vine damage much more quickly. The wet soil reduces oxygen in the root zone and prevents the uptake of water by the roots. The vine suffers and eventually succumbs to some climatic challenge such as drought or winter cold. Figure 4-4 shows a strip of dead or dying vines in the midst of an otherwise healthy vineyard. Their condition is due to an area of poorly drained soil.

If your vineyard site has a high water table or imperfectly drained soil, deal with it by laying drain tile to a depth of 24 to 31 in. (60 to 80 cm). This is best done before any vines are planted, but can also be done in existing vineyards.

Dealing with Physical Barriers

Many vineyards are planted on land that was previously cultivated in field crops such as corn. Such sites usually suffer from a hardpan layer in the soil about 12 to 18 in. (30 to 46 cm) deep. This hardpan layer impedes growth of the vine's roots down into the subsoil. Vines planted on these sites cannot reach down into the subsoil repository of nutrients and moisture. Moreover, with their roots confined to the shallow surface zone of the soil, these vines are vulnerable to extreme cold soil temperatures. If you choose a site such as this for your vineyard, it is crucial that you break up the hardpan layer by deep subsoil plowing before planting the vines.

Controlling Disease

Foliage damaged by disease cannot possibly function as well as healthy foliage. Photosynthesis and carbohydrate production is reduced. If damage due to disease is significant, the vine will be poorly prepared for the winter and winter injury will result. Different parts of the cold climate grapegrowing world have different disease problems. For example, Downy Mildew is a major and often debilitating problem for certain grape varieties in Minnesota, but in Latvia and Estonia, where temperatures are perhaps too cool for Downy Mildew growth, the disease is unknown. Because of this, we will make no attempt here to recommend a spray program. Check out local sources of information on specific spray recommendations for your area. We will, however, emphasize the importance of understanding your local disease problems and the weather conditions under which they occur, and the proper timing of sprays to control diseases. Here are a few rules to follow:

1. **Apply a Dormant Spray.** Many fungus diseases overwinter on the canes and under the bud scales. When the buds break and shoots begin to elongate, these spores are released. Under the right conditions of moisture and temperature, they are released to infect the growing shoot. Thus, if you had fungus in your vineyard last season, we highly recommend applying a dormant spray the following spring at the scale crack stage of growth. This will reduce the amount of overwintering fungus spores. Lime-sulfur is the classic spray material for this, but copper compounds are also effective for some diseases such as Powdery Mildew.

2. **Spray Early.** Begin your normal fungus control sprays when the shoots are only 3 in. (8 cm) in length. Try to get in two sprays before bloom and two right after bloom. The second of these must be applied before the clusters of tight-clustered varieties close up. Once the clusters close up, there is no way to get spray material on the interior side of the berries. If there is no disease in your vineyard at this point, you are probably home free for the season and can anticipate some disease-free fruit.

3. **Pay Attention to Weather Conditions.** Certain diseases such as Downy Mildew require free moisture on the foliage for a period of time combined with a certain amount of warmth in order to germinate. If the weather forecast predicts that such a period is coming, then be proactive. Apply an appropriate protective spray to your vines before the bad weather comes. If rain and warm weather catch you by surprise and fungus breaks out in the vineyard, then quickly applying a spray material that has "kickback", can actually eradicate a fungus outbreak. Waiting until the weekend will not do. Most eradicant fungicides are effective only if applied within 12-36 hours after the infection period. Timing is everything.

4. **Apply Extra Sprays to Susceptible Varieties.** Some varieties are especially susceptible to infections of certain diseases. Plan to apply extra sprays to these varieties to prevent disease from starting.

References

Bailly, D. Winter cover: Alexis Bailly Vineyard. *Notes from the North*. Minnesota Grape Growers Association, Minneapolis, MN, 12-3, 1986.

Fisher, K. H. Drainage for optimum vineyard root growth. *Wine East*. 10-20. March/April, 1997.

Macgregor, D. Editor's notebook. *Notes from the North*. Minnesota Grape Growers Association, Minneapolis, MN, 6-3, 1981.

Wang, L.X. Grape culture in Inner Mongolia of China. *1989 Annual Report of the Minnesota Grape Growers Association*. 21-25, 1990.

Chapter 5

Sites for Northern Vineyards

Vitis amat colles wrote Plinius, which means the vine loves the hills. He was right. The vine does love a hillside. As you will see later in this chapter, hillside sites offer some very special benefits for cold climate viticulture. However, selecting a vineyard site in regions of severe winters and short growing seasons is a bit more complicated than Plinius's famous observation might lead us to believe. After all, his baseline was southern Italy; our's is Minnesota, Quebec, and Latvia.

Other factors must be considered in addition to slope and elevation. First we must consider regional weather and climate. This includes winter temperatures, spring and fall frosts, the heat and sunshine available spring through fall in the local region surrounding the vineyard. Second, the climate of a specific vineyard site can be better or worse than the surrounding region. Climatic variations, both favorable and unfavorable, will occur within the same region due to the characteristics of the specific vineyard site. Slope, elevation, soil, windbreaks, bodies of water, and forests all will have climate-modifying effects.

Regional Weather and Climate

The first step in evaluating a new vineyard site is to examine the weather of the region in which it lies. This will get you thinking about which grape varieties might grow and fully ripen in the area, whether or not they will need winter protection, and how they will have to be trained. Investigating your regional climate also will highlight any major problems with spring and fall frost susceptibility and lack of heat for inflorescence and ripening.

Local vineyard sites with advantageous characteristics, such as good elevation, south slopes, and wind protection can sometimes offset these regional climate shortfalls. Your investigation of regional climate will tell you exactly how much of a climate shortfall you will have to make up for with outstanding vineyard site features. It should focus your search for real estate.

The Limits of Winter Cold

Every book on viticulture that we have seen has set a severe limit on the extremes of winter temperature under which grape growing can occur. In fact, the limits of winter cold accepted in most viticulture circles would virtually eliminate most of the regions we address in this book. We may be skeptical about attempting to start a vineyard in regions that regularly experience –45 °F to –50 °F (–43 °C to –45 °C) temperatures, but we wouldn't rule it out, and we are quite comfortable with grape growing in areas that have experienced –40 °F (–40 °C). Milder is better, of course, but it is not required. It is more important to us that you, as prospective growers, develop a realistic, accurate picture of your winter climate. Once you understand that, you can make good decisions about the requirements for specific sites within the region as well as what kind of viticulture will be possible. So how do you go about obtaining a good picture of winter cold in a particular local region? You should, in your assessment of the winter climate in your region, consider data on the following variables.

Absolute Cold

Look at annual minimum temperatures for the past 50 years. In how many years out of every five does the coldest temperature drop to –40 °F (-40 °C) or colder? Minus 31 °F (-35 °C) or colder? If the annual minimum temperature is much colder than –31 °F (–35 °C) more than once every ten years, then you should probably consider only varieties that fall in the highest hardiness category shown in Table 3-1 in Chapter 3. Alternatively, realize that you will have to provide winter protection in order to grow more tender varieties.

Temperature Fluctuations

As we discussed in Chapter 2, the vine attempts to increase its level of acclimation to cold as the temperature drops. Cold acclimation is a physiological process that is limited in how quickly it can occur. If decreases in temperature are large and sudden in onset, the acclimation of the vine will probably not keep pace. Winter injury often occurs in these situations. Recall also from Chapter 2 that some *Vitis* species (e.g. *Vitis amurensis*) and their hybrids have a shorter period of endodormancy than other species. This means that they are ready and willing to start emerging from winter dormancy if the right conditions prevail, even if winter is not over. Sudden mid or late-winter warm spells provide the right conditions for these species and hybrids to arouse from dormancy. Once a vine is deacclimated, a return to normal winter temperatures can cause severe injury.

Therefore, another site analysis task is to examine daily temperature data and look for major temperature fluctuations. How would you characterize the winters in the prospective area? Does it get cold in November, gradually get colder, and stay cold until March (as in the Siberian steppes)? Or, are there significant periods of rapid thawing, followed by rapid cooling (e.g. Minnesota, Latvia, Estonia)? Look also at the periods of time immediately preceding the coldest single temperatures recorded each year. Note how quickly the temperature fell during these cold snaps to reach these low temperatures. The more rapid the drop in temperature, the more severe the potential for winter injury. How rapid is rapid? Vines are severely challenged by a drop of 1.5 °F to 2 °F (about 1 °C) per hour or 40 °F to 50 °F (20 °C to 30 °C) in 24 hours. If rapidly falling temperatures like this are at all common, then you probably are looking at a pretty tough site. Superhardy *riparia* hybrids or heavy winter protection are ways to cope.

Snow Cover

Good annual snow cover pretty much guarantees good protection for the roots of the vine. In contrast, vines of many varieties can suffer severe root injury if the lack of snow cover is combined with extremely cold temperatures. In your analysis look for these severe winters, with little snow cover. If they occur at all frequently, your options might be to grow only varieties in the highest hardiness category or to graft your vines on super hardy rootstocks (see Chapter 4). If you plan to grow tender varieties and protect them, realize that in open winters, dirt alone will not be sufficient protection. In the absence of significant snow cover, a mulch will have to be applied on top of the dirt to prevent deep freezing.

Autumn Rainfall

Wet autumn conditions delay vine hardening for winter. Recall from Chapter 2 that the vine naturally stops meristematic growth in the late summer and early fall, shifting from carbohydrate consumption to carbohydrate storage for winter. Wet conditions in the fall serve only to encourage continued growth and delay hardening. In the fall, the vine tries to reduce its water content in preparation for winter cold. Wet conditions tend to make this difficult. So, check out the rainfall, particularly during the month of September, when vines growing in short season areas must finish ripening their fruit and wood.

Drought also can interfere with the vine's preparation for winter. Under severe droughty conditions in the late summer and fall, the leaf stomata close to reduce transpiration. These conditions slow carbohydrate production and storage. The vine goes into the winter without adequate carbohydrate reserves, making it susceptible to injury.

Sources of Data

An approximate picture of winter severity can be developed using daily temperature averages across many years. This information is readily available in various almanacs and reference books and would suffice for a quick estimate of winter conditions. However, in most areas, historically average results will be misleading. Individual years will vary from the average and include some years that were much colder and some that were milder. The prospective grower must ask, "In how many individual years out of ten, twenty, or fifty did conditions occur that would have injured a particular variety and caused a loss of crop?" You may even wish to look at hourly temperatures for those periods of severe temperature fluctuation that you identify.

Some excellent climate databases now are available on the internet. The best one in the United States is operated by the six U.S. Regional Climate Centers and can be found at: http://www.wrcc.sage.dri.edu/rcc.html. Each Regional Climate Center maintains historical weather data for literally hundreds or even thousands of stations in the region. You usually can find data for a station near your vineyard site. Historical data are available on temperature extremes, precipitation, date of first and last freeze, frost-free season, and growing degree days for base temperatures of 40 °F (4.4 °C), 45 °F (7.2 °C), and 50 °F (10 °C). If you wish to view hourly temperatures for a station near you, you should access the database at the National Climatic Data Center, found at: http://www.ncdc.noaa.gov/ol/ncdc.html. Here you will also find data on additional weather variables of interest to grape growers including humidity, visibility, wind speed, wind gusts, snow depth, and frequency of fog, rain, snow, and hail.

If your site is outside the United States, you might consider accessing the climate database maintained by Columbia University International Research Institute for Climate Prediction, found at: http://ingrid.ldeo.columbia.edu/. This database includes weather data for 8,000 stations worldwide, summarized daily and monthly. The items of data available are similar to those included in the National Climatic Data Center database.

But be careful. Official temperature monitoring stations are frequently located in or near a large metropolitan area or a major airport. Winter temperatures measured in cities or at large municipal airports typically are 5 to10 °F (2.8 to 5.5 °C) warmer than temperatures in outlying areas. Anyone with a vineyard even slightly outside the city heat shield will experience colder temperatures than the city. For example, Tom's vineyard is located in rural Hugo, Minnesota, about 30 miles northeast of Minneapolis-St. Paul International Airport and five miles from any significant municipal build-up. Winter temperatures measured at this site are routinely 6 to 8 °F colder than those recorded by the National Weather Service at the airport. This temperature differential is mostly important in assessing the absolute low temperatures for a prospective site. If you are working with temperature data recorded in a municipal or built-up area, add this temperature differential to the official recorded minimum temperatures. You may be shocked by the result, especially if you have lived in the city your whole life. But it is better to be shocked before you plant any vines than after!

Phenological Observations

Phenological observations of other plant species are not sufficient in themselves for assessing winter conditions in a region but can serve to validate conclusions drawn from temperature records. One of the best indications of winter severity is the kind of fruit crops and perennial landscape plants that are commonly grown in a region. For example, peaches provide a benchmark on the low end of winter severity. If you can grow peaches in a region, you can probably grow most of the tender grape varieties discussed in the appendix to this book without winter protection. *Forsythia* is another benchmark perennial, that will not flourish in a landscape if winters drop below –30 ℃ with any frequency. The varieties of apples that grow also provide important benchmarks. Cultivation of Red Delicious is possible only in regions that do not experience the –30 ℉ (–34 ℃) winter. In Minnesota, Regent apple is cultivated only in areas that rarely drop below –31 ℉ (–35 ℃). Talk to orchardists and nurseryman and find out how well these benchmark crops perform in your area.

The Limits of Frost

As grape buds open, they become increasingly susceptible to spring frosts. Some critical temperatures for spring freeze injury of grape buds were determined by Dr. Stan Howell at Michigan State University using Concord grapevines. These critical temperatures are shown in Table 5-1. Howell's results show that when buds are swelled so that green tissue is visible, and free moisture is present, temperatures only a few degrees below freezing (25 to 26 ℉ or -3.5 ℃) will damage them. The crop is reduced in both quantity and quality. Some regions are inherently frostier than others. Therefore, in considering a site, it is important to determine whether spring frosts will severely limit the vineyard's potential.

Stage of Bud Development	Definition of Stage	Moisture Status- Wet	Moisture Status- Dry
Scale Crack	First visible indication of growth; small crack appears between bud scales	21.7 ℉ (-5.7 ℃)	15.1 ℉ (-9.4 ℃)
First Swell	"Cotton tip" stage; bud has swelled out of bud scales and is globular, pale brown and fuzzy; no green yet	24.1 ℉ (-4.4 ℃)	17.8 ℉ (-7.9 ℃)
Full Swell	"Green tip"; bud has elongated to 1.5 to 2 times as long as wide; one or more bulges of leaf tissue show green	25.7 ℉ (-3.5 ℃)	19.2 ℉ (-7.1 ℃)
Burst	"First leaf"; leaves have separated at the tip, exposing the growing point; no leaf has yet made a right angle to the stem	26.4 ℉ (-3.1 ℃)	20.1 ℉ (-6.2 ℃)

Table 5-1. Grape bud development stages and approximate tolerance to spring freezes in Concord grapes (from Howell, 1981).

Estimating Spring Frost Susceptibility

Susceptibility to frost in a region can be estimated using daily temperature records and a few facts about how developing grape buds respond to mild spring temperatures. Three pieces of information are needed:
1. 50 ℉ date (10 ℃ date)
2. Estimated bud swell date
3. Average date of the last killing frost

1. Compute the 50 °F (10 °C) Date. Assume that grape vines begin to push buds in the spring when the average daily temperature reaches 50 °F (10 °C) [1]. Before this date, frost is no threat. To compute the average daily temperatures, simply add the low temperature for the day to the high temperature for the day and divide the result by two: (high + low)/2. Do this for each day in the early spring. The calendar date at which the average daily temperature first reaches 50 °F each spring is called the 50 °F date.

2. Estimate Bud Swell Date. Bud swelling does not occur suddenly on the 50 °F (10 °C) date. It requires about seven days of warm weather or about 40 to 50 degree days (°F) or 24 to 29 degrees days (°C) of accumulated heat. The Bud Swell Date can be estimated in either of two ways. A crude approximation can be made by simply adding seven calendar days to the 50 °F (10 °C) Date. Crude, because after that first day with an average temperature of 50 °F, mild days may occur infrequently. In the north, it is not uncommon for bud swelling to take 12 to15 days, rather than seven. A more precise method to determine Bud Swell Date is to use average daily temperatures to actually compute degree days.

You can compute degree days in the following way. For each day following the 50 °F (10 °C) Date, first compute the average daily temperature (high + low)/2. Then subtract 50 °F (10 °C) from each average daily temperature. The difference is the degree days or heat accumulated on that day. Summing these degree day values, day after day, represents the total heat accumulated for that period. The date on which this sum reaches or exceeds a value of 40 degree days (°F) or 24 degree days (°C) is a good estimate of the Bud Swell Date for grapevines. Figure 5-1 shows an example of how to compute degree days.

Date	Daily High (°F)	Daily Low (°F)	Average Daily Temperature (H-L/2)	Average Daily Temperature minus 50 °F	Degree Day Accumulation (Degrees F, Base 50 °F)
30 April	70	40	70+40/2 = 55	55 - 50	5
1 May	57	45	57+45/2 = 51	51- 50	1
2 May	54	50	54-+50/2 = 52	52 - 50	2
3 May	67	47	67+47/2 = 57	57 - 50	7
				Total Degree Days 30 April-3 May	15

Figure 5-1. Example of degree day computation.

[1] Some selections of *Vitis amurensis* and their hybrids (such as many of the Baltic varieties discussed in Chapter 3) begin growth at average daily temperatures as cool as 44-46 °F (6-8 °C). Thus, if you are considering a planting of these early-budding varieties, your analysis of site frost susceptibility should use an average daily temperature of 45 °F (7 °C) rather than 50 °F (10 °C). Note that once these early budding selections have started growth, they may also continue bud swell and development at cooler temperatures than more standard grape varieties (see "Computing Bud Swell" on this page). Be conservative in your computations of bud swell date if you are considering these varieties.

3. Date of Last Killing Frost. This can be obtained from daily temperature records for an area. Grape buds that are swelled so that green tissue is beginning to show will freeze around 25 to 26 °F (-3 to -3.5 °C), particularly if moisture is present. The last date in the spring on which such a freeze has occurred in the region is the Date of Last Killing Frost.

4. Putting It All Together. Figure 5-2 shows a sample analysis of spring frost susceptibility in three regions of varying suitability to grape growing.

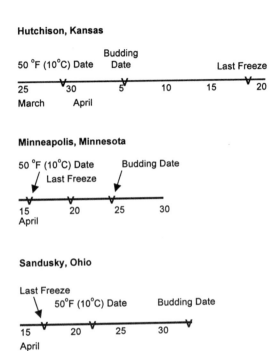

Figure 5-2. Plots of spring frost susceptibility at three vineyard sites (from Macgregor, 1978).

In the first case, Hutchison, Kansas, the Date of the Last Frost occurs well after the estimated Date of Bud Swell. In the year shown in the figure, the vines would have suffered severe frost injury. The third case, that of Sandusky, Ohio, illustrates the very benign spring frost situation typical of that region. The presence of open water on Lake Erie virtually eliminates late spring frosts, with last frost occurring weeks before the 10 Degree (°C) Date. Minneapolis, Minnesota lies in between these two extremes. In the year shown, the vine would have escaped injury. However, the date of the last frost is very close to the period of bud swell. This region is marginal for spring frost susceptibility. Analysis of additional years would be required here. This is precisely the kind of region where factors of vineyard site would be of great importance in avoiding frosts.

5. One Year or Many? This frost susceptibility analysis can be done using daily temperature data averages across many years. Information from almanacs and reference books would suffice for a quick estimate. However, in marginal areas, such as Minnesota, historically average results may be misleading. The average results may look a lot like the

Minneapolis data shown in the figure. On average, the last frost may well precede the Bud Swell Date. But the individual years that went into computing this average will vary from the average, and include some years that were frostier and some that were less frosty. The prospective grower must ask, "In how many individual years out of ten, twenty, or fifty did frost occur after the 10 Degree (°C) Date or the Bud Swell Date? In how many years out of ten or twenty would I have lost my grape crop to spring frost?" If you are considering a marginal area for a vineyard site, it is well worth the additional effort to dig out the daily temperature data for specific years and compute frost susceptibility on an annual, rather than average basis.

Estimating Fall Frost Susceptibility

A killing frost in the fall will halt both the ripening of the fruit and, worse yet for winter hardiness, the maturation of next year's fruiting canes. The latter profoundly affects the ability of the vine to prepare properly for the winter. The fall frost susceptibility of a region has great implications for variety selection. In regions with high susceptibility to early fall frosts, vineyard site variables such as elevation and slope will become extremely important in selecting a specific vineyard site.

You can find temperature data from which to estimate fall frost in almanacs and reference books. Just as you estimated spring frosts, you can average temperatures across many years to get a rough idea of regional susceptibility to early fall frost. However, in marginal areas, it is worthwhile to examine individual years and determine how many years out of ten or twenty early frosts will likely occur, force a premature harvest, and cut short the vine's winter preparations.

The Limits of Sun, Heat, and Growing Season

In the spring, sufficient heat and sun are needed to ensure a normal rate of shoot growth and flower development, culminating in successful pollination and fruit set. As the summer progresses, heat and sun are responsible for building sugars in the ripening grapes, reducing acidity, and developing color and flavor components. By August, heat and sun become important for cane maturation and winter preparations. A sufficiently long growing season ensures that all these growth and ripening processes have time to proceed to their optimal conclusion.

Heat for Early Season Growth, Bloom, and Set

Discussions of heat requirements for grape production usually center around the topic of heat and fruit ripening. Relatively little attention has been paid to the vine's requirements for heat during the spring and early summer period of growth, bloom, and fruit set. This is not an issue in most of the classic grape growing regions of the world, but it is a topic worthy of some attention when selecting a site on the northern fringes of grape growing.

Cold and Early Shoot Growth.

Prolonged temperatures of 59 °F (15 °C) or cooler during the period between bud burst and bloom reduce nutrient uptake and slow the rate of shoot growth in most grape varieties. Extremely cool temperatures, 35 to 43 °F (2 to 7 °C), during the period of early shoot growth will actually slow vine photosynthesis by up to 70%, depending on grape variety. When the weather warms up, the vines recover quickly from these cold spells. The only consequence is that bloom is delayed, but this can be significant. If early frosts limit your growing season in the fall, then a delayed bloom may shorten the time from fruit set to harvest to such an extent that the grapes cannot possibly ripen fully. Grape growers in the Baltics face this problem almost every year.

Cold During Bloom.

Cold weather that occurs either immediately before or during bloom can have significant and irreversible effects on the grape crop. Dr. Mark Kliewer at the University of California-Davis has been studying this problem for many years. Working with *Vitis vinifera* vines, he found that a period of 50 to 55 °F (10 to 13 °C) just before and at the beginning of anthesis (pollen release from the flower anthers) resulted in a nearly complete loss of pollen germinability and poor fruit set. He also found that conditions such as heavy overcast, which severely reduce the light intensity, make the effects of cold on fruit set even worse.

Unfortunately these are sparsely researched problems. There are no recommendations for heat accumulation during this early part of the grape growing season. Moreover, there are large species and varietal differences in tolerance to spring and early summer cold and heat requirements for growth and bloom. If you are planning to grow vines in a region that you suspect is prone to spring and early summer cold, it is well worth your time to carefully examine daily temperature records for this period between bud burst and bloom. Look for prolonged periods of cool weather with daily highs under 59 °F (15 °C) and short bursts of cold weather with daily highs of 35 to 43 °F (2 to 7 °C) or cooler. Look especially at temperatures around bloom time. You will have to use a little imagination here. To identify bloom time each year, assume that vines will bloom approximately eight weeks after bud burst. Note also if it was cloudy or rainy around this time. Look at 20 years or so of weather records for this period. In how many years out of 20 would conditions have been cool and overcast during bloom? Your results will tell you a lot about what kind of site you need to find and what varieties will have a chance of succeeding in your area. If you find that your site is cold during early growth and bloom, look into the Baltic grape varieties, which have been developed to succeed under these conditions (see Chapter 3).

Heat Accumulation and Ripening

Experience with the classic *Vitis vinifera* wine grapes in both Europe and North America suggests that the best white wines are produced in regions with a total heat accumulation of 1000-1250 DDC (1800-2250 DDF). The best reds are produced in regions that receive 1150-1500 DDC

(2070-2700 DDF) of heat. This assumes a growing season of 180 days and at least 1250 hours of sunlight.

That said, we still find successful vine growing, often on a large scale, in regions with lesser amounts of heat and a shorter frost free season. How do they do it? First, they plant grape varieties that are well-adapted to ripening under cool conditions or during short seasons. Minnesotans admit that we will never ripen Cabernet Sauvignon here like they do in Bordeaux! Yet our grapes of varieties such as Foch, LaCrosse, St. Croix, and St. Pepin ripen quite nicely. As we showed in Chapter 3, grape varieties are available that will ripen in regions with as little as 700 DDC (1260 DDF) of heat. Secondly, successful growers in cool or short season regions use vine training and summer pruning techniques that maximize the use of available sun and heat for ripening. Chapter 6 discusses training systems for northern regions. Chapter 7 discusses summer pruning techniques to enhance ripening and wine quality. Thirdly, cool climate growers pay very special attention to characteristics of the local vineyard site, the climate within the vineyard, in order to compensate for regional shortfalls in heat, sun, and growing season.

The Climate Within the Vineyard

Is commercial grape growing possible in Riga? If, by clever vineyard site selection, one could raise the daily average temperature of Riga, Latvia by just 2 °C (3.5 °F) during May through September, that area would have heat comparable to Zurich, Switzerland, Mt. Vernon, WA, and Plymouth, England, all areas of extensive short-season commercial vine growing.

Consider a classic study reported by Dr. Norbert Becker at the State Wine Institute in Freiburg (Baden), Germany. For several years, Dr. Becker closely monitored 12 vineyards in Baden, some with good sites and some with poor ones. Every year, he examined vine performance and quality of the harvest at these sites. A sample of his results on fruit quality, comparing two of these 12 vineyards, is shown in Figure 5-3. The first vineyard stood on the lower part of a southerly slope, well-situated for high solar gain. The second one was located at a higher elevation than the first, but on a plateau that was exposed to the wind. The total heat summation, from March to October, was 14% higher on the first site compared to the second one. But heat summation during the period of ripening, from September into October, was 57% higher on the first site! As shown in the figure, this had a considerable impact on quality. Fruit from the first vineyard attained a much higher sugar level with lower acidity than fruit from the second site. The first site produced Kabinett grade wine, which sold for approximately twice as much as the Tafelwein produced at the second vineyard. As you can see, good site selection makes for good vineyards in otherwise poor climatic regions.

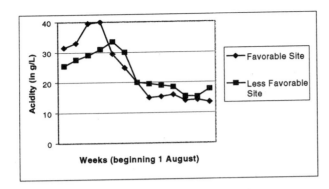

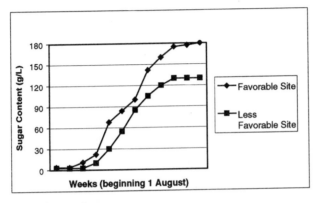

Figure 5-3. Sugar accumulation and acid reduction in grapes growing on a good compared to mediocre site in Baden (from Becker, 1988).

Slope and Row Orientation

If you looked at the regional heat accumulation data for the Rhein River Valley, you would conclude that there is no way varieties like Riesling should mature there. In fact, you might guess that potatoes are a good crop for this region. Yet the greatest Riesling wines in the world are produced along the north bank of the Rhein between Wiesbaden and Koblenz at a latitude of nearly 50 degrees. South slopes are magical! There is no other explanation. Where the Rhein River turns to the west at Wiesbaden, all the vineyards on the north side of the river slope dead south. This slope advantage makes up for the generally unacceptable cool climate in this region.

South slopes provide the heat to finish ripening. Figure 5-4 shows the amount of solar energy striking sloped sites each month of the growing season and compares these sites to a completely flat vineyard site. The latitude is about 48 °N. You can see that south slopes have an advantage in solar reception throughout the growing season. However, the advantage is especially pronounced during the autumn months of September and October. This is precisely the period of time when grapes need heat to finish ripening properly for wine. A south slope of only 15 degrees receives 22.5% more solar radiation during mid to late September compared to a level site. A north slope of 15 degrees receives 30% less radiation in September than a level site and 50% less than the 15 degree south slope.

Then how do you orient the rows of vines? How to orient rows of vines is a timeworn argument. Consider the path of the sun during the summer over a vineyard planted on a south sloping hill. The sun actually rises to the north of east during the summertime in the northern mid-latitudes.

Rows that run east to west will first be illuminated, row by row, on their north sides, as the sun rises in the morning sky. Gradually as morning arrives, the sun will move around to the south sides of these east-west rows. The south sides of the rows will be illuminated. The north sides of the vines will be in shade. Late in the day, the reverse effect happens. The sun drops across the sky and sets north of west. How about rows planted in a north-south direction? As the sun rises, only the eastmost row of vines will get direct sun radiation. The other rows, to the west of the eastmost row, will be shaded. As the sun swings around to the southeast and rises in the morning sky, both sides of the rows will be illuminated for a period of time during the midday. Late in the day, the vines again grow more shaded as the sun moves into the western sky and a lower altitude.

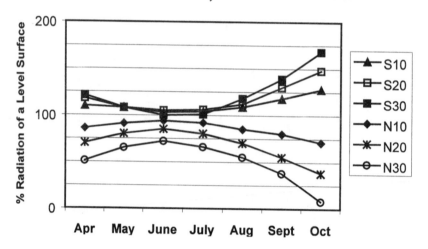

Figure 5-4. Amount of solar radiation striking sloped sites compared to level ground (from Koblet, 1985).

So which row orientation is best? It is pretty much a toss-up. East-west rows get more morning sun. Photosynthesis is greatest in the early morning, before the midday heat causes the leaf stomata to close up. On the other hand, north-south rows get more prime midday sun and heat. We recommend that you resolve the dilemma of row orientation by taking into account the issue of wind in the best way you can.

Wind

A vineyard that is well protected from the wind and located on a good sunny site will have a special warm climate on sunny days. On calm sunny days in such protected sites, the temperature of the leaves and fruit will be as much as 18 °F (10 °C) higher than the air temperature. This is a huge advantage for growth and ripening of fruit in otherwise cool regions. Strong wind destroys this ripening advantage. The wind also retards transpiration from the leaves and slows vegetative growth.

How much wind is too much? German viticulturist, Dr. Norbert Becker, reports that in Germany, winds of no more than 4.5 miles/hr (2 m/sec) blowing in the direction of the rows or of more than 9 miles/hr (4 m/sec) blowing across the rows will destroy this warm local climate. It is startling how easily the wind can upset the best-planned vineyard site! In order to counter the effects of wind, Dr. Becker recommends that growers orient vineyard rows at a 45 to 90 degree angle to the prevailing summer winds. Never orient your vineyard rows parallel to the wind direction. Also, if you plant on an open and potentially windy site, plant a dense windbreak along with your vines. Denmark, for example, is famous for its Baltic and North Sea winds. Understanding the deleterious effects of wind on vine growth and ripening, especially in cool climates, one grower there planted 15,000 trees and shrubs around a new vineyard of 10,000 square meters (about 2.4 American acres). Plant fast-growing trees and shrubs that have dense canopies, such as poplars, timber willows, Amur maple, and red pine. Be sure to plant the windbreak close enough to the vineyard that you begin to enjoy benefits from it within 3 to 4 years of planting. There are many good references on designing windbreaks. Find one and use it.

Slope, Elevation, and Frost

Some telling observations have been made about slope, elevation, and cold air:

1. A slope of only 1.5 to 3 percent (roughly 0.5 to 1 meter rise per 30 meters of run) will cause cold air to flow out of the vineyard instead of settling.

2. Differences in elevation as small as 20 feet (6.2 meters) have been found to result in 1 °F (0.56 °C) cooler temperatures on average at the lower site.

3. In the fall, night temperatures can vary as much as 16.2 °F (9 °C) between sites at the foot of a hill and those on the side or top of the hill. Frost can arrive three weeks earlier on a low-lying site compared to a hillside site.

Towering hills and river bluffs are nice but are not required for your vineyard site. On the other hand, we have seen few vineyards in the north that do not suffer in some way from being situated on flat or low ground. A moderate slope and some elevation above the surrounding terrain should be your goal in seeking a vineyard site almost anywhere. Drive around your region early in the morning on a cool foggy day or in the evening just as the temperature drops and fog begins to form. The frost pockets will be obvious. They are the first places to fill up with fog. Note the hills and knolls that stick up out of the fog. These may be the best vineyard sites in the area.

Figure 5-5 shows three particularly well-chosen vineyard sites: one in southern Latvia, the second near Lake Temisquemingue in northeastern Ontario, and the third near Lake Pepin in southern Minnesota. All three sites benefit from their height above the surrounding terrain and from their position on a slope. The vineyards in Latvia and Minnesota have a southern exposure. The Ontario and Minnesota sites are located close to large bodies of water which provide additional frost protection for the vines.

a.

b.

Figure 5-5. Three excellent cold climate vineyard sites: a) near Rezekne, Latvia, b) near Lake Temisquemingue, Ontario, and c) near Lake Pepin in Minnesota. Photograph of Ontario vineyard courtesy of Dr. Helen Fisher, Vineland, Ontario.

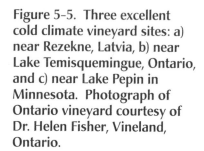

c.

Soil Versus Climate

The soil distinguishes the wine, right? So, here in the north country, should you base your selection of a vineyard site on soil chemistry? Just how important is soil versus climate for producing high quality wine grapes? This is another age-old debate.

About ten years ago, Dr. Klaus Wahl, at the Bayerische Landesanstalt fur Weinbau und Gartenbau in Wurzburg (Franken), Germany, set out on an extremely ambitious experiment to answer the classic soil versus climate question. His idea was to grow vines in each of the major soil types found in the region, but to grow them all in the identical local climate. With climate the same for all the vines, any differences between the wines then could be attributed entirely to the effects of the different soil types. But how can one possibly do that? He did it the old fashioned way, by brute force.

Dr. Wahl constructed large concrete containers, 168 of them in all, on the same vineyard site in Marktheidenfeld, Germany. Then he had soil carefully excavated from seven different vineyard sites around Franconia, each with a different soil type. The soil was hauled to Marktheidenfeld and placed in the concrete containers, with 24 containers of each type of soil. Vines of Muller-Thurgau and Silvaner were planted in the containers and all grown in exactly the same way. As the vines matured over the years, yield, sugar and acidity of the fruit were recorded. Wines were produced from vines growing in each soil type and evaluated in rigorous taste tests. He then compared the results to assess which soil types, if any, produced wines that were significantly different or better than the others in terms of aroma, taste, or acidity.

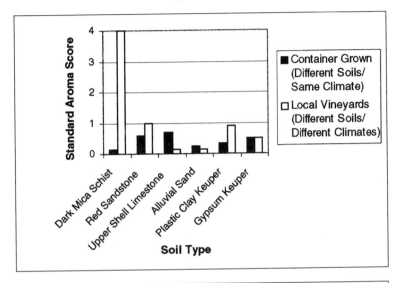

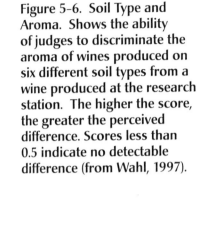

Figure 5-6. Soil Type and Aroma. Shows the ability of judges to discriminate the aroma of wines produced on six different soil types from a wine produced at the research station. The higher the score, the greater the perceived difference. Scores less than 0.5 indicate no detectable difference (from Wahl, 1997).

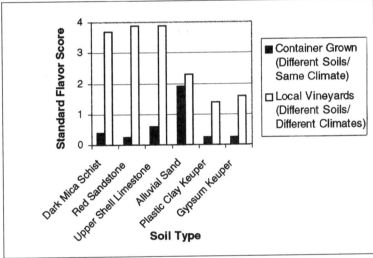

Figure 5-7. Soil Type and Flavor. Shows the ability of judges to discriminate the flavor of wines produced on six different soil types from a wine produced at the research station. The higher the score, the greater the difference. Scores less than 0.5 indicate no detectable difference (from Wahl, 1997).

Wahl found that soil type had a significant impact on vine yield, with alluvial sand and red sandstone producing the smallest annual crops and soils of mica-schist rock (Urgstein) and plastic clay keuper (Lettenkeuper) the largest. That finding is not surprising since sandy soils lack the organic material to bind minerals and nutrients, and are notorious for low fertility. Their ability to hold moisture during droughty periods is poor and they do not trap and hold heat very well. Heavier soils like clays tend to produce larger crops because they have a much larger natural capacity for binding nutrients, better water-holding capacity during dry times and, once they warm up in the early spring, better maintenance of heat.

Wahl's study also found that soil affected the acidity of the fruit. The alluvial sand and red sandstone soils produced fruit with significantly lower acid, but they also produced the lowest yields. Limestone and

Lettenkeuper consistently produced grapes with higher total acidity. But how about the things classically associated with soil, aroma and flavor? In most years, the tasting panel in the study found that soil type had no effect on wine aroma and taste as judged by the tasting panel. The most significant aromatic differences due to soil type occurred in the year 1991, as shown in Figure 5-6. As you can see from Figure 5-6, two soils, those derived from red sandstone and upper shell limestone, produced wines that could be discriminated on the basis of wine aroma from the wine produced on the lower shell limestone soil at Marktheidenfeld. While statistically significant, the differences in wine aroma were small. The wine produced on the three other soils could not be discriminated from those grown on Marktheidenfelde limestone.

The largest differences in flavor due to soil type were noted by judges in 1989. The black bars in Figure 5-7 show the results for these container grown vines. Even in this year, only two wines, those produced in the containers of upper shell limestone and alluvial sand, could be discriminated from the Marktheidenfeld wines based on their flavor. Again, the differences are not large.

Wahl was now ready to explore the relative effect of climate on wine quality. He returned to each vineyard from which he had mined soil several years before for the container plantings--seven soil types, seven vineyards, each vineyard with its own local climate, as defined by wind, humidity, rainfall, nighttime and daytime air temperature, and amount of sunshine. Grapes were harvested, made into wine, and evaluated. These wines, the product of soil plus climate, were compared with each other and the differences between them measured. The white bars in Figure 5-6 and Figure 5-7 illustrate the results. Wines from six different Franconian vineyards are compared to wine from Marktheidenfeld. The figures show that these wines, influenced by local climate, differ enormously from the one produced at Marktheidenfeld, particularly in terms of flavor. Compared to the differences in aroma and flavor produced by soil type alone, the amount of variability due to climate is staggering.

Dr. Wahl emphasizes that the large variations in wine aroma and flavor are related to the significant differences in local climates around Franconia. Sites with more heat and sun tended to produce more developed varietal flavors and aromas. In other regions, climate influences may be smaller and soil influences may be greater. Also, all of Wahl's wines were made with the same technique and style. It is possible that other techniques or styles of winemaking would have better highlighted the influences of soil on flavor and aroma. So we must be cautious not to overgeneralize here. What we can conclude from this study is that for marginal grape growing regions, we may need to put the importance of soil in perspective. Soil affects yield and, to a lesser extent, acidity. In some regions, it also contributes to the distinctive aroma and flavor of wines. But, in general, in regions short on sun and heat, its effects on wine quality are probably not as great as those of local climate. On the northern fringes of grape growing, let local climate drive your site selection decisions. Then, for distinctive and high quality wines, take advantage of a good local climate by applying good cultural practices (which we will discuss in Chapters 6 and 7).

References

Regional Climate and Site Selection

Macgregor, D. (Ed.) *Comparative climatology and vineyard microclimatology for northern areas. A posthumus condensation of writings by research climatologist Elias Amdur*, Eden Prairie, MN, 1978.

Vineyard Site

Becker, N. Site selection for viticulture in cooler climates using local climatic information. In: *Proceedings of the International Symposium on Cool Climate Viticulture.and Enology*. D.A. Heatherbell, P.B. Lombard, F.W. Bodyfelt, and S.F. Price (Eds.). Oregon State University Technical Publication No. 7628. Eugene, Oregon, 20-43, 1985.

Becker, N. Site and climate effects on development, fruit maturation and harvest quality. In: *Proceedings of the International Symposium on Cool Climate Viticulture and Enology*. R.E. Smart, R.J. Thornton, S.B. Rodriguez, and J.E. Young (Eds.). New Zealand Society for Viticulture and Oenology. Auckland, New Zealand,13-16,1988.

Koblet, W. Influence of light and temperatures on vine performance in cool climates and applications to vineyard management. In: *Proceedings of the International Symposium on Cool Climate Viticulture.and Enology*. D.A. Heatherbell, P.B. Lombard, F.W. Bodyfelt, and S.F. Price (Eds.). Oregon State University Technical Publication No. 7628. Eugene, Oregon, 139-157, 1985.

Koblet, W. The influence of geographical and topographical factors on the quality of the grape crop. In: *Proceedings of the International Symposium on Cool Climate Viticulture.and Enology*. D.A. Heatherbell, P.B. Lombard, F.W. Bodyfelt, and S.F. Price (Eds.). Oregon State University Technical Publication No. 7628. Eugene, Oregon, 169-180, 1985.

Wahl, K. and Patzwahl, W. Beziehungen zwischen Boden und Wein. *Rebe und Wein*. 304-309, September, 1997.

Frost Tolerance

Johnson, D.E. and Howell, G.S. Factors influencing critical temperatures for spring freeze damage to developing primary shoots on Concord grapevines. *American Journal of Enology and Viticulture*. 32-2,144-149, 1981.

Effects of Early Season Cold

Balo, B. Mustardy, L.A., Hideg, E., Faludi-Daniel, A. Studies on the effect of chilling on the photosynthesis of grapevine. *Vitis*. 25, 1-7, 1986.

Buttrose, M.S. Vegetative growth of grapevine varieties under controlled temperature and light intensity. *Vitis.* 8, 280-285, 1969.

Ewart. A. and Kliewer, W. M. Effects of controlled day and night temperatures and nitrogen on fruit-set, ovule fertility, and fruit composition of several wine grape cultivars. *American Journal of Enology and Viticulture.* 28-2, 88-95, 1978.

Haesler, C.W. and Fleming, H.K. Response of Concord gapevines to various controlled day temperatures. *The Pennsylvania State University Bulletin.* 739,1967.

Roubelakis, K. A. and Kliewer, W.M. Influence of light intensity and growth regulators on fruit-set and ovule fertilization in grape cultivars under low temperature conditions. *American Journal of Enology and Viticulture.* 27-4, 163-167, 1978.

Chapter 6

Training and Pruning Vines in the North

A favorable climate and a good site set the stage for a successful vineyard. But this potential will be realized only if the vine is grown in such a way that its fruit and foliage intercept the sun's energy effectively. Thoughtful training and balanced dormant pruning are the basic tools for achieving this goal. Skillfully trained vines, with good fruit and foliage exposure, will intercept the maximum amount of radiation possible. They will make the most out of the heat and sun that is available and maximize the chances for fruit to ripen. Conversely, the advantages of a south slope or a heat-rich summer climate can be negated by poor vine training that results in shaded fruit and foliage.

This chapter reviews some principles for training and balanced pruning that, if carefully applied, will result in vines that make the most out of the sun and heat available on your site. The chapter also provides some ways in which you can easily measure how well you have done your task of pruning and training.

Training Vines in the North

Dozens of ways have been invented to tie grapevines on trellis structures: Pendelbogen, Halbogen, Kniffin, Geneva Double Curtain, Te Kauwhata Three Tier. These present growers with a perplexing set of options. Which of these training methods best exposes the vine to the sun and yet is suitable to the needs of northern grape culture? Through the pioneering research of the late Prof. Nelson Shaulis of Cornell University, Dr. Richard Smart from New Zealand, and Dr. Andrew Reynolds of Brock University, Canada, we now understand which of these training systems provides good exposure to the sun and fosters good fruit quality. With these results in mind, we can focus here on the issues of adapting good training systems to northern grape varieties and viticultural practices.

Answering three basic questions about your vines will help sort out the useful options.

1. Are you growing varieties that will require winter protection?

2. How does the vine want to grow? Are its shoots rambling and horizontal in nature or even "droopy"? Or, do the shoots grow straight up?

3. Are your vines moderately or extremely vigorous in growth?

Trunk	The relatively permanent above-ground stem of the vine
Cordon	Permanent horizontal extension of the trunk along a lower, middle, or top wire
Head	The top of the trunk from which canes or spurs grow
Cane	A mature woody shoot after leaf fall
Spur	A cane pruned to four or fewer buds
Shoot	A green growth from a bud having leaves, tendrils, and fruit

Table 6-1. Terms for Vine Training.

Training for Winter Protection

Many a Minnesota grower has lamented the late autumn task of wrestling with bulky vines to lay them flat on the ground for winter covering. As one end of the bulky trunk is pinned down, the other end pops up. To the sounds of cracking wood, the grower finally twists and bends the vine into submission. Pinned flat on the ground, it now can be covered with soil or mulch.

Tender varieties can be successfully grown with a very short trunk or even no trunk at all. Figure 6-1 shows one of these methods, the Low Cordon. Figure 6-2 shows another method, the Low Head or Gavot style of training. A third method, the Mini J, shown in Figure 6-3, uses longer, flexible trunks and doubled-up canes on a low wire for good production. We recommend that tender vines be trained using one of these three methods.

Low Cordon. In the first method, which we will simply call a Low Cordon, the trunk is allowed to grow only to a bottom wire set at 4 to 6 in. (10 to 15 cm) above the ground. A permanent horizontal cordon grows out from the low trunk in both directions along this very low bottom wire. There are short spurs all along the cordon. In this system, only the bottom one or two buds on each spur need to survive the winter. Shoots are trained to grow straight up from the spurs through a series of parallel catch wires. Some extra work is involved to position shoots between the catch wires. During the winter, the cordon and lower two or three buds on each hardened off shoot are protected by a mound of dirt 12 to 15 in. (30 to 40 cm) deep. We have seen this method used successfully all over the north, from Denmark to Belarus. It works for many tender varieties including Ravat blanc, Bianca, Reform, Seyval blanc, Millot, Castel, Rondo.

Figure 6-1. Vines in Denmark trained to a Low Cordon. Note permanent cordon on low wire, very short spurs, and new shoots growing straight up.

a.

b.

Figure 6-2. Seyval vine trained to Low Head (Gavot) style in Quebec: a)Spring shoot growth from spurs. b) Pruned dormant vine. Note catch wires for the shoots at height of 2.5 ft. (0.8 m).

Low Head Training. The second method, Low Head Training, is widely used in the commercial grape growing region around Montreal, Quebec. It is also known as the Gavot style of training in France. The vines have virtually no trunk, only 3 to 6 in. (7.6 to 15.2 cm), with a head trained close to the ground. There are no cordons. Rather, six to eight short spurs are left directly off the stubby trunk. It grows as a bush, so to speak. As with the Low Cordon, the shoots must be trained to grow straight up and spread out evenly over the trellis for good sun exposure. For the winter, a hill of soil 12 to15 in. (30 to 40 cm) deep covers the head and the lower 2 to 3 buds on the canes. Since these canes are pruned to short spurs in the spring, only the bottom 2 to 3 buds need to survive the winter. Large-clustered, upright-growing varieties like Seyval are well adapted to this style of training. Small-clustered, rambling varieties such as Foch are not.

Both of these methods spare the grower from the task of cutting vines down from the trellis and pinning them to the ground. It also spares the vine from all the twisting, cracking, and bending that occurs during the pinning task. The grower has more time to do a careful job of hilling up soil around the vine or to mulch. Upright varieties, such as Seyval, naturally adapt themselves to these methods. Their shoots will grow naturally, with little assistance from the grower, straight up and through the trellis catch wires. Less upright varieties, such as many of the French-American hybrids, tend to wander, rather than grow upward. Getting them to cooperate will require extra effort at positioning and tying.

The fruit in these very low systems hangs very low on the vine, with most of the foliage above it. You must keep the fruit well-exposed to sunlight and air by means of hedging when the shoots have passed the top wire and by removing basal leaves around the clusters (see Chapter 7). Care also must be taken to insure that the low-hanging fruit does not actually touch the ground, which would make it vulnerable to rots and mildews.

Mini J-Style Training. The third method for training winter tender vines, the Mini J-Style system, was developed in Minnesota as an alternative to the Low Cordon and Low Head systems for varieties such as Seyval and Chardonnay. As shown in Figure 6-3, several trunks are grown in a J shape with the first 3-4 feet (1.0-1.3 m) following close to the ground (but not actually touching the soil) and then curving up to a head at the bottom wire. The bottom wire is at a height of about 2 feet (0.6 m). Four canes are grown from this head and also tied to the bottom wire, two canes on the left and two on the right. Shoots grow up from the canes on this low wire and are placed between catch wires before reaching the top wire of the trellis. The fruit is well-placed just above the bottom wire in good position for green pruning and harvesting. Hedging and leaf removal (see Chapter 7) is essential in this system to prevent shading of the fruit from the foliage above.

Note that in a Mini J two canes in each direction are literally tied together along the same wire. This approach assumes that in the tender grape varieties for which Mini J training is well suited, there will be always be some winter injury. With say 50% dead buds, one cane will provide insufficient growth and production, but two canes together will have more normal production. In years with less injury, the crop has to be adjusted by a combination of shortening canes during dormant pruning and cluster thinning (see Chapter 7).

Figure 6-3. Mini J style training for tender varieties.

One of the ongoing tasks with this Mini J training is trunk renewal. In the fall, the Mini J vine is pruned, bundled and pinned flat on the ground for covering. This works well with young and flexible trunks, but is increasingly difficult as trunks get older. Each year plan to cultivate one strong sucker growing from the base of the vine to use as a replacement trunk. When trunks reach an age of five years they usually have to be replaced.

J- Style Training. Some vigorous vines with rambling growth habits, such as Joffre and Foch, simply refuse to accept these low head training or Mini J systems. For these vines, you may have to resort to the J system of training, shown in Figure 6-4. As in the Mini J system, a trunk is grown in a J shape, with the first 4 ft. (1.3 m) following close to the ground. In J style training the trunk curves up to a head at the top wire of the trellis. Canes and spurs are grown from this high head along the top wire. As in the Mini J, vines trained to a J are prone to developing a bulky trunk within five years of planting, making it difficult to pin them flat on the ground. Trunk renewal is key to successfully using this system.

Figure 6-4. J style training. Note the long curved trunk with head and canes on the top wire.

Training Winter Hardy Varieties

One of the great pleasures of growing winter hardy grape varieties is that training is not constrained by the demands of winter protection. You can choose from the entire palette of training systems, and focus all your training efforts on maximizing solar energy reception. Bulkiness is no longer an issue. In fact, research has shown that older wood (trunks and cordons) produces better quality wine. For this reason, and for their demonstrated superior sun exposure, we recommend that hardy vines be grown on cordon systems.

Single Bilateral Cordon. Shown in Figure 6-5, single, bilateral cordons can be positioned on either the middle wire or top wire of the trellis. Vines with a droopy, horizontal growth habit, such as Sipaska, Kay Gray, or St. Croix, should be trained with a cordon on the top wire. The shoots will grow out from the spurs along the cordon and naturally hang down, like a curtain. The fruit remains near the top wire, with most of the foliage below it. The result is excellent exposure of the fruit to the sun. The shoots do not hang down perfectly on their own. They have to be combed down several times during the season to achieve a uniform drooping curtain of foliage.

Hardy vines with a more upright growth habit, such as Prairie Star, are better-suited to a low to middle wire cordon system. Their shoots will naturally grow straight up through the catch wires. Hedging the tips of the shoots above the top wire, before they begin to tip over and shade the fruit and foliage below, is essential. Prairie Star shoots have a tendency to break off in a stong wind. Low or middle wire cordon training with good catch wires for the upward growing shoots will virtually eliminate this problem.

a.

b

c

Figure 6-5. Top wire bilateral cordon: a) Dormant vine pruned to short spurs. b) Spring shoot growth from spurs along the cordon. c) Vine in full leaf (shoots have been trimmed or hedged for sun exposure)

Double Cordon (Geneva Double Curtain). Training vines to a divided trellis doubles the amount of space in which the vine can grow and improves sun exposure without taking any more vineyard space. Carefully monitor the vigor of your vines. If your vines show signs of outgrowing a single cordon training system, switch them over to a top wire double cordon system.   Use a divided trellis, a trellis with arms, as shown in Figure 6-6.

How will you know that the vine has outgrown the single cordon system? First, some varieties, such as Sipaska, Troubador, and other first generation riparia hybrids, produce rather small clusters. Yet they have great vegetative vigor. Mature vines of these varieties are capable of producing a tremendous amount of high quality fruit if they can be pruned to a large number of buds. The only way to achieve the desired number of buds per meter on these varieties is to double the amount of cordon using a divided trellis.   Other varieties, such as Sabrevois are so vigorous vegetatively that the foliage overcrowds a single wire system and shades the fruit. Double cordon training will accomodate the vigor.

Figure 6-6. Divided trellis and double cordon training. New shoot spring shoot growth along the two cordons.

A Few Other Training System Considerations

The three basic training questions presented at the beginning of this chapter are the most important for northern growers. A few other factors, of lesser relevance to northern situations, are still worth mentioning. For instance, on Low Head and Low Cordon systems, the fruit hangs on the vine within 1 ft. (0.3 m) of the ground. It is harder for people to pick and easier for critters to pick (especially wild turkeys). The low fruit and foliage on these vines also tends to get in the way of sprayer-applied herbicides such as glycophosphate. So, if you choose one of these low training systems, you must think well in advance about how you will control weeds around these low-growing vines without injuring them and how you will harvest the fruit. Figure 6-7 shows a vineyard "scooter" invented by Rejean and David Guertin in Quebec that allows a worker to sit comfortably and move easily along the rows of low head-trained vines.

Figure 6-7 Rejean and David Guertin's scooter designed for comfortable pruning, cluster-thinning and harvesting of low trained vines.

Growth Versus Crop Production (Balanced Pruning)

"How many buds should I leave?" This is a timeworn question among grape growers worldwide. More grape growers are confused about balanced pruning than any other aspect of grape growing. The creative pruning formulas, discussed below, reduce pruning to simple mathematics. These formulas are a good place to start, but they provide only general guidance. They will need to be adapted to your specific varieties and vineyard situation. Apply the formula for a year, observe and assess the results, record notes and modify the formula for next season.

Pruning Formulas
Estimate Bud Count From Desired Crop Weight. A mature hybrid vine of the sort we recommended in the Varieties chapter of this book, can be expected to yield 10 to 20 lb. (4.5 to 9 kg) of well-ripened fruit. So, as a starting point, figure a crop of 13 lb. or 6 kg for an average healthy vine with no winter injury. This amount of fruit will be the product of the weight of one cluster multiplied by the number of clusters per shoot multiplied by the number of shoots (or the number of dormant buds left on the vine after pruning). Typical cluster weights for many varieties are given in the Varieties Appendix of this book and can be readily plugged into this formula. For the number of clusters per shoot, assume three clusters per shoot for varieties with small clusters. For large-clustered varieties, such as Seyval, assume two clusters per shoot, because, in the

North, you will cluster thin these varieties (see Chapter 7 on thinning). Let's take the red wine variety Rondo as an example:

$$\frac{\text{desired crop (6000 g)}}{\text{cluster weight (120 g) X number per shoot (2)}} = \text{number of buds (25)}$$

The cluster weight used in this example came from the section on Rondo in the Varieties Appendix of this book. The number of clusters per shoot assumed that we would thin down to two clusters per shoot on Rondo. The resulting recommendation is that we prune to approximately 25 dormant buds on this Rondo vine.

Estimate Bud Count From Pruning Weight. One way to strike a balance between vegetation and fruit is to balance their weights. The closest you can come to actually weighing vegetation is to weigh the woody material pruned from the vine. Prune with a scale in your pocket! (A fisherman's scale works nicely) A timeworn formula for French-American hybrid varieties holds that you should leave 20 buds for the first 1 lb. (0.5 kg) of prunings and 10 buds for each 1 lb. (0.5 kg) of prunings thereafter. We have found this formula to be way too conservative, especially when applied to small-clustered varieties. Applying this formula to a variety such as Sipaska would result in about half the crop necessary to balance this vigorous vine's vegetative growth. The old formula would produce a vine that is rampantly out of balance. So, reserve this formula for large-clustered varieties, where it gives more accurate results.

Shoots Per Meter. Recent research views balanced pruning in terms of sun exposure. Simply put, the grower asks "How many shoots can I have growing on a vine in the given space on the trellis and still have good sun exposure of fruit and foliage?" That's the number of buds you want to leave when you prune. Some classic research by Dr. Andrew Reynolds, Brock University, suggests that for low to medium vigor vines, 20 to 26 shoots per meter (3.25 ft.) of trellis will achieve good sun exposure and a good balance between crop and vegetation. The exact number of shoots will depend on the vigor of the variety on your site. For varieties with high vigor, remember that you can easily double the number of shoots per meter of trellis within the same space by moving to a divided trellis and Double Cordon training system.

Observe, Record, and Adapt
These pruning formulas provide only a starting point for pruning activity. Using one or several of these formulas is much better than guessing. But the first year you use the formula, don't be surprised if the result is something other than perfect. It is extremely important that you observe that result and measure how well crop and vegetation are balanced on your vine. Record that information and use it to adjust the pruning formula for the next season. Within one or two seasons, you will be able to adjust the formula to the varieties you grow and to your specific conditions of growth and vigor.

A. Standing away from the canopy

1. **Canopy Gaps.** Look through the canopy, from one side of the vine to the other. Estimate the extent of gaps or open places through the canopy:

-About 40%   10
-About 50% or more   8
-About 30%   6
-About 20%   4
-About 10% or less   0

2. **Leaf Size.** Examine the basal-mid leaves on the shoots; focus on the exterior leaves on the vine. The leaves are:

-Slightly small   10
-Average   8
-Slightly large   6
-Very large   4
-Very small   2

3. **Leaf Color.** Examine the basal leaves in fruit zone. The leaves are:

-Green, healthy, slightly dull and pale   10
-Dark green, healthy, shiny   6
-Yellowish green, healthy   6
-Mildly nutrient deficient   6
-Unhealthy, with marked necrosis or chlorosis 2

B. Standing at the Canopy

4. **Canopy Density.** Look from side to side through the vine in the fruit zone. Estimate the number of leaf layers:

-About 1 layer or less 10
-About 1.5 layers   8
-About 2 layers   4
-More than 2 layers   2

5. **Fruit Exposure.** Estimate the portion of fruit on the vine that is exposed to sun. Remember to consider both sides of the vine:

-About 60% or more exposed   10
-About 50% exposed   8
-About 40% exposed   6
-About 30% exposed   4
-About 20% or less fruit exposed   2

6. **Shoot Length.**

-About 10-20 nodes long   10
-About 8-10 nodes long   6
-About 20-25 nodes long   6
-Less than about 8 nodes   2
-More than about 25 nodes   2

7. **Lateral Shoot Growth.** Look at the point along the lateral shoots where they would be hedged or trimmed in late season. If laterals have already been trimmed, look at the diameter of the trimmed stubs:

-Limited or no lateral growth   10
-Moderately vigorous lateral growth   6
-Very vigorous lateral growth   2

8. **Growing Tips.** Examine all shoots on the sample vine. Estimate the proportion of shoots with actively growing tips. Make allowance for trimming or hedging if that already been done. The proportion of shoots with growing tips is:

-About 5% or less   10
-About 10%   8
-About 20%   6
-About 30%   4
-About 40%   4
-About 50% or more   0

Total Points   =   ____

Total Points/80 =   ____%

Figure 6-8. Vineyard scorecard for assessing vineyard potential to produce quality wine grapes (Richard Smart, 1990).

Dr. Richard Smart, a viticulture consultant from New Zealand, has developed a convenient, easy-to-use scorecard for measuring the potential of a vineyard to produce quality wine grapes. The scorecard is shown here in Figure 6-8. Most of the measures in Smart's scorecard relate directly to the issue of growth, fruit and vegetation balance, and sun exposure. Use the scorecard between veraison and harvest to measure the success of your dormant pruning and vine management. A score of 80 (a score of 10 on each of the 8 measures) is perfect. Note the results and adapt your pruning next year. We realize that you may not have time to literally score a sample of your vines using these measures. But try to commit these eight measures to memory. Then, at the very least, use them to guide what you look at and note as you work in your vineyard. Finally, if the majority of shoots are less than 11.8 in. (30 cm) long, or if the vines are clearly diseased, chlorotic, necrotic, or excessively stressed, then do not score the vineyard.

All Canes Are Not Created Equal

Which canes are the best ones to select for fruit production? Dr. Stan Howell at Michigan State University and Dr. Nelson Shaulis at Cornell University conducted some now famous research to answer this question. Their findings have become axioms for grapevine pruning. The best canes for winter hardiness and fruitfulness are those with the following characteristics:

1. well exposed to sunlight
2. dark-colored periderm
3. medium (6 to 7 mm or about 1/4 in.) diameter
4. lack persistent lateral shoots

When you prune, look for canes that meet these criteria.

Double Pruning to Reduce Frost Risk

In the spring, bud development depends upon 1) the position of the bud along the cane and 2) the length of the cane. Apical buds, the ones at the ends of the canes, begin growth in the spring at the same time regardless of the length of the cane. The proximal or lower buds on the canes, however, are delayed in opening in direct proportion to cane length. The longer the cane, the more delayed are these lower buds.

This delay can be used to your advantage to reduce the threat of spring frost injury. If you live in an area plagued by spring frost injury to emerging buds, consider one of the following alternatives. First, consider pruning vines to fewer but longer canes to delay budbreak in the lower buds. Alternatively, prune twice. Prune once early in the spring to trim out all but the selected canes. After budbreak, prune the selected canes down to the desired number of buds. The long canes left after the initial rough pruning will delay the opening of buds on the lower portion of the cane and reduce their susceptibility to frost.

Special Considerations

Training Young Vines. In northern regions the first heat wave of the summer usually arrives in June. The growth in the vineyard is nothing short of phenomenal during this period. Dealing with this burst of growth, particularly among the younger vines, requires a great deal of attention to summer training activities, such as suckering, pinching, green pruning, and tying. The form that these young vines will have for the next year or so is largely determined by the training activity during these hot weeks in late June and early July. Some principles and techniques for developing a good vine structure are:

1. Get the vines trellised and climbing. Vines were meant to climb, not crawl on the ground. Lying on the ground, vines put all their growth into producing lateral shoots at every node. This is at the expense of the growing tip at the end of the main shoot (destined to become the trunk). Get the vines trellised early and staked or tied up on a piece of twine.

2. Grow one trunk at a time. You may eventually want to grow multiple trunks on your vines. However, it is difficult for a young vine to develop two trunks simultaneously. Pick out the strongest and best-placed shoot growing out from the base of the vine and focus your training efforts on that one. Most of the other shoots (i.e. suckers) that grow out from the base should be removed. However, you should leave two or three of these sucker shoots intact, just in case something happens to the main shoot. Wind, for example, often foils even the best attempts to develop a strong main shoot. These two or three sucker shoots should be kept short, about 2 to 3 nodes long, by pinching them back regularly. This will minimize their competition with the main shoot.

3. Break off persistent laterals. As the main shoot grows up it will begin to develop lateral shoots at each node. The best-placed of these lateral shoots will eventually become the fruiting canes or the cordons on the vine. Thus, the well-placed lateral shoots, those that sprout out right at the level of wires on your trellis, should be encouraged. The rest of them, however, should be severely pinched back or removed.

4. Top off above the top wire. As the main shoot grows up, continue to tie it to the wires or twine to prevent breakage in the wind and to maintain a nice form. When the shoot is about 18 in. (45 cm) above the top wire, it can be topped. Make the topping cut through the first node above the wire. This will leave a good 6 in. (15 cm) piece of vine above the wire with which to secure the trunk at pruning time next year. Topping the main shoot like this will force the vine's growth into the lateral shoots just below it. These lateral shoots will become the new canes for the young vine. If you plan cordon training for the vine, the selected laterals will become the permanent bilateral cordons.

Now, depending upon the training system you plan for the vine, the term "top wire" can be a taut wire only 6 in. (15 cm) above the ground (for low training systems), a middle wire 3 ft. (1 m) above the ground (for low-middle cordon vines) or a high wire 6 ft. (2 m) above the ground (for high cordon training systems). Topping the main shoot to force selected lateral growth is done in the same way no matter how high or low the vine will be trained.

Figure 6-9. Trimming laterals and topping a young vine.

Retraining Winter Injured Vines

At some time, everyone in the North is faced with the prospect of retraining grapevines that have been injured by severe winter cold. Repairing damaged vines takes some extra time and effort and a lot of careful observation and attention to the vines' growth. Injured vines that are not repaired and retrained will be unfit to face the next winter and unproductive in subsequent years. Instructions for assessing the extent of vine injury, including photographs of live and injured buds, canes, and trunks, were presented in Chapter 2. Some guidelines for retraining winter-damaged vines are presented below.

1. Delay pruning. If your examination of buds indicates that vines of a particular variety have suffered more than 50% primary bud injury, then delay your dormant pruning. These vines should be tied up to the trellis sometime before bud break, in early to mid April, but with very little pruning. Leave even the laterals and root suckers attached. In early May, after the vines have budded out, re-assess the damage. The surviving primary buds are growing vigorously at this time, the secondaries less so, and the tertiaries are only beginning to push. Therefore, it is relatively easy to make the discriminations necessary for bud counts. In some cases, you may be pleasantly surprised to find more buds pushing open than you had anticipated. Shorten up some canes here and there or remove some laterals or root suckers to account for growth.

2. Maximize leaf area. The healing and repair of injured cambium tissue depends, critically, upon sufficient vine photosynthetic activity. This can be encouraged by maximizing the leaf area of the injured vine. As a rule of thumb, if more than 50% of the primary buds on a vine have been killed, simply don't prune that vine in the spring. It will need all of its live buds to produce something close to a normal amount of foliage. If the vine is damaged, but with less than 50% dead buds, prune more lightly than usual, leaving extra buds in proportion to the amount of damage.

As the season goes on, you should keep other things in mind. First, on heavily damaged vines, let all the root suckers sprout up, rather than strip them off. The root suckers can help with the leaf area problem and are essential for replacement trunks. Out of these many suckers, some will be better placed than others to serve as future trunks. Select these out, tie and train them up. If the other suckers get too vigorous, simply pinch them back at their tips. Pinching back will temporarily slow their ability to compete with other suckers that you are trying to grow into new trunks. Second, vines with less than the normal amount of live buds will tend to grow with extreme vigor from the remaining ones, producing some massive bull canes. If you notice that a few shoots are dominating and developing in this manner, pinch them back at their tips, repeatedly, over a period of weeks. This will force laterals to grow out from the shoot, which will harden off better in the fall and be a much more useful fruiting cane the following year.

3. Control vigor. Grapevines are extremely vigorous plants that will re-grow readily after winter injury. A danger is that the injured vine, growing from fewer points than normal with the same root capacity, will be excessively vigorous, producing soft wood that fails to harden off properly in the fall. To avoid overly vigorous vines, wait until well after bud break to remove damaged trunks and canes. Cutting them off at the outset will only encourage rampant re-growth. Also, keep in mind that the nitrogen requirement of an injured vine will be less than a normal vine. Thus, following a severe winter, you should initially withhold nitrogen fertilizers from vines that have suffered either dead trunks or more than 50% dead buds. Observe their re-growth for the first three weeks or so after bud break. If growth is vigorous, you won't need to provide nitrogen this season. If shoot growth appears to be poor, however, you can apply some nitrogen at this point.

4. Manage crop load. Achieving a good balance between vegetative growth and crop load on damaged vines can be a real challenge, especially in varieties that have suffered heavy primary bud damage. These varieties will fruit, for the most part, from secondary buds. Secondaries are only 50% to 70% as productive as primaries. Thus, in your dormant pruning, you will have to leave nearly twice as many nodes as usual in order to achieve the same crop load. You can take advantage of some production from root suckers to help with this. The key is to provide for enough of a crop to balance out the vigorous vegetative growth you will get without overcropping these already stressed vines. If your dormant pruning happens to leave too many clusters and the vines appear overcropped, clusters can be removed right up to veraison in order to achieve a better balance.

5. Select best shoots to retain. By mid to late June, you will begin to have some idea about which shoots are going to be useful as permanent replacement parts (new trunks, cordons, and canes) for your damaged vine. Make sure you get these trained up and tied into the trellis so they get good sun exposure and harden off well. If your vines did not have multiple trunks in the past, now is a good time to correct that. Plan to train up and foster two or three sucker shoots to become future trunks.

References

Bordelon, B. Dealing with winter-injured vines. Presentation to the Spring Symposium of the Minnesota Grape Growers Association, 1995.

Howell, G.S. and Shaulis, N. Factors influencing within-vine variation in the cold resistance of cane and primary bud tissues. *American Journal of Enology and Viticulture*. 31-2, 158-161, 1980.

Reynolds, A.G., Pool, R.M., and Mattick, L.R. Effect of training system on growth, yield, fruit composition, and wine quality of Seyval blanc. *American Journal of Enology and Viticulture*. 36-2, 156-164, 1985.

Reynolds, A.G., Pool, R.M., and Mattick, L.R. Effect of shoot density and crop control on growth yield, fruit composition, and wine quality of Seyval blanc grapes. *Journal of the American Society for Horticultural Science*. 111-1, 55-63, 1986.

Reynolds, A.G., Wardle, D.A., and Dever, M. Shoot density effects on Riesling grapevines: interactions with cordon age. *American Journal of Enology and Viticulture*. 45-4, 1994.

Reynolds, A.G., Edwards, C.G., Wardle, D.A., Webster, D.R., and Dever, M. Shoot density affects Riesling grapevines I. Vine performance. *Journal of the American Society for Horticultural Science. 119-5, 874-880, 1994.*

*Reynolds, A.G. an*d Wardle, D.A. Impact of training system and vine spacing on vine performance and berry composition of Seyval blanc. American Journal of Enology and Viticulture. 45-4, 444-451, 1994.

Reynolds, A.G., Edwards, C.G., Wardle, D.A., Webster, D.R., and Dever, M. Shoot density affects Riesling grapevines. II. Wine composition and sensory response. Journal of the American Society for Horticultural Science. 119-5, 881-*892, 1994.*

Reynolds, A.G., Wardle, D. A., and Naylor, A.P. Impact of training system and vine spacing on vine performance and berry composition of Chancellor. American Journal of Enology and V*iticulture. 46-1, 88-97, 1995.*

*Smart, Richard. Canopy microclimates an*d effects on wine quality. In: Advances in viticulture and enology for economic gain. In: Proceedings of the Fifth Australian Wine Industry Technical Conference. Perth, Australia. T.H. Lee a*nd T.C. Somers (Eds.). 113-132, 1984.*

*Sma*rt, R.E. Principles of grapevine canopy microclimate manipulation with implications for yield and quality: a review. American Journal of Enology and Viticulture. 36-3*, 230-239, 1985.*

*Sma*rt, *R.E., Dick, J.K. Grave*tt, I.M., and Fisher, B.M. Canopy *management to impr*ove grape yield and wine quality-principles and practices. South African Journal of Enology and Viticulture. 11-1, 3-17, 1991.

Smart, R.E. Sunlight into Wine. Winetitles, Adelaide, Australia, 88 pages, 1991.

Chapter 7

The Ripening Grape: Veraison to Harvest

For thousands of years, farmers, their families and friends have celebrated the grape harvest even more than the harvest of other crops. Basic food crops such as corn or dried beans or potatoes, provide sustenance, plain and simple food for this winter and, in good years, perhaps even for the next. Grapes, on the other hand, have the potential to be transformed into a beverage that lives for years, perhaps decades and, when consumed with these simple foods, renders them infinitely more interesting.

The enthusiasm for the harvest, however, is dampened when the crop is of poor quality. All too frequently, we see grapes that are ripened poorly, the result of careless vineyard practices or premature harvest.

This chapter describes some vineyard practices that will help you develop the best possible chemistry in your grapes during the growing season. Also, for those attempting to grow grapes in extremely cool or short season areas, we discuss some ideas for artificially manipulating the vine microclimate to enhance ripening. Finally, the chapter concludes with some guidelines for determining when grapes are ready for harvest.

Wine Quality and Vineyard Practices

Wine quality begins in the vineyard. Select a vineyard site with a good climate for ripening grapes. Plant grape varieties that have the ability to ripen fully in your climate. Place vines on a training system that accommodates their vigor. Control disease. Prune to balance fruit and vegetative growth. These principles and practices are basic to producing high quality grapes for wine. Apply them and you are well on your way to producing high quality wine grapes. But there is yet another level of vineyard techniques to be mastered, techniques that fine tune the grape's chemistry and encourage uniform and full maturation of the grape berries.

The Quest for Uniformity

Uniformity of the fruit and evenness of ripening hold the key to high quality wines according to Zelma Long, President and Winemaker of Simi Winery, Healdsburg, California. For over a decade, she has studied uniformity of ripening in the vineyards at Simi Winery. A sample of her data, shown in Figure 7-1a and 7-1b, shows the problem. To create the upper of these two plots, Long collected four hundred grape berries at random from Cabernet Sauvignon vines that had been grown using standard vineyard practices. She then measured sugar content (in degrees Brix) of each individual berry. She counted and plotted the number of berries out of the four hundred that contained various amounts of sugar (17, 18, 19, ... 27 °Brix). Long repeated the same analysis, shown in the lower plot, for a group of Cabernet Sauvignon vines that had been given special attention to encourage evenness of berry ripening.

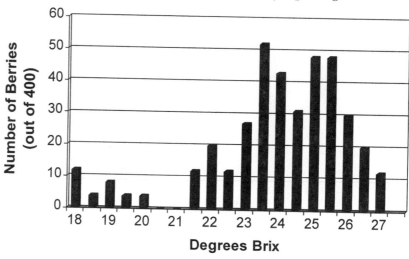

Figure 7-1a. Sugar content of a sample of individual berries collected from poorly managed vines. (from Zelma Long, 1996)

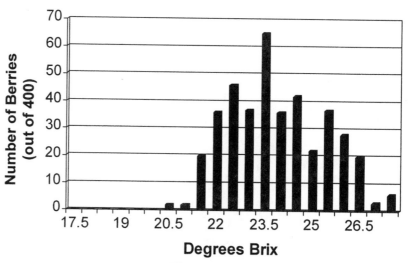

Figure 7-1b. Sugar content of a sample of individual berries collected from well managed vines. (from Zelma Long, 1996)

Both plots dramatically show that, under most conditions, grape berries in the same cluster and within the same vine or local planting of vines will not ripen to the same degree. Instead, there is a wide range of sugar content among the berries. Now let's focus on the upper plot for a moment. Sugar varies from underripe at 17 °Brix to overripe at 27+ °Brix.

The average sugar content of the combined lot of four hundred berries is around 24 °Brix, which is excellent for red winemaking. But don't be deceived by this statistical average. Looking at the chart, you can see that very few individual berries actually contained that nearly optimal content of sugar. It is merely the statistical average of combining lots of extreme highs and extreme lows.

Compare the upper to the lower plot now. Berries in this sample ranged from 19.8 to 27+ °Brix, and the average sugar content is about the same as the upper plot. However, one look at the distribution tells you that this average is from a truly well ripened sample of berries. A high proportion of the berries have something close to this optimal sugar content. The variance in sugar content among these berries is about half the variance among the berries in the upper plot. While there are some berries at each extreme, they are few in number. Further, the lowest sugar content is now 20, not 17 °Brix. One would have to call this a much more evenly ripened sample of berries than that illustrated in the upper plot.

The plots shown in Figure 7-1a and and 7-1b deal with sugar content as a measure of ripeness. But with these wide variations in sugar content can come wide variations in other aspects of grape chemistry. Look again at the figure, and imagine that the plots showed the variations in berry flavor and aroma instead of sugar content. For a single variety, they could range from "veggie" on the underripe side to "stewed prunes" on the overripe side, or from "neutral fruity" on the underripe to "Welch's Grape Juice" on the overripe.

Look at the plots again and imagine the range of acidity that goes with these variations in berry ripeness. Berries on the left side of the plots would have a preponderance of malic acid, with its sharp flavor compared to overripe berries toward the right extreme that might taste a bit flat.

Now think about this for a moment in terms of the interspecific hybrid grape varieties. The variety Kay Gray is overripe for winemaking and already has developed an undesirable flavor by the time it reaches 20 °Brix. A typical sample of Kay Gray berries that averages 17 °Brix will contain some portion of overripe berries that have this undesirable flavor. The more unevenly the grapes have ripened in the vineyard, the more likely the must will contain a larger portion of these overripe berries. The wine will prove it! For another example, consider a wine produced from grapes of the Frontenac variety. Frontenac tends to have a herbaceous flavor when less than fully mature. The wider the variability in ripeness of these grapes at harvest, the more unripe herbaceous-tasting berries will be fermented in the must. Again, the outliers in an unevenly ripened batch of grapes ruin the wine.

Techniques for Quality Enhancement

So, what can we do as grape growers to make sure our grapes ripen more evenly, with most of the fruit right around the preferred degree of ripeness that produces quality wine? Several vineyard practices, commonly referred to as summer training and pruning, have the potential to improve grape uniformity, full maturity, and wine quality. In fact, the berries shown in the even ripening sample graphed above were the result of applying these practices. Summer training and pruning require good timing and good observational skills. However, they are easy to apply in the vineyard and will improve the quality of your wines.

Train to Encourage Even Shoot Growth

This is a sequel to the story we told in Chapter 6. Shaded shoots tend to be stunted and produce low quality fruit. How can you prevent that? In Chapter 6, we discussed the importance of placing the vine on a trellis and training it in a manner that can accommodate its vigor. For vigorous varieties, a divided trellis may be necessary. Early in the summer, through the period of rapid shoot growth, you need to pay attention to how and where the shoots are growing. A vigorous vine whose trunks and canes are well arranged on an appropriate trellis after skillful dormant pruning still has the potential to run amuck during the growing season. If its shoots are left to grow wherever they please, many will grow into positions where they shade other shoots, including fruit. The shoots must be placed into more desirable positions and tied to the trellis wires. On high cordon training systems, shoots must be "combed" down into a vertical position several times early in the season. The result will be an orderly canopy and good fruit exposure.

During the period of rapid shoot growth, roughly from early June to mid-July in most areas, you should walk through the vineyard about once a week to and tie up and comb unruly shoots. Significant gains in sugar content and reductions in acidity, both important for northern winemaking, will result from shoot positioning.

Remove Weak Clusters and Shoots

Weak shoots produce poorly ripened fruit and wines that are herbaceous and low in color and phenols. In fact, most of the unripe berries depicted in Zelma Long's plot of uneven ripening likely came from weak shoots. On a healthy, vigorous vine, the weak shoots that need to be removed will become apparent between berry set and veraison. Often you will find them growing in the interior of the vine, where they have sprouted from trunk buds, winter-injured wood, or tertiary buds that were slow to push open and late to bloom. By veraison, they will be hopelessly shaded and stunted, yet still trying to ripen some poor fruit.

Remove Suckers

Aside from training up one or two suckers each year to serve as spare parts, or using them to help invigorate a badly winter-injured vine, there is no reason to keep them. Fruit borne by suckers will not be in a zone where you can easily care for it and ripen it. So, here is another task to do on your weekly vineyard walks. While you are tying up shoots, you can also pull off suckers.

Remove Basal Leaves

Vines with well-exposed foliage produce fruit with more sugar and less acid than vines with shaded foliage. That's practically an axiom in today's grape growing. But, given good leaf exposure, does it matter if the clusters themselves are well exposed to the sun? Over the past decade, this question has been studied by several grape researchers, most notably, Andrew Reynolds of Brock University, Werner Koblet at the Swiss Federal Station-Wadenswil, and Janice Morrison at University of California-Davis. The answer to the question is clearly, "Yes, fruit exposure matters." But it is not so important for higher sugar and lower acidity. Direct exposure of the fruit cluster to the sun barely affects sugar and acidity in most years. However, it has significant effects on the build-up of color pigments and tannins (anthocyanins in red wine grapes) and flavor compounds (terpenes and phenols). Well-exposed fruit may have as much as 30 to 50% greater accumulation of these compounds than shaded fruit. The color will be better in reds, and the mature fruit flavor and aroma typical of the grape variety will be more prominent in both reds and whites.

So, how can you get the clusters better exposed to the sun? Assume that the fruit clusters are well located in the first place due to good training and pruning practices and not buried deep in the vine canopy. The only leaves really shading the cluster, then, are those growing right around it. These basal leaves are the oldest leaves on that shoot. So old that by veraison, they are producing very little photosynthate for the vine. Removing them will in no way interfere with the vine's vitality. Therefore, during the two weeks preceding veraison, remove the bottom two or three leaves on the shoot. The cluster is opened up to more direct sun exposure and will gain in color, tannins, and flavor. Moreover, if basal leaf removal is done consistently throughout each vine in the vineyard, the resulting crop will be more uniformly ripe. Note that leaf removal can be overdone. It is not necessary to strip off all the basal leaves. Especially in northern areas with intense sun and high summer temperatures, the clusters can be damaged by excessive direct sun exposure. Confining leaf removal to two or three basal leaves will achieve the desired effects on quality without over-exposing the fruit.

Remove (thin) Clusters

When we prune a vine during the dormant season, we try to leave just enough buds to produce the right amount of fruit. Dormant pruning is absolutely important, but it is an imprecise way of controlling crop load. The fruitfulness of many of these hybrid varieties is not well known. For example, there are no set rules for pruning bud counts on the likes of Sipaska, Kay Gray, and E.S. 5-3-89 growing in places like Hugo, Minnesota, Dunham, Quebec or Litchfield, Maine. The grower has to make an educated guess. Further, even if dormant pruning is delayed until spring, and a winter injury survey has been done, the grower still cannot perfectly account for buds that are winter injured and the associated crop loss. The rule of thumb is to err on the generous side and leave extra buds, but the result often is too much poorly ripened fruit. This is especially problematic in varieties such as Seyval that have a natural tendency to overbear.

Given the imperfect result of dormant pruning, how can you make crop load adjustments during the growing season? Cluster thinning usually provides the answer. Once the flowers appear on the vine, you can get a much better idea of crop load. From the data provided in this book (Varieties Appendix) you know how heavy the clusters will be on different grape varieties. Aim for a crop of 10 to 20 lbs on a mature grapevine. Figure how many clusters add up to that amount of crop. Remove flower clusters until you arrive at this number, but do not remove them at random. Start with the distal flower cluster, the one farthest out along the shoot. Remove that distal cluster on all the shoots. If you have not reached your number, go through and remove the next most distal flower cluster. Never remove the basal or bottom-most flower cluster. It will always become the biggest and best-ripened cluster on the shoot.

As a general rule, we recommend that you thin clusters right after fruit set. In some varieties, this timing tends to encourage a somewhat looser cluster which is easier to spray and care for than a very tight one. In all varieties, this post-bloom cluster thinning will tend to promote uniformity in the fruit, improved sugar-acid balance and earlier ripening. Earlier ripening is an additional bonus that comes with cluster thinning. Cluster-thinned vines may ripen fruit up to a week earlier than unthinned vines. In northern regions, this can make the difference between ripening a late season variety such as Seyval and not ripening it.

Technique	Effect on Quality				
	Increases Sugar	Reduces Acidity	Increases Color, Tannins, and Aroma	Eliminates Poorly Ripened Fruit	Increases Fruit Uniformity
Position shoots	X	X		X	X
Remove weak shoots				X	X
Remove suckers				X	X
Remove basal leaves			X		X
Thin flowers/clusters	X	X			X

Table 7-1. The effects of various uniformity-enhancing vineyard practices.

Ripening Grapes at Extreme Cool Sites

So what can you do to obtain more fully ripened grapes for winemaking if you are one of those zealots growing vines in the extreme cool environs of Finland, Norway, the Urals, or the north shore of Lake Superior in the United States? The summer pruning practices described in the previous section will be extremely important for you. But there are some other techniques to consider as well, particularly if you are growing vines on a small scale. During our fall of 1998 travels in the Baltic countries and

Belarus, we observed a lot of creative and highly specialized approaches to the problem of ripening grapes in extreme cool climates. The best of these are described below.

Techniques to Enhance Solar Gain

Walls. In very cool climates, nothing much can beat the presence of a massive brick or stone wall to increase heat gain. Dark colored walls absorb heat and release it into the vineyard during the evening. White walls intercept the sunlight and reflect it back onto the vines. While in the Baltics we saw both approaches used with good results.

Figure 7-2. A vineyard in Latvia with an ideal system for ripening grapes in an extremely cool climate: a light-reflective wall, floating row cover for autumn frost protection, and vines trained at an optimal angle to sun.

Plastic and Reflective Mulches. Recent studies in France show that covering the soil around the vines with black plastic as a way to promote ripening is overrated. In fact, in these studies, black plastic mulch had almost no effect at all. The only mulch that was even moderately effective was aluminum foil which that reflects and scatters sunlight back into the vine and onto the fruit clusters. A new self-reflecting mulch called SRM-Red™ has proven useful in ripening early tomatoes and strawberries. SRM-Red™ works by reflecting infrared light up into the plant. Trials with grapes have not been reported, but growers in the very coolest regions for ripening may wish to experiment with this material. Remember that only low head trained vines, with the fruit relatively close to the ground, will benefit from a reflective mulch. Vines on higher training systems will not.

Specialized Trellises. The interception of sunlight can be increased by optimally orienting the vine toward the sun. This means orienting the vine to the south. Also, the angle of the vine toward the sun can be manipulated to some advantage. The sun's radiation is greatest when it strikes foliage and fruit at right angles. The more we can orient the vine at right angles to the sun's rays, the more energy it will intercept. The optimal angle of the vine to the sun will depend upon your latitude. For example, assume that the sun is 45 degrees above the horizon at midday on midsummer. Spreading the vine out on a divided trellis that is at a 45 degree angle to the ground will place it at right angles to the sun during the period of peak radiation. An excellent trellis system that illustrates this principle was devised by Andrash Fazekash in Gulbene, Latvia, and is shown in Figure 7-2. Note the wall in the background and the use of a floating row cover for early autumn frost protection.

Techniques for Frost Protection

Floating Row Covers. In the Baltics we often heard growers lament, "If I could just get by that first frost in early September, I would have two more weeks of nice weather for ripening." Early killing frosts that cut short the ripening season are the norm for many northern growers. One possible solution is to cover your vines with a material that provides some frost protection. A wide variety of horticulture fabric materials now are available that, under the right conditions, can provide up to 10 °F (5.5 °C) of frost protection. That is usually enough to survive an early frost and extend the growing season. These materials are so lightweight that they virtually float over the vine and do not need to be supported.

Be aware that all of these row cover materials will cut down on the amount of solar radiation striking the vines underneath. Generally, the better the frost protection afforded by a material, the less its light transmittance, leaving you with a tradeoff. You can avoid an early frost by using the cover. But will the additional radiation gained by extending the season exceed the radiation lost by virtue of the cover's less than perfect transmittance of solar energy? It is probably a good tradeoff if you can extend your ripening season by 1 to 2 weeks of sunny weather.

Tuffbell™ is the one product we have found that claims to combine good transmittance (92%) with good frost protection (up to 10 °F or 5.6 °C). This fabric consists of two layers of a finely netted material, rather than spunbonded polypropylene. Its absorption properties allow moisture to freeze within the row cover and form a protective shield over the crop, much like an igloo.

Table 7-2 provides data on several commonly available floating row cover materials. These are usually available in widths ranging from 10 to 65 ft. (3 to 20 m) and in lengths ranging from 20 to 2600 ft. (6 m to 800 m).

Product	Material	Weight Oz./yd^2 (g/m^2)	Light Transmittance	Degree of Frost Protection
Typar T-518	Spunbonded Polypropylene	1.25 (41.2)	70%	Up to 6 °F (3.6 °C)
Agribon 19	Spunbonded Polypropylene	0.55 (17.6)	85%	Up to 4 °F (2.3 °C)
Agribon 30	Spunbonded Polypropylene	0.90 (29.4)	70%	Up to 6 °F (3.6 °C)
Agribon 50	Spunbonded Polypropylene	1.5 (49.4)	50%	Up to 8 °F (4.5 °C)
Agribon 70	Spunbonded Polypropylene	2.0 (65.9)	30%	Up to 10 °F (5.6 °C)
Tuffbell	Netted Material		92-95%	Up to 10 °F (5.6 °C)

Table 7-2. Some commonly available floating row cover materials.

Spraying for Frost Protection. Several new products are available on the market today that can provide some protection against frost injury. These materials have not been systematically tested in vineyards, but they are worthy of experimentation in very cool regions where frost threatens to damage emerging shoots in the spring. One of these new products is Frost Shield™. This material is a microscopically thin pro-polymer that forms a permeable protective coating on developing buds or on the foliage and fruit of your vines. This film inhibits water loss and slows the rate of cooling caused by evaporative transpiration. The internal temperature of the plant remains above the freezing point. Product specifications for Frost Shield™ indicate that you can expect protection down to 25 to 28 °F (-3.9 °C to –2.2 °C). A spray of Frost Shield™ needs 4 to 6 hours to dry completely. When dry, it is very resistant to rain. Another product to try is Anti-Stress 2000™, a latex-based material produced by Polymer-Ag, Inc. This product has produced excellent results in apple orchards in the United Kingdom, providing protection of apple blossoms at temperatures of 25 to 28 °F (-3.9 °C to –2.2 °C).

Vine Growing in an Unheated Plastic House

If all else fails, you can almost guarantee good ripening of your grapes if you simply grow them in an unheated plastic house. University of Helsinki researcher Meeri Saario reports that the seasonal heat accumulation in her unheated plastic house just outside Helsinki nearly equals the heat accumulation in Minneapolis, Minnesota. The plastic house accumulates 75 to100% more heat than an outdoor site in Helsinki. In the extremely cool environs of Helsinki, the plastic house extends the grape growing season by about one month in the spring and one month in the fall. Saario grows many Minnesota grape selections under plastic and harvests them in excellent condition. This is a drastic approach but well worth the effort if your ripening conditions are extreme and there is no other way to gain sufficient heat for ripening even the earliest grape varieties.

Enough grapes to supply a home winery producing about 27 gallons (100 l) of wine per year could be grown in a plastic house measuring about 20 x 40 ft. (6 m x 12 m). The height of the plastic house should be at least 13 ft. (4 m) to allow ventilation space above the vines and to serve as a temperature buffer. Good ventilation is essential in the plastic house to prevent mildew and to allow excess heat to dissipate in summertime. A door on each end of the plastic house and a window in the roof serves this purpose well. If the plastic house is set up on well-drained soil, the vines can be planted directly into the soil without concern about excess wetness. Vines can be extremely vigorous in the plastic house. Be prepared to manage the vines for good light exposure by positioning the shoots, removing weak shoots, and removing leaves around ripening clusters. Finally, winter temperatures inside the unheated plastic house are about the same as temperatures outside, so choose varieties that are winter hardy for your area.

When to Harvest

Depending on the location and the grape variety, the developing grape berries reach veraison by mid-July to mid-August. This is the date of first noticeable color change in the grape berry. Veraison is an exciting time to the grapegrower because it marks the beginning of a whole host of physiological changes in the grape berry that, within six to eight weeks, will result in ripe grapes for harvest. Sugar content begins to increase. Acid content begins to decrease. Coloration appears. Varietal flavors develop. The berries soften. The seeds turn from green to brown. All of these are potential indicators of grape ripeness. How do we measure them and interpret them? How do we know when the grapes are ripe?

Sugar Content

Sugar content increases in the grape berry following veraison and eventually levels out at season's end. If we were to harvest the grapes based on sugar content alone, then we would look for a sugar content of about 21 to 22 °Brix in grapes intended for white table wines and 22 to 24 °Brix for red wines. But there are many examples of how sugar content alone can fool you about ripeness. Sugar can be at these ideal levels while acidity is still too high or pH too low for fine winemaking. The perception of sweetness in the grapes may actually be enhanced by the high acidity. Don't be fooled by this. Don't harvest based on a quick subjective perception of sweetness.

In some varieties, particularly muscat types, the full floral varietal aroma and flavor develop a week or two after the accumulation of sugar begins to slow up. Harvesting based on sugar content alone would be premature. Waiting a week or so would have some significant benefits for wine quality. *Labrusca* types present quite the opposite problem. Most *labrusca* grapes will never reach these optimal sugar levels no matter how long you let them hang on the vine. They struggle to reach 18 to 20 °Brix. The longer you let them hang, the stronger the *labrusca* flavor gets. Allow these to ripen to 17 to 18 °Brix and then harvest them before the intense flavors develop.

The best way to measure sugar content in the vineyard is with a hand refractometer. Considering the variation in sugar content among berries even in the same cluster, measuring one berry will not do. Rather, you should make refractometer measurements of sugar content on at least six to ten berries taken from different parts of the cluster and compute an average sugar content.

Acidity

Grape acids decrease as the grapes ripen. This decrease in acidity often continues for a week or two after the berries have developed sufficient sugar for fine winemaking. Resist the temptation to harvest based on sugar alone. If some warm autumn days follow, then significant natural reductions in acidity will occur. The natural reduction of malic acid is particularly important to the winemaker. As we will discuss in Chapter 9, wines with an excess of malic acid will tend to taste green and sharp, and the sharpness will not disappear with time. Red wine musts can be put through malolactic fermentation to reduce the malic acid content during winemaking. But this usually is not an option for fruity, floral whites. Malolactic fermentation reduces the freshness and fruitiness. Malic acid in these fruity whites should be reduced, naturally, in the vineyard, by means of a well-timed harvest. Barring a heavy frost, it is well worth waiting for this natural late-season drop in malic acid before harvesting your grapes.

Titratable acidity, the combination of tartaric and malic acids, can be measured in juice samples by doing a simple acid-base titration with sodium hydroxide. A standard method for this test is included in most beginning texts on winemaking.

pH

Acids are compounds consisting of hydrogen ions (H+) bound to negatively charged ions, such as carboxyls (COOH-). Our perception of tartness or acidity in wine comes from these hydrogen compounds. In solution, acidic compounds more or less break apart or dissociate. Strong acids, such as sulfuric acid, are the most broken up, having a high percentage of free floating H+ ions. Weaker acids, such as those found in grape juice, have relatively few free H+ ions in solution. The more free floating hydrogen ions there are in the solution, the more tart the solution tastes to us. Hydrogen ion potential, or pH, is a measure of how many hydrogen ions are combined as acids versus how many are floating free. The more free floating hydrogen ions there are, the lower the pH and the higher our perception of acidity. Conversely, the more the hydrogen is combined into acidic compounds, the fewer the number of free floating hydrogen ions and the higher the pH. pH is an excellent measure of grape ripeness. Depending on the variety, ripe grapes will have a pH of between 3.00 to 3.55. A portable "pH pen" with sufficient accuracy for assessing grape ripeness can be purchased for around $75 (US).

Color and Tannins

Anthocyanins are the pigments that give the grape berry its characteristic blue-black color. Anthocyanins also are responsible for the red color and astringency or mouth feel of red wines. Anthocyanins increase after veraison at an almost identical rate to that of sugar. Do you actually have to measure anthocyanin content, then, to determine ripeness? Not really. Since they are so similar in their development, harvesting at an optimal sugar content usually ensures a sufficient content of anthocyanins, as well.

Flavor Components

Taste the ripening grapes periodically. Crush some berries between your fingers and smell the juice. The first year you grow a variety, leave some clusters to hang late into the autumn. Continue to taste them and see what kinds of varietal flavors develop and how intense they are. After doing this for several years, you will learn how the flavor and aroma of each variety develops and changes as it ripens. These sensations will become benchmarks for judging ripeness.

But how do you know when varietal flavor and aroma have reached an appropriate level for fine winemaking? At least for the highly-flavored grapes of the *labrusca* and muscat types, full varietal flavor tends to develop late in the ripening period, often after other indicators of ripeness, such as sugar, acidity, and pH, have reached their optimum harvest values. For muscat grapes, this suggests that patience is the best policy. You will prematurely harvest if you pick the grapes solely on the basis of sugar and acidity. If you wait an extra week or so you can reap the benefits of flavor and aroma compounds that develop late. For *labrusca* grapes, the message is quite the opposite. If you let them hang until sugar and acidity are optimal, you will harvest some extremely foxy grapes. If you harvest them early you may have to chaptalize the must and/or modify must acidity, but the must will tend to be fruity, rather than foxy.

Texture Changes

Ripe grapes pull away from the stem easily. Unripe grapes do not. Bite into the grape berries as they ripen and you will notice texture changes from veraison to full ripeness. The grape berry softens as it ripens. In fully ripe grapes the skin collapses easily to the bite and the pulp is viscous, not watery.

Color of Seeds

Fully mature grapes have brown seeds, not beige or tan. This is about as simple an indication of ripeness as you can find. Check the seed color. If the seeds are not brown, the grapes probably are not quite ripe.

Grape ripeness should be assessed based on a composite of the ripeness indices described above. Some of these are easily measured using instruments (refractometers, pH meters, etc.), but some can be assessed only by the human senses. Do not fall into the trap of technology and consider only the things that can be measured with an instrument. These quantifiable things are very important, but, in addition, try to spend time in your vineyard so you can taste, smell, and observe the changes in the grape berries that only people can detect. Figure 7-3 provides a checklist that will help you apply these subjective sensory criteria for grape ripeness. Take this checklist with you to the vineyard when you evaluate grape ripeness and memorize it through practice. Only with these observations in hand can you interpret the true ripeness of the grape for winemaking purposes.

Attribute	Description/Sensation	Points
Color	Green (lack of color)	0
	Color change; translucent	1
	Fully mature color	2
	Over mature color	1
Ease of removal of berries from pedicels	High resistance of pedicels	0
	Moderate resistance	1
	Little/no resistance	2
Texture upon touch	Firm	0
	Soft/elastic	1
	Shriveled; loss of shape	0
Texture-initial bite		
Ease of skin collapse	High resistance to pressure	0
	Moderate resistance	1
	Low resistance	2
Mechanical features of pulp	Thin, watery	0
	Viscous	2
	Jelly-like	1
Aroma	None	0
	Characteristic varietal aroma	2
Flavor upon chewing		
Initial character (upon chewing)	Unripe; green; bland	0
	Some varietal character	1
	High varietal character	2
Flavor release from skin	None	0
	Typical varietal character	1
Aftertaste	None	0
	Bitter; Astringent; phenolic	0
	Typical varietal character	1
Maximum Total Score		**15**

Figure 7-3. The Eschenbruch checklist of subjective criteria for evaluating grape ripeness (from Reynolds, 1996).

Note: These criteria for ripeness do not apply to *Vitis labrusca* hybrids which usually require harvest earlier than these criteria would suggest.

References

Harvest Quality/Vineyard Practices

Gu, S. Shoot thinning , shoot positioning, and leaf removal. *Vineyard and Vintage View*. Murli Dharmadhikari (Ed.) 13-5, 1-3, 1998.

Jackson, D.I. and Lombard, P.B. Environmental and management practices affecting grape composition and wine quality: a review. *American Journal of Enology and Viticulture*. 44-4, 409-430, 1993.

Koblet, W. and Perret, P. Translocation of photosynthate in grape vines. *Vinifera Wine Growers Journal.* Winter, 211-218, 1979.

Koblet, W. Canopy management in Swiss vineyards. In: *Proceedings of the Second International Cool Climate Viticulture and Enology Symposium.* Auckland, New Zealand, 161-164, 1988.

Long, Z. Manipulation of grape flavor in the vineyard: California North Coast region. In: *Proceedings of the 6th Australian Wine Industry Technical Conference.* 82-88, 1986.

Long, Z. Developing wine flavor in the vineyard. *Practical Winery and Vineyard*. July-August, 6-9. 1997.

Morrison, J. The effects of shading on the composition of Cabernet Sauvignon grape berries. In: *Proceedings of the Second International Cool Climate Viticulture and Enology Symposium.* Auckland, New Zealand, 144-146,1988.

Peterson, D. Cluster thinning to control crop size. *Fruit Grower*. August, 34, 1997.

Reynolds, A.G. and Wardle, D.A. Impact of various canopy manipulation techniques on growth, yield, fruit composition, and wine quality of Gewurtztraminer. *American journal of Enology and Viticulture*. 40-2, 121-129, 1989.

Reynolds, A.G. and Wardle, D.A.. Influence of fruit microclimate on monoterpene levels of Gewurtztraminer. *American Journal of Enology and Viticulture*. 40-3, 149-154.,1989.

Reynolds, A.G., Sholberg, P.L., and Wardle, D.A. Canopy manipulation of Okanagan Riesling vines for improvement of winegrape quality. *Canadian Journal of Plant Science*. 72, 489-496, 1992.

Reynolds, A.G., Wardle, D.A., Hall, J.W., and Dever, M. Fruit maturation of Okanagan Riesling grapes: Effect of site, year, and basal leaf removal. *Fruit Varieties Journal*. 49-4, 213-224, 1995.

Reynolds, A.G., Wardle, D.A., Hall, J.W., and Dever, M. Fruit maturation of four *vinifera* cultivars in response to vineyard location and basal leaf removal. *American Journal of Enology and Viticulture*. 46-4, 542-558, 1995.

Reynolds, A. G. and Wardle, D. A. Impact of viticultural practices on grape monoterpenes and their relationship to wine sensory response. *Proceedings of the 4th International Symposium on Cool Climate Viticulture and Enology*. 1-17, 1996.

Reynolds, A.G., Wardle, D.A., and Dever, M. Vine performance, fruit composition, and wine sensory attributes of Gewurtztraminer in response to vineyard location and canopy manipulation. *American Journal of Enology and Viticulture*. 47-1, 77-92, 1996.

Rojas-Lara, B.A. and Morrison, J. C. Differential effects of shading fruit or foliage on the development and composition of grape berries. *Vitis*. 28, 199-208, 1989.

Season Extension with Soil and Row Covers

Agent, O., Baldy, C., Robin, J.P., Boulet, J.C., Sanon, M. and Suard, et. B. Effects of artificial soil covers on the internal temperatures of grape berries during the grape maturation. *Journal International des Sciences de la Vigne et du Vin*. 29-3, 131-142, 1995.

Appropriate Technology Transfer for Rural Areas (ATTRA). Report on season extension in horticultural crops. 1999. See at http://www.attra.org

Evaluating Grape Ripeness

Coomb, B.G. and Iland, P.G. Grape berry development. In: *Proceedings of the Sixth Australian Wine Industry Technical Conference*. 50-54, 1987.

Hrazdina, G. and Keller, M. Physiological changes during development and ripening in grape berries-indices to assess ripeness. *1996 New York Wine Industry Workshop*. Geneva, New York, 68-74, 1996.

Reynolds, A. G. Assessing and understanding grape maturity. *1996 New York Wine Industry Workshop*. Geneva, New York, 75-88, 1996.

Chapter 8

Getting Started

Growing high-quality wine grapes in a cold climate is a remarkable and difficult feat. To make it worthwhile, the winemaker needs to know how to get the best from the hard-earned harvest. The next chapter starts with the fundamentals of winemaking, which serve to minimize common mistakes. This is enough knowledge to make drinkable wines with many cold climate grape varieties in good years. If you settle for drinkable wines, however, you will be missing much of what these varieties have to offer.

We hope that you will set lofty winemaking goals and will commit a moderate amount of money to equipment. We assume that you want to minimize the formal study of the underlying science that guides modern winemaking practice. Finally, we assume that you have tried winemaking at least a few times and that you already own one or more basic winemaking texts. If not, you should. We recommend *Grapes into Wine by* Philip Wagner, *Modern Winemaking* by Philip Jackisch, and the second edition of *Home Winemaking Step by Step* by Jon Iverson. They cover basics that we do not and are valuable references. *Modern Winemaking* is currently out of print but may still be available from some sources. Finding a copy would be well worth the search. You should also own at least one book on wine tasting (see Chapter 14).

The routine part of winemaking, avoiding major mistakes by following basic winemaking procedure, is laid out in the next two chapters. Even good home winemakers sometimes stray from sound basic procedures. The result is problem wines. Sound procedure is the foundation of successful winemaking. It relies on the right chemistry and good sanitation to avoid problems that would require much more detailed knowledge to fix. In other words, you don't need to know all of the details when everything is going right.

Sound procedures are essential but will rarely be enough to bring out the best in a wine. Rather, making outstanding wines requires the ability to analytically taste a young wine and make judgments to enhance and balance it. Later chapters will tell you when judgments are likely to be required and how to gain the needed experience to make them.

Cold climate winemaking is mainly *vinifera*-style winemaking with some minor adaptations. We can readily apply most of what has been learned over thousands of years about winemaking with *vinifera* varieties in a wide range of climates, but we must watch out for the chemical quirks sometimes found in hybrid grapes. Wines produced from many of the recommended hybrid grape varieties require more balancing or shaping, augmenting or suppressing, than wines produced from *vinifera* grapes. Typically, less is known and written about making wine from hybrid grape varieties. In the case of some Baltic and even some of the Minnesota varieties, practically nothing is known. The winemaker is truly on his or her own! Unlike winemakers in the Napa Valley or Bordeaux, you are probably not living in a winemaking community where a neighbor can give expert advice. Simply put, we cold climate winemakers are an obscure minority group. We've got to stick together and learn from each other when we can.

Most winemakers working with hybrid grape varieties will not be making wine on a commercial scale, which has drawbacks and a few advantages. You will probably be working with more primitive equipment and, unless you make a point of it, will not have a sterile, well-laid out work area that promotes sound winemaking practice. Your costs per bottle of wine will be higher in dollars and time. To your advantage, cost per bottle may not be so critical if you are making only a few cases per batch. You also will not have the dual tyranny of dealing with a morass of legal requirements, or with aiming to please the palates of the public.

Equipping and Stocking the Basic Home Winery

A visit to ten home winemakers' facilities would probably show ten different ways to set up a work area. Likewise, the amount invested in equipment would probably vary by at least a factor of ten. Achieving quality as a home winemaker is hard enough even when you have all of the equipment and supplies you need. Plan to spend $US 500 or more. If this gives you pause, consider watching or helping a winemaker who is already well equipped. Seeing equipment in use will give you a clear picture of its relative value. Consider also that the dollar investment is dwarfed by the investment of time and effort needed to become a competent home winemaker.

Fruit Crushing and Pressing
The cheapest and simplest way to crush grapes is to put them in a large food grade plastic bucket (a primary fermenter) and crush them by hand or tread on them with very clean rubber boots. You can also use a large nylon mesh press bag to press out the juice by hand. If you make your own bag, make it strong and big enough to fit over a five-gallon bucket. A large, strong colander is useful for allowing the last of the juice to slowly drain off. This approach works with batches of five gallons or less, but most winemakers will want a crusher/destemmer and a wine press as volume increases.

Must Containers

Buy at least one ten-gallon (35 l) or larger food grade plastic primary fermenter with a cover. Grape acids can leach nasty chemicals out of the wrong kind of plastic. Primary fermenters are nothing more than bucket-like containers with covers that close tightly enough to keep out fruit flies. The ten-gallon size is right for 5 to 7 gallon (19 to 25 l) batches of wine. If you plan always to work with three-gallon (10 l) batches or less, then you can work with much cheaper five-gallon (20 l) food grade plastic buckets.

Secondary Fermenters

Five gallons or 20 liters usually becomes the standard batch for home winemakers. You are likely to need a number (roughly double what you think) of five-gallon glass carboys and maybe a few three-gallon carboys. You may want a few plastic five-gallon carboys for short-term storage or cold stabilization when there is the possibility of the wine freezing. One-gallon (3.9 l) glass jugs, usually available without cost, are handy for small batches. You will need a good supply of airlocks and stoppers. Most five-gallon carboys take a size 6.5 stopper, while gallon jugs usually require a size 7.5 or 8. When in doubt, order a range of sizes.

Transfer (racking) Equipment

A handy siphon can be made by squeezing a six or seven foot (2 m) length of food grade 3/8 inch (1 cm) clear plastic tubing over a two foot (60 cm) length of polyvinyl chloride (PVC) pipe. Have several on hand.

Measuring Equipment

Hydrometer
Thermometer (preferably floating)
Acid test kit
SO2 test kit (Titrettes)
Measuring spoons and cups
Kitchen scale

Bottling Equipment

Wine bottles
Bottle closures (preferably corks)
Bottle corker

Other Equipment (we find essential but many others don't)

CO^2 tank (to help minimize oxygen contact)
Refrigerator (to control cool fermentation temperature and allow for easy cold stabilization)
Hot pad or electric blanket (to control warm fermentation temperature)
pH meter (to measure the acidity that affects wine chemistry)
Wine thief (to convieniently way draw wine samples)

Chemicals and Supplies You Will Need

Potassium metabisulfite (or Campden tablets)

Yeast cultures

Yeast nutrient

Pectic enzyme

Tartaric acid and Citric acid

Acid reduction chemicals: Calcium carbonate, Potassium bicarbonate

Fining chemicals: Sparklloid, Bentonite

Potassium sorbate

Glycerine

Polyclar

Soda ash

Other Equipment and Expenses

Some would include a filter in a list of essentials but we do not. Good filters can easily cost $US 500. Even disregarding cost, they trade improvement in clarity for a slight loss of flavor and aroma. They can be very good at drastically reducing the amount of yeast cells remaining in a wine, which can be an advantage. If we were commercial winemakers, we probably would want a good filtration system.

One final cost that should be added to the list is tuition, which includes money for buying exemplary commercial wines and reference texts and for attending commercial tastings. If you plan to make a concerted effort to become a good winemaker, you should allow a fair amount of money for continuing education. Most dedicated amateurs have more than $US 1,000 invested in equipment and supplies and produce enough good wine to make the expenditure worthwhile.

The Basic Home Winery: an Efficient Work Area

Winemaking is messy, requires moving of heavy containers, and has a way of sprawling out into more space than you would think possible. Good planning, however, can hold the headaches to a minimum. Here are activities that have specific work area requirements.

Crushing and Pressing

Have a convenient way to wheel grapes to the work area. You will want to avoid stairs whenever possible. Whenever you crush or press, you will probably get some crushed grapes or juice on the floor and walls. The juice is sticky and stains readily. We press on a patio-like area outside the basement door whenever weather allows. Otherwise, we haul the containers of grapes into the basement work area. The concrete floor is sealed but still tends to stain unless it is quickly cleaned up. Any crushing or pressing should be near water access for easy rinsing. Don't try this in cramped quarters. This requires space.

Temperature-Controlled Areas

Ideal fermentation temperature for red wines approaches 85 °F (30 °C), so you need a warm spot for one or more of your primary fermenters. If you keep the fermenter off the floor in an area of 70 °F (21 °C) or above, you can usually warm the must enough with an electric blanket or a heating pad. White wines should typically ferment near 55 °F (13 °C), which can be achieved in some cool basements during the winter. An old refrigerator with shelves removed, that can be set from 25 to 55 °F (-4 to 13 °C), solves the problem. It also comes in handy for cold soaking (Chapter 10) and cold stabilization (Chapter 9), which requires temperatures approaching 25 °F (-4 °C). None of these activities is particularly messy, nor does it require much space.

Racking and Bottling

Racking is usually done by placing the full carboy on a stable work surface, roughly three feet (1 m) high, and then siphoning. A five-gallon (18.9 l) glass carboy filled with wine weighs about 52 lb (24 kg) - plastic carboys weigh about ten pounds (4 kg) less - so you don't want to do this on a slippery floor, or with a bad back, or with bad lifting technique. If the weight is a problem for you, there are many adaptations to make this less of a problem. Bottling and racking have enough similar requirements that the same work area can be used for both. Racking and bottling do not seem like messy jobs, but invariably something will spill, squirt, or break, so it should be done in an area that is easily cleaned up. Also, you should be near a laundry tub or a sink to rinse carboys and siphoning equipment.

Washing and Drying

A surprising amount of a winemaker's time goes into rinsing out equipment, carboys, and bottles. Laundry tubs work fine for most things. If you use recycled bottles, you will need a place to store bottles upside down for the few days it takes them to dry. Some avoid these steps and buy new bottles, but at eighty cents per bottle, most winemakers prefer recycling.

Laboratory for Testing and Evaluation

Comfort, good lighting, and easy access to test equipment are required. The lab and testing area can be small, but it should be close to where you store the wines you want to test. This area often impresses guests who wonder about how serious you really are about winemaking, so make it look like a compact science lab. Exotic glassware and electronic test instruments should be prominently displayed, whether or not you ever use them!

Wine Cellar

This is yet another area to show off to your guests. Stable, cool temperature, from 50 to 65 °F (10 to 18 °C) is optimal, with as little variation as possible. Absence of light and extreme vibration are also very important. This is a good place to store stable carboys of wine. Do not try to squeeze by with minimal storage space. The need for wine cellar space is easy to underestimate.

General Storage

Cases of empty bottles, extra carboys, and all of the equipment and supplies that do not have a designated spot all seem to sprawl out and colonize far more space than you would think possible. None of these things has unusual storage requirements, and they are relatively lightweight, so store them out of the way whenever you can.

Now that you know the specifics of the required areas, the next task is to be sure that you can readily move heavy, bulky things from one work area to another. A good plan and some inventiveness will minimize workflow problems and hold down the sprawl to a tolerable level.

Becoming a zealous home winemaker probably will take more dedicated space than you had originally planned. It would be very difficult to find enough space in an apartment with no basement work area. The money invested, space consumed, and mess to be contained is roughly comparable to buying a few basic power woodworking tools and using them in your basement.

Enough said about the logistics and mechanics of outfitting and setting up a winemaker's work area. Let's go on to the winemaking.

Chapter 9

Staying on the Path of Established Winemaking Practice

Good winemaking combines following mundane winemaking procedure with subjective, artistic judgments. We will start with the mundane, because it is the foundation of winemaking. Our model, referred to here as "staying on the path," is a vastly simplified approach to winemaking. Its' simplicity lies in practices that will help you avoid common problems, most of which would require experience and additional knowledge to solve. Following the model of 15 basic points would seem like a fairly forthright thing for amateur winemakers to do, yet there are constant pressures to violate the model. Two things account for much of this. First there is the delay in seeing the consequences of our mistakes. It can be many months until it becomes apparent that something has gone wrong with the wine, without any obvious connection to a winemaking mistake. Second, many of us are not by nature meticulous and detail oriented. Strictly following basic procedure is not, for us, the appealing part of winemaking, but we push ourselves to do so, because we know that good results rest on this foundation.

While it is unlikely that you can get away with making an exceptional wine without following the fundamentals, occasionally you can make an exceptional wine by doing nothing but following the fundamentals. Our first truly good wine, made in 1991, is a case in point. It was a Muscat Canelli, made from frozen juice ordered from Peter Brehm, who brokers premium quality frozen juice and crushed grapes from the West Coast of the United States. Our winemaking contribution was to "stay on the path" and not make mistakes. What emerged, without any special creativity from us, was a wonderfully aromatic, fruity, high acid wine that the wine judges loved. We have seen similar examples from other relatively new winemakers who were extremely careful and produced some exceptional wines without applying any of the artistic shaping that you will learn about in subsequent chapters.

Our exceptional results required not only sound basic procedure but also exceptional grapes that yielded a wine requiring almost no balancing or blending. There is more to learn about winemaking than following the fundamentals, but none of the artistry will matter if you do not "stay on the path."

Simply put, "staying on the path" consists of establishing an environment where the yeast of your choice can thrive and turn the grapes into wine with minimal competition from spoilage agents. Very simple! Yet this is where most amateur winemakers go wrong by taking shortcuts, ignoring steps, or not being careful enough.

The Critical 15 Steps

1. Have a Plan

Ideally, you should make a written outline listing the sequence of what you will be doing and what equipment and supplies you will need before harvesting or receiving your grapes. Learn as much as you can about the grapes that you will be using. Consider what style of wine is typically made from this grape and anything unusual about this harvest that would cause you to handle it differently. Talk with somebody who has made a good wine from this variety.

2. Start With Good Sanitation

Anything that your grapes or juice will touch should be sanitized. Commercial wineries normally use steam or very hot water at temperatures of 165 °F (75 °C). Home winemakers can use a sulfite solution as a practical alternative. One teaspoon per gallon (1.7 g/l) of potassium metabisulfite and four teaspoons of citric acid per gallon (5 g/l) in water works well for general sanitation. Be sure to thoroughly dissolve the metabisulfite powder in water before adding the acid. Otherwise the acid solution will drive off some of the free sulfite gas (the active form of sulfite) before it can dissolve. Chlorine bleach solution can work for cleaning floors and other winery surfaces but otherwise has many drawbacks. Soap or detergent should be avoided because they leave residues that can impart off odors and flavors to the wine. It is good practice to mix a gallon or so of sulfite solution and have it handy for sterilizing anything that will touch your must or wine.

3. Work With Chilled Grapes in Good Condition

For temperatures above 50 °F (10 °C), the speed of most chemical reactions affecting grapes doubles for each 10 °C, almost always to your detriment. Your plan should help you minimize grape handling time from crush to fermentation. The exception is covered in Chapter 10, which describes the cold soak process. Also, you will want to minimize oxygen contact with the crushed grapes, particularly white wine grapes. The tannins in red wine grapes offer some early protection against oxidation. Siphon, don't pour, juice from white grapes. When working with a variety that oxidizes readily, consider adding a small amount of ascorbic acid or blanket the juice being siphoned with carbon dioxide.

4. Use Sulfite

Treat the crushed grapes or juice with 50 ppm of sulfite to stun or kill wild yeasts and spoilage organisms as well as to reduce the vulnerability to oxidation. Some expert winemakers avoid this step when they know that the grapes are in prime condition, with no broken skins or disease. Amateurs who want to hold sulfite levels to a minimum should use about 30 ppm, rather than forgoing sulfite at this stage.

5. Add Pectic Enzyme

Pectic enzyme should be added to break down the pectins in the grapes or juice. It will help extract color out of red grapes, might give you slightly more juice yield when pressing whites, and will minimize one cause of cloudiness in both whites and reds.

6. Measure the Sugar Level (Brix)

Measure the sugar content of the must with a hydrometer or a refractometer and correct it to a level that will produce the desired amount of alcohol for the style of wine you are making. The desired Brix level can range from 18 to 30 °Brix. Most wine styles, however, call for about 12 % alcohol. This requires a must corrected to 1.087 Specific Gravity or, if you are measuring with a refractometer, about 21.2 °Brix.

7. Measure the Acid Content

Measure the acid content of the must with a pH meter to be sure you are starting with a pH between 3.0 and 3.55 or, if you have only an acid test kit, within the range of 0.7 to 1.2 g/l of titratable acidity. Acidity, as measured by pH, affects many aspects of wine chemistry (particularly stability), while titratable acidity affects how acidic the wine tastes. Unfortunately, the two measures correlate only roughly. Most home winemakers do not measure pH, so they run the risk of being off the path without knowing it. Here are two rough indicators that tell you that the pH is probably in a safe range. If the yeast starts OK, then the pH is probably 3.0 or more. If the total acidity starts above 1.0 g/l, then the pH is probably below 3.6.

8. Inoculate With a Properly Started Yeast

You want to grow a huge population of viable yeast cells that will overwhelm the competition, because the slower starting spoilage organisms are always waiting for an opportunity. Sprinkling dry yeast on top of the must is not the way to do it! Dehydrated yeast needs to be carefully reactivated before it can thrive in a high sugar environment. First, the yeast needs to be rehydrated in water of about 100 °F (38 °C). Let the temperature of the rehydrating yeast gradually drop to about 70 °F (21 °C) during the approximately 30 minutes it takes to become viable. Once viable, the yeast cells need to feed within an hour or they will starve. Add two or three parts of room temperature juice to one part of yeast solution. Add the fermenting yeast to the main batch after 4-12 hours, when fermentation is obvious.

9. Add Yeast Nutrient

The yeast will start by feeding on available amino acids in the must and the nutrient you have added. But they could begin starving if they run low on nutrient. This adversely affects fermentation chemistry. By the time you detect symptoms such as off odors and/or slowed fermentation, your wine already may have lost some quality highlights and gained some problems we path-bound winemakers will not experience. Please note in Chapter 11 that some yeast varieties have much higher nutritional demands than others.

10. Ferment Whites Cool and Reds Warm

Room temperature works fine for the first day of fermentation after the yeast has been hydrated. But temperature should be carefully managed soon thereafter for best results. Cool temperature fermentation preserves the aromatics that give fruity white wines their character. It also allows some wine yeasts to produce fruity esters in higher volume than they would at warmer temperatures. Warm temperatures help to extract color, tannin, and flavor from the skins of reds. The peak temperature only needs to be maintained for two or three days before it can be allowed to gradually cool back to room temperature.

11. Smell, Taste, and Watch What is Happening

The time during fermentation and the month thereafter are periods of active change. If you pay close attention, you will soon learn what a normal fermentation and stabilization process looks, smells, and tastes like. Any major deviation from the typical pattern is most likely the sign of a problem. If you are alert to their onset, problems usually can be controlled with minimum damage. Be aware that yeast varieties often differ in their fermentation vigor, fermentation aroma, and rate of foaming. Likewise, white and red wines differ in their patterns of development because of fermentation temperatures and presence of tannin. This is not as complicated as it sounds. Just make a habit of paying close attention to your wine during fermentation and stabilization times, and learn from it.

12. Control Sulfite Levels Carefully

Sulfite usage requires precision and timing. Too much sulfite inhibits key biological and chemical processes. Not enough free sulfite leads to uncontrolled growth of spoilage microorganisms and rampant oxidation. So how much is the right amount? Presuming normal "on the path" chemistry, you should add 50 ppm at crush. Another 50 ppm should be added as fermentation gases dissipate or malolactic fermentation ends. At each racking, add 25 ppm of sulfite.

If you observe spoilage or early oxidation problems, add another 25 ppm of sulfite. Finally, add sulfite as needed at bottling to bring free sulfite levels to 80 ppm for sweetened table wines, 60 ppm for dry whites, and 40 ppm for dry reds. The malolactic fermentation reference in Chapter 11 describes an exception to this guideline.

Sulfite dissipates during fermentation, rackings, and in storage. It is sometimes difficult to know exactly how much free sulfite remains in the must or wine. In order to know the amount of free sulfite remaining in the wine, measure it using a simple one step sulfite test sold as Titrettes™. Then you can add precisely the amount of sulfite that you need to bring the level up to the standards described above.

13. Standardize the Routine Part of Winemaking
Keep written records so you know what you have done and when you have done it. Not only does this allow you to replicate success, it will allow you to rule out a lot of potential causes if something goes wrong.

14. Do not Bottle Unstable Wines
Chill (cold stabilize) all white wines to below 32 °F (0 °C) for three weeks to precipitate potassium bitartrate crystals. Clarify any haziness or cloudiness by fining, filtering, or waiting for the particles to settle.

15. Keep Wine Handling to a Minimum
While you should never skip purposeful steps, remember that each racking risks potential exposure to spoilage agents and too much oxygen. Sometimes you can combine steps in a single racking. Following a plan and standard procedure will help you minimize handling.

When you follow these 15 critical steps, you minimize your chances of making the typical mistakes of home winemakers. We reluctantly admit to still have an occasional problem wine in which the problems stem from not adequately following one of the 15 steps. We less reluctantly note similar problems in the results of other winemakers. Even if you do not manage to flawlessly adhere to the 15 steps, your winemaking should be free of fundamental mistakes and their resulting problems.

Chapter 10

13 Keys to Winemaking Quality

Chapter 9 has shown that you can avoid many common winemaking problems by following the rules. The rules, or "staying on the path," provide the foundation of good winemaking. So far, so good! Usually though, an experienced winemaker wants to build on that foundation and shape the wine into something special. This is done by bringing out the best a grape has to offer and showcasing its highlights. Faults should be masked or eliminated. Finally, missing highlights can sometimes be added by blending.

Before looking at what the winemaker does to shape the wine, let's acknowledge that most of the shaping has already occurred by harvest time. If the grower has done a good job and the season has been kind in yielding optimally ripened grapes, the winemaker's main task is to not get in the way of what is already there. When this happens, the winemaker holds meddling to a minimum by thinking, "Let the wine become what it wants to be." However, in the North, grapes often are not optimally ripe and a more manipulative role is required of the winemaker.

The 13 variables that the winemaker controls are, in some ways, an odd conglomeration. Manipulating some of these variables requires almost no judgment after you have a bit of experience. Others require winemaking judgments that will continue to improve throughout your winemaking career. We have presented the variables in the order in which you will encounter them. The decisions that require judgment gained over time are marked with an asterisk *.

Winemaking Keys

1. Selecting a Wine Style *
Making a decision about winemaking style is probably the most important of any of the 13 key winemaking variables. Certainly it requires the most judgement and experience. Choosing the best winemaking style for a grape depends on harvest conditions and the typical characteristics of that grape variety. Winemaking style decisions are most easily made knowing

how good wines have been balanced and applying that balance. If you know that high acid, fruity wines, balanced with a hint of residual sugar (Germanic-style) are often made from the St. Pepin grape, then this style is probably your best choice. Cold hardy grapes often lend themselves to making Germanic-style whites and medium bodied reds. Other varieties such as Foch can (and should) be made into different styles of wine depending on their ripeness. The idea of a winemaking style may be new to you. Either be patient, or do a quick skim of Chapter 11.

What can go wrong in selecting a wine style? You could downplay the assets of the current particular harvest and actually accentuate its faults, the exact opposite of what a versatile winemaker should do.

2. Harvesting Grapes*

Try to minimize all the ways grapes can deteriorate, from the moment of harvest until fermentation starts. Assuming that you have made a good decision about when to harvest (see Chapter 7), the way you harvest the grapes can either preserve the quality or degrade it. Harvest clusters that are nearly free of damage, such as breaks or punctures in the berry skins. Grapes in good condition will need less sulfite throughout the winemaking process and will yield a softer, more elegant wine. You may even want to sort out the best clusters and ferment them as a vintner's reserve. Harvest the grapes at as cool a temperature as possible and as gently as possible.

What can go wrong with the harvest? Hail, disease, wasps, birds, or raccoons can damage the fruit. Try to harvest the least damaged fruit and treat it as your vintner's reserve. Badly damaged fruit can introduce huge populations of acetobacter and wild yeasts (see Chapter 12) that can ruin your wine. Grapes infected with Powdery Mildew (Oidium) will produce wine with mildew flavors and aromas. All of these negative biological reactions are accelerated in grapes that are harvested at warm temperatures.

3. Enzymatic Fermentation (Carbonic Maceration)

Carbonic maceration depends on grape enzymes, rather than yeast, to begin the fermentation process. It requires whole uncrushed berries and an oxygen-free fermentation environment for the enzymes to convert sugar into alcohol and CO_2. About one week after carbonic maceration is started, the alcohol level will reach 2% and the whole berries will rupture from CO_2 pressure and cellular deterioration. The must should be pressed at this time and immediately inoculated with the yeast of your choice. Once yeast fermentation is active, malolactic bacteria should be introduced.

Partial carbonic maceration is a modified method that starts with 20% of the clusters crushed and inoculated with yeast and 80% whole clusters. Gently load whole clusters on top of the fermenting must. Blanket the must with CO_2 to push out the last of the oxygen and seal the primary fermenter with a tight cover. The actively fermenting must soon generates enough CO_2 at room temperature to protect the whole berries from oxygen contact. This gives it a safety advantage over the standard carbonic method. Apart from starting with 20% fermenting must, procedures are the same for both methods.

Carbonic maceration saves work. You do not have to crush and destem the grapes and there is no need to punch down the cap (see winemaking key number five on skin contact.) The real advantage though, is that it produces fruity esters distinct to the process and most evident in Nouveau Beaujolais wines. Also, carbonic maceration usually helps you avoid the herbaceousness produced by some varieties like St. Croix and Foch, particularly when Foch is not fully ripe. Do not use carbonic maceration for wines that you expect to be complex and long-lived.

What can go wrong with enzymatic fermentation? If oxygen is present, acetobacter will be busy producing volatile acidity, and you will smell vinegar. If it is pronounced, all is probably lost. However, a minute amount of vinegar aroma in a carbonic-style of wine is acceptable. Treat it with 50 ppm of sulfite and store it in a topped off carboy. Blending may be an option.

4. Crushing
Ideally, a crush would rupture all berry skins, but not tear stems or break seeds. Walking on the grapes with clean rubber boots in an open vat works well. You will want to switch to a mechanical crusher-destemmer if you are making five gallon (20 l) batches or more. You might want to first blanket the loaded vat with CO_2 to minimize oxygen exposure. Destem crushed red wine grapes immediately.

What can go wrong with the crush? If you are using a mechanical crusher, setting the rollers too close together can break seeds and tear stems. This can add a pronounced bitterness to the wine.

5. Skin Contact*
The general rule for white wines is to press out the juice with no skin contact. Many white musts, pressed from northern hybrid varieties, tend to oxidize readily and have skins that can impart an herbaceous character. However, there are times when up to 24 hours of skin contact under controlled conditions can intensify a pleasant varietal character and enhance the body and mouthfeel in white wines, and possibly increase juice yield by up 10 %. This method is called "cold soak." If you try the cold soak method, be sure the fruit is not damaged or diseased. Make sure the stems are lignified (woody). Taste them. If they have an obvious bitter taste, or are vegetal, you need to either remove them immediately after the crush or abandon the cold soak plan.

Red wines, on the other hand, usually derive their color, aroma, and flavor from the skins, so skin contact often extends throughout most of the fermentation process. Ideally, grapes should be chilled to 50 °F (10 °C) or less, crushed gently, sulfited to a maximum of 30 ppm, blanketed with CO_2, and treated with pectic enzyme. Pectic enzymes are all but inactive at temperatures below 50 °F (10 °C). So, we are stuck with a balancing act. We must hold back some chemical and microbial processes, but encourage others. While cold-soaking reds will not, in most cases, do any harm, the skin contact that matters is during fermentation. Punching down the cap twice a day optimizes extraction by keeping the skins in contact with the juice and the ever-increasing alcohol in the must.

What can go wrong with skin contact? Skin contact for whites is a measure of the winemaker's boldness. If words like " harsh," "rough," "stemmy," "bitter" come to mind as you taste your wine, then you were too bold! Some of this harshness may soften with time, but if these characteristics are pronounced, you may want to consider choosing an alternative, less fruity style. Have another winemaker, whose judgment you value, taste the juice at this point. Tasters who know only finished wines usually cannot help at this stage. You might want to consider a style that uses a warmer fermentation, followed by malolactic fermentation, followed by oak.

Another problem with cold soak processing is that a wild yeast fermentation can start. Not only will this interfere with the settling process, but the wild yeast may also impart undesirable flavors and aromas. If all of this sounds too hazardous to you, then forego the cold soak of whites for now and try it when you have more experience. Extended skin time for cold hardy reds is generally not warranted because more than ample color is readily extractable. The desirable tannins, which leach out slowly, are usually not present for extraction in grape hybrids.

6. Pressing
Press both reds and whites with a minimum amount of pressure. If you have a convenient way of separating out the free run juice without going through the press, do it. If the stems are still in your crushed pulp, they will aid in the flow of juice. Some winemakers add rice hulls as a press aid to ease juice flow. After flow has all but stopped, ease off the press, break up the press cake, and press again.

Keep the juice from this final press run for a separate fermentation. It is usually too harsh to blend back with the free run and first press juice. Occasionally, it can be used as a positive blending component for another wine.

A large, fine-meshed nylon press bag is a good alternative to a press for small batches. You can clean a bag faster than a press, but the juice yield may suffer.

Chill and settle all of your white press runs for twelve to twenty-four hours. Then rack them off the sediment and into a fermenter.

Red wines are typically pressed before fermentation is completed, as Specific Gravity approaches 1.000. But there are regular exceptions to this rule, as you will see in later chapters.

What can go wrong with pressing? You can be too greedy and try to squeeze out the last ounce of juice. Note that this is no real problem if you have kept your final press run separate. Your "white" juice may become orange-pink in color if you didn't clean your press well enough after pressing the last red. The off color can probably be stripped out with Polyclar, but you have been issued a color-coded warning ticket!

7. Selecting a Yeast

The yeast you select is determined by the winemaking style and, to a lesser degree, by the grape variety. While there is some overlap, white and red wines usually call for different yeast selections.

Our yeast choices for white wines are:

Premier Couvee (also known as *Prise de Mousse* and *EC 1118*) ferments cleanly and vigorously, even at low temperatures. It often imparts citrus-like aroma and flavor. It has high alcohol tolerance and is low foaming. It is good with all winemaking styles but, because of its cold and SO_2 tolerances, is hard to stop when you want to retain residual sugar. If we had only one yeast to work with, this would be it.

Pasteur Champagne (*UCD 595*) is closely related to *Premier Couvee*, with which it shares most characteristics. It is more neutral in aroma and flavor and it foams more. It is less vigorous and has more compact lees.

Cote de blancs (*Epernay 2; Fermiblanc Arom* or *FB-500* is very similar) is a low- foaming, slowly fermenting yeast, with a lot of floral and fruity aromas, particularly when the wine is young. Its low alcohol tolerance and susceptibility to cold shock make it easy to stop when residual sugar is desired.

71-B (*INRA 1122*) produces high-ester nouveau-style wines. It metabolizes up to one third of malic acid present in juice (compared to about 15% with other yeasts) and is useful if you are not planning a malolactic fermentation. This yeast is a very heavy feeder and will need at least double the nutrient of any other yeast.

K1-V116. The "K" is for its killer factor, which quickly overruns wild yeasts. It can ferment to 20% alcohol with proper nutrition.

D47 is another "killer" that produces enhanced mouthfeel and fruity flavors in some varieties.

Wadenswil is very cold tolerant and low foaming. Used with Riesling and Gewurztraminer, it could be tried with Germanic style cold climate white wines.

M2 is a selection offering enhanced pure fruit character and mouthfeel. We have not personally sampled wines made from this selection, but it has much promise for both white and red hybrid varieties.

Our yeast choices for red wines are:

Pasteur Red is a very good all-around choice for red wines. It foams a bit, but not enough to be a problem.

Lalvin BM 45 is a recent and promising selection that produces good mouthfeel and soft and aromatic fruity notes. It is a slow starter and makes relatively high nutrient demands.

Premier Couvee, Pasteur Champagne, 71B, and K1V116 all can be used to ferment reds if you need what they have to offer. Generally though, they will not be as good as *Pasteur Red* and *BM 45* at extracting color and tannin from skins.

What can go wrong with yeast selection? Your choice may bring out weaknesses or downplay strengths. You must know what wine aromas and flavors you are trying to enhance or suppress to take advantage of specific yeast characteristics. Using a yeast that extracts color well and readily ferments to dryness is probably the wrong choice for a white wine for which you plan to stop fermentation. If you lack the facilities to ferment at very cool temperatures, choosing a yeast that depends on cool fermentation to emphasize fruity aromatics will probably yield disappointing results. Premier Couvee is a good, all-purpose selection if you are uncertain about making a choice. Do not choose Premier Couvee if you intend to stop fermentation by cold shock because it is extremely cold-tolerant.

8. Starting a Yeast

Ideally, you want the preferred yeast population to explode and rapidly overwhelm all of the nasty competition such as wild yeasts and molds. Yeast cells subdivide with increasing difficulty in response to alcohol toxicity so you want to start with a large population. While starting a yeast properly is simple, it goes contrary to some old practices still used by some home winemakers.

Yeast cells are not ready to work as they come out of the package. Most would be killed by contact with the sugar in grape juice or by temperature shock. Once they are hydrated and are not subjected to sudden temperature change, yeast cells are very resilient. Start by hydrating the dried yeast in an ounce or two (100-200 ml) of 100-105 °F (40 °C) non-chlorinated water. Let it stand for 30 minutes, then stir in to a few ounces of room temperature juice. Allow the yeast to grow for at least four hours in the must. When it is obviously fermenting actively, add it to your main batch of must. Make sure that the temperatures of the yeast starter and the must are approximately the same. Once the main batch is fermenting, you can safely raise or lower the fermentation temperature for desired results. Add yeast nutrient.

What can go wrong with starting a yeast? If the yeast fails to start in the temperature-adjusted juice, the juice may have too much free SO_2.

The simplest thing to do is to give it another day to start fermenting. If that doesn't work, reinoculate. It is possible that the yeast is no longer viable, particularly if you've had it around for a number of years or are using a previously opened packet.

Fruits like cranberry, *Sorbus* or Rowan, and rhubarb have chemistry that tends to inhibit yeast growth, but this seems unlikely with any grape. Wine yeast thrives in an acidic environment of pH 3.0-3.8 compared to its competitors, and with sugar up to 24 °Brix. Higher sugar concentrations will impede yeast, as will a very low pH. The worst, and least likely cause is that the grapes have picked up traces of a fungicide, like Benlate, that will inhibit yeast growth.

9. Time on the Lees

Style normally determines whether or not one should allow the wine to rest on the lees. We are reluctant to let any wine rest on gross lees (fruit pulp, stems, seeds). Fine lees (mainly dead yeast cells) look much like a thin layer of flour on the bottom of the carboy. Wines headed for malolactic fermentation frequently are left on the fine lees. Fruity, Germanic whites usually are not. The fine lees promote lactic bacterial growth, and foster the onset of malolactic fermentation. On the other hand, any wine that can be called "crisp" probably will not benefit from lees contact.

For neutral or more complex white wines, clean lees contact can add a supple, creamier mouth feel. The ultimate expression of this process comes with barrel fermentation, where oak contact, malolactic fermentation, and lees contact are all part of the maturation process. Unfortunately, few home winemakers make wine in large enough batches to make this method practical. Gently stir the lees every few weeks unless you are determined to make a wine with an absolute minimum of processing. Stirring will yield a bit more lees character.

Reds intended to be drunk while still very young and fruity should be racked as soon as they fall clear. Heavier reds can rest on lees for months with out being disturbed.

What can go wrong while on the lees? Your wine can pick up off flavors from the gross lees, particularly if the juice did not settle well. Wines can quickly develop a strong hydrogen sulfide (rotten egg) odor, which requires prompt remedial action.

10. Malolactic Fermentation

Consider malolactic fermentation for any non-Germanic style wine where the malic acid quality is not an asset. Almost all cold climate red wines, in which the sharpness of malic acid is rather unpleasant, will benefit from malolactic fermentation. In whites, however, our preference is for crispness. So, often we will leave malic acid in some fairly neutral white wines. In general, a malolactic fermentation will enhance softness and complexity of the wine but with some loss of fruitiness.

Malolactic bacteria should be introduced as the yeast consumes the last of the sugar. If residual sugar is present, malolactic bacteria will sometimes feed on it, with unpleasant results. The most convenient and reliable way to introduce malolactic bacteria into a must or wine is with one of the new direct addition dehydrated cultures. For malolactic bacteria to start their work quickly, sulfite levels must be below 30ppm and the temperature rather warm, above 70 °F (21 °C).

What can go wrong with malolactic fermentation? If wild malolactic bacteria were at work instead of the commercial inoculant, there's no saving it. This is highly unlikely however, because commercial strains are more vigorous. Secondly, commercial malolactic bacteria cultures have kind of a sauerkraut-and–pork-chop smell. Wild strains have definite off smells that you would not confuse with a commercial one. A more likely problem is that the malolactic fermentation stops, probably because the wine is too cold. As long as you haven't added SO_2, malolactic fermentation should start again if you warm the wine to above 70 °F (21 °C). Another mistake is to bottle the wine before it has completed malolactic fermentation, with a free SO_2 level too low to inhibit refermentation. Under favorable temperature conditions, it will start up again in the bottle. If you are blending a wine that has undergone malolactic fermentation with one that has not, you need 60 to 90 ppm to prevent further malolactic activity in the bottle.

11. Oak and Other Non-Grape Additives*

Oak flavoring in the form of chips or granules can sometimes enhance a white that has gone through malolactic fermentation to give it a little tannin, more mouth feel, and more complexity. Remember that oak competes with fresh, fruity character. Oak is routinely added to medium and full bodied reds.

The effect of oak addition is relatively quick and easy to test. Draw off a pint and add a teaspoonful of oak granules to it. After one week, the wine has absorbed all the flavors it is going to absorb. This proportion should seem far too oaky, so you will see what over-oaking does to your wine. You can now compare the full spectrum of oak treatments, from no oak to too much oak, and decide how much, if any oak you want. Oakiness mellows a bit with time. Our bias is to favor fruit over oak, so our oaking usually is light-handed. Ideally, you should make one bottle of your chosen blend with oak addition and set it aside for a month to allow the flavors and aromas to marry.

Glycerin is about the only other additive that you might consider adding to a white wine. It is a natural product of fermentation, with more glycerin being found in high alcohol and carbonic maceration wines. Glycerin adds body and masks bitterness. It is a non-fermentable sweetener, but its sweetness is almost undetectable at the prescribed usage. Be cautious about how much glycerin you add because some of the harshness you are countering from the acids and tannins will soften over time. If you add half of what your immediate tasting is telling you, it will be about right. Three ounces (90 ml) per five gallons (18.9 l) is the absolute limit we would use.

Finally, 1/4 teaspoon (0.6 g) of powdered grape tannin per five gallons (18.9 l) of a white wine sometimes can be used to aid in clearing the wine and to add a hint of astringency. Red wines often can benefit from tannin addition if more tannin fits the intended style.

What can go wrong with oak or additives? You can overdo it or try to add qualities that did not fit with the wine's style.

12. Blending for Balance*
Even a young, simple wine should display interesting characteristics from the beginning of the tasting experience to the middle mouth to the finish. If it doesn't, you should look for ways to fill in the holes. The flavors and aromas of white wines tend to be much more delicate than reds, so you need a much lighter hand in blending. It helps to grow grapes with a specific style in mind, so you have some natural pairings.

What can go wrong with blending? Your wine might be technically balanced but have confusing and conflicting tastes and aromas. This is a mistake that all blenders need to make in order to learn that all seemingly good blending combinations do not work. Once you gain more experience with your grape varieties and know what you want in a style, this is unlikely to happen. Practice, practice, practice.

13. Aging
Most of our cold climate white wines will be ready to drink within a year. Oaked wines put through malolactic fermentation sometimes can benefit from two years of aging. Beyond that, only cold climate reds and high acid or high alcohol dessert wines are likely to continue improving.

What can go wrong with aging? Wide heat variation, exposure to light, and vibration are all storage problems inhospitable to aging. If you bottled your wines at a high pH (not enough acid), a low alcohol level, or with not enough free SO_2, your wines may not keep for a year. Even if you do everything right, the hybrid grape varieties for white wine mostly do not produce long-lived wines. One mistake that cannot really be blamed on the winemaker is drinking the wine at the wrong time. Style should give you some strong clues on when to drink wine. Most home winemakers that we know drink their wines very early, which is fine for fruity wines and for unstable wines that would fall apart prematurely. If you have made a really well balanced tannic "vintner's reserve" red wine though, you may be drinking it too soon to fully appreciate your own artistry. If the wine has exuberant fruit, but seems sharp due to tannin and acid, you are probably drinking it too soon. If the fruit is gone, so is any chance that this wine will age well. Another, admittedly rough, guide is that when a half full bottle has sat open for hours and is getting better, then it probably will improve with age.

So there you have it, the winemaker's art in greatly simplified form. Good procedure, combined with a bit of experience, is sufficient to master some of these winemaking variables. Others (marked with the *) require more experience and judgement based on a skilled evaluation of the color, smell, and taste of the fruit, must, and wine. The next four chapters will describe the winemaking skills acquired with experience, and how to go about developing them.

Chapter 11

Winemaking Styles

Once you have learned how to avoid basic mistakes and make sound wines, you are free to focus on the artistic part of winemaking. You can use the variables described in the last chapter to amplify and suppress sensory elements with a preconceived pattern in mind, described here as "style." Styles are shorthand summations of time-honored, successful winemaking patterns. The patterns suggest the type and amount of acid to aim for in each style. They approximate what tannin, alcohol, and residual sugar levels will be required. They tell us what aroma and color intensity to seek. The concept of style assumes that acid, tannin, alcohol, and sugar levels are not "mix and match" elements but work together in predictable ways. For example, a high acid wine is usually best made with low tannin and alcohol levels and will probably have some residual sugar. High acid and high tannin do not go well together unless there is something unusual about a wine to mediate the conflict between the two.

The grape variety you are working with will often strongly influence style choice, which is why we will recommend grape varieties to go with each style. A wine from the St. Pepin grape variety, for example, almost always is made as an acidic, fruity wine. A Foch wine, by contrast, can be made in five different styles, depending on harvest parameters. With most other varieties though, usually you will have to choose between two closely related styles, depending on grape ripeness. You may favor one style over another but be cautious of personal biases. Forcing a grape into a style that does not fit will not take full advantage of a grape's potential.

Most style choices must be made very early, because this choice will influence or dictate harvest parameters, skin contact, yeast selection, and fermentation temperature. Sometimes if a wine does not live up to expectations a style can be shifted in midstream. Late induction of malolactic fermentation, oak addition, and blending are all examples of ways to shift a lighter, fruitier style toward a more neutral, complex wine. Generally though, it is best to know from the beginning which style will best fit your wine.

Allow yourself some time to get familiar with the elements and examples of classic styles. Try at least one commercial example of each style. Choose wines from cool climate regions when you can. A good wine store should be able to recommend a good, moderately priced example of each style. Dessert wines have a higher "moderate" price. Any expenditure on such a noble exercise should be viewed not as an extravagance but as tuition. Try to evaluate each wine as if it were your own.

Classic Styles

Germanic Style Whites

Aromatic fruitiness and crispness are the prominent features of Germanic style white wines. This style requires a balance between relatively high acid and some residual sugar of 1 to 3.5 %, and alcohol of 9.5 to 11.5 %. This requires grapes ripened enough to develop pronounced varietal flavor. Residual sugar should be just high enough to bring out fruit flavor but not leave a sweet aftertaste. Malolactic fermentation is not normally used because it will reduce the fruitiness. Blending should respect the featured grape's varietal character. The grapes should be picked cool, pressed cool, settled from the pulp cool, and fermented cool. When well made, Germanic style white wines are among the best wines made from cold climate grapes. Many good commercial examples are available. Avoid those relatively low in acid and high in sugar.

Alsatian Style Whites

Alsatian wines are made with the same grape varieties as those used for Germanic style wines but with a vastly different approach. Alsatian style whites are typically made bone dry, with relatively high alcohol to balance the acidity. They are much heavier and more full-bodied than Germanic style whites. This can be a good approach if you live in Alsace, or maybe New Zealand. Varieties grown in the most northern areas, however, are likely to fall short of the lush fruitiness required to make this style work well. See the discussion of "full-bodied white varietals" below. These depend more on complexity than the lush fruit required for Alsatian style whites.

Neutral Whites

Neutral is defined here as meaning subdued in flavor and aroma. Sometimes neutral grapes can achieve a pleasant fruitiness when ideally ripe, or they can be blended with a more fruity white grape variety. Neutral grapes, on the other hand, have more to offer when they are made into a less flamboyant wine more easily matched with food. Neutral white wines are finished with a bit less acid, no residual sugar, and alcohol in the 11.5 to 13% range. Techniques routinely applied to reds, such as malolactic fermentation, blending, resting on the lees, and exposure to oak often works well with neutral whites. Ripe grapes with an excess of malic acid can be made into an acceptable neutral white wine because the malolactic fermentation process will soften and reduce the acid. Try a commercial Seyval as an example.

Full-bodied White Varietals

Commercial Chardonnay typifies this style. These wines emphasize complexity, with a winemaking approach more befitting a red wine than a white. They are high in alcohol (12.5 to 13.5%) and often are subjected to cold soaking before pressing, extended lees contact, malolactic fermentation, and some oak. Virtually no residual sugar, but high alcohol, and glycerin make these wines full-bodied. There must be enough tartaric acid in these wines to balance the high alcohol.

Dessert Whites

These wines are typified by high sugar and concentrated fruit. They are richly aromatic. This is achieved in either of two ways. Traditionally, dessert wines are produced from very ripe or even overripe grapes, with high sugar content and highly concentrated flavors and aromas. More recently, some excellent dessert wines have been produced by removing ice from the partially-frozen juice of normally ripe fruit. A well-made Sauterne or a German Beerenauslese will show you what the goal is here.

Sparkling Wines

This style lends itself to cold hardy grapes that are a bit low in sugar and a bit high in acidity. Unfortunately, the process of making sparkling wine is tedious enough that very few home winemakers try it more than once. We claim no expertise here. *Modern Winemaking* and *Home Winemaking Step by Step* both cover it well.

Rose´

Cheap commercial examples give a limited sense of what this style can be. This wine can be made by immediately pressing the juice off the skins of red wine grapes, with limited skin contact time of three to twenty-four hours. Occasionally, it is made by adding a small amount of red wine to a white wine for a hint of color and tannin. This style is made as though it were a fruity white, with fresh fruit apparent in the nose, crisp acidity, no malolactic fermentation or oak, 9.5 to 12% alcohol, and just enough residual sugar to bring out the fruit.

Fruity Reds

Simple fruit flavor and aromas are highlighted in this style, with the consequent sacrifice of complexity and aging potential. Because tannins are relatively low, acids should be higher than in other reds. Alcohol rarely should exceed 12%. The carbonic maceration process (see Chapter 10) results in fruity reds with a characteristic "nouveau" aroma. The goal here is to preserve the fruity aromatics but not necessarily maximize tannin, so you should keep the fermentation cool and minimize oxygen contact. Avoid extended skin contact, malolactic fermentation, and addition of oak. Properly ripened grapes are particularly important for this style in order to foster fruitiness and to avoid extreme malic acid character in the wine. (See Chapter 10 about malic acid reduction by yeast selection.)

Medium-bodied Red Varietals

Some red wine zealots would consider this the beginning of the red wine section. These wines should have enough middle tannin to require some aging, which enhances their structure and complexity. Virtually all should be put through malolactic fermentation, most should be oaked, and no residual sugar should be apparent on the palate. Alcohol should be about 12.5%. Blending, preferably done after a year of aging, often enhances the character and structure of medium reds. Unlike the fruity reds, a medium bodied red wine will have some roughness and harshness that needs time to mellow. Trying to tame the harshness too early can rob the wine of highlights that would have appeared a year or two later. Do not confuse harshness with pronounced bitterness, which is likely to remain a major flaw, even after many years of aging. The aroma should be clearly characteristic of the primary grape variety, providing that the variety has an aroma worthy of highlighting. Total Acidity can be higher than you think when tasting it as a young wine but not above 0.7%.

Rhone Style Reds

These wines are blends that aim for a medium-bodied wine that features complexity and balance, as opposed to pronounced varietal character. This style comes as close as a winemaker ever gets to "inventing" a wine. When done well, it combines positive attributes of different varieties in a way that makes a markedly better wine than any of its constituents. This style is described more fully in Chapter 16.

Full-bodied Red Varietals

Full-bodied reds require fully ripe grapes with rich ripe aromas and flavors, and with substantial tannin. This style is more typical of grapes grown in warm to hot climates, so we are reaching a bit to even mention it here in the North. Blending and grape tannin addition are likely to be required for Northern grapes.

Late Harvest Reds

These wines require luscious, concentrated fruit flavors and aroma, from grapes pushing the limits of ripeness. Alcohol should be high to volatilize the aromatics of ripe fruit. While aroma is important in all styles, it is what makes this style special.

Generic Wines

Many wines are made that do not fit any of the classic styles described above. They are generic wines, sometimes called "house wines" or "everyday wines." They are typically well-balanced blends that are in no way offensive but do not offer much in the way of highlights.

What can go Wrong with Wine Style Selection?

If you try to mix and match elements of style, you have strayed "off the path" and the wine judges will get you! For example, a crisp, fruity white wine seems odd if it also has high alcohol. You may have intended to stop fermentation to leave residual sugar but without success. The sugar turned into alcohol! Or, you may find that a wine has gone through malolactic fermentation against your intention and now is flabby, rather than crisp and fruity.

If you have chosen a style that amplifies the grape's good qualities and doesn't try distorting the grape into something it can't be, nothing should go wrong here. But don't despair! There will be plenty of chances to go astray later.

Chapter 12

Indications of Problems: What Can Go Wrong?

Chapter 9, "Staying on the Path," shows how you can avoid most common winemaking problems by using standardized winemaking practice. Sound winemaking procedure does not prevent all problems, however, just as automotive preventive maintenance does not keep your car from ever breaking down. Problems arise, partly because the path of sound winemaking practice is very narrow. Typically, we are working to favor our chosen yeast, bacteria, and enzymes over spoilage organisms that may thrive under nearly identical conditions. Likewise, each harvest presents somewhat different conditions that could cause problems. Finally, winemakers may try to get by with shortcuts or simply make mistakes. Winemakers must learn how to recognize problems and know what to do about them. Let's look at the problem-causing culprits, how they do their dirty work, and what can be done to minimize damage.

Unwanted Guests

Acetobacter
These bacteria are all around us but their favorite hangout is damaged fruit. They convert alcohol into acetic acid and ethyl acetate in the presence of oxygen.

Acetic acid smells like vinegar. It is one of the few acids found in wine that has an odor and is volatile, hence the term "volatile acidity." Acetic acid is present in virtually all wines and, when it is below the human perceptual threshold of about 0.1%, is not a problem. If you have a wine that is not far above the threshold, you may want to try a test blend with another wine to bring it down to an acceptable level. Adding a wine with high volatile acidity to an actively fermenting one may succeed in driving off most of the volatile substances. Such blending efforts, of course, run the risk that you will be producing only bigger quantities of moderately bad wine.

Acetobacter is relatively easy to thwart in all wines except those made by the carbonic maceration method. Treating moderately damaged fruit with 50 ppm of sulfite twelve hours before inoculating with your chosen yeast will, in most cases, prevent acetobacter from getting started. Acetobacter also requires oxygen and temperatures above 70 °F (21 °C), so keeping oxygen away after fermentation and storing in cool conditions offers further insurance. If oxygen is not kept away from a carbonic maceration fermentation, then acetobacter is very likely to thrive.

Ethyl acetate smells like nail polish remover. It is an ester that is formed by the interaction of acetic acid and alcohol. Most esters that develop in wine have pleasant, fruity aromatics, but the smell of nail polish remover tells us that ethyl acetate is a rude exception. Humans are six times more sensitive to ethyl acetate than to acetic acid, so losing this odor in a blend is unlikely.

Lactic Acid Bacteria

Of the many strains of lactic bacteria, most must be considered spoilage organisms. Wild lactic bacteria seem to be obsessed with hanging out in warm places with adequate oxygen, consuming malic acid, and producing foul odors. Not the kind of helpers a winemaker seeks out! Some strains can produce acetic acid, with the resulting increase in volatile acidity and the nail polish remover smell of ethyl acetate. Other strains produce a dairy-product-gone-wrong aroma, or a mouse urine aroma. Other signs are the development of bitterness or a slimy, oily feel. The only good things that can be said about wines showing signs of wild malolactic activity is that pouring them down the drain will be an easy decision. Plus, you will be highly motivated to avoid a repetition of the problem. Even selected strains of lactic bacteria are capable of producing problems if given a chance. The bacteria will degrade potassium sorbate, producing a distinct geranium leaf smell. This may not sound so bad compared to some of the vile aromas noted above, but it is a fault with no remedy.

Proper use of sulfite will prevent wild lactic bacteria from degrading your wine. If a commercial strain of lactic bacteria gets a good head start, it will crowd out the wild bacteria. After the chosen bacteria have converted the malic acid, all danger of wild malolactic infection is gone. Once you use a commercial strain of lactic bacteria, it is likely to remain in your winemaking area, ready to attack new sources of malic acid. Keep this in mind when working with wines you do not wish to go through malolactic fermentation.

Wild Yeast Strains

Yeasts vary considerably in the environments that they will tolerate and, likewise, they vary in the results they produce. Here are the problem yeasts most often encountered.

Film yeast. This one is readily identifiable by a pale-colored surface film. This develops after fermentation is completed and the wine has access to oxygen. If left untreated, film yeast will oxidize the wine, consume alcohol and malic acid, and produce acetic acid and ethyl acetate. If you check your carboys every few weeks for film, you will be able to catch it before wine quality is degraded. Wine stored at cool temperatures, in full containers, with adequate sulfite, and at least 11% alcohol are less likely to have the problem. Some film yeasts, however, are quite tolerant of sulfite. The most effective treatment we have found is to fill the carboy within an inch of the top. Then, after all film has floated back to the top, douse a small paper towel in ethanol or vodka and clean the remaining top inch of exposed glass within the neck of the carboy. Be sure the surface of the airlock is also sanitized with a heavy sulfite solution. Dribble a tiny bit of the ethanol into the wine. Alcohol will remain on the surface long enough to kill any floating yeast before dissipating. Misting the surface of the wine with a spray bottle of alcohol or sulfite solution also works well.

Brettanomyces. This microorganism is likely to eventually show up in wines you have aged for a while. Its characteristic odor is "barnyard," but it also can have a mousy, burnt plastic, or even a medicinal smell. Normally, it is very slow to develop. If you keep up the sulfite levels during storage and are scrupulous about sanitation in the winery (brettanomyces does not come from the vineyard), you may never encounter it in your wine. Once started though, only tight filtration is likely to stop it.

The keys to minimizing wild yeast problems involve good all-around winery sanitation, making sure that the chosen yeast gets a quick and vigorous start, managing oxygen contact, and maintaining a good sulfite regimen.

Cork Taint
Cork taint usually smells "musty" or "like a concrete basement" and the aftertaste will probably be musty also. This comes from a fungus growing on or in (can you guess?) corks. Expect cork taint to affect individual corks but not the entire batch. The problem is much less likely when you buy good corks, store them in a dry place, and soak them for a few hours in a sulfite solution of about 300 ppm. Do not use chlorine!

Winemaking-related Problems

So far, all of the described culprits have been unwanted invaders, but problems originating with the grapes, or off flavors and smells from lax winemaking practice, can also degrade wine quality. Some of the most common examples follow.

Uncontrolled Oxidation
Telltale signs of oxidation are browning and a rapid softening of formerly crisp acidity in white wines, sherry-like or "nutty" nose, and a bitter finish in both whites and reds. Once you learn to recognize the nose of an oxidized wine, you will be able to identify it at a relatively early stage. All wines need small amounts of oxygen at just the right time. Too much oxygen, however, results in the excessive development of aldehydes, a family of organic chemicals that are an intermediate step between sugar and alcohol. Unless you have set out to make a sherry, excessive

oxidation usually will ruin your wine. Minimal oxygen contact and sound sulfite usage are the key prevention measures for whites. Red wines can withstand more oxygen contact than whites due to the protection afforded by their grape tannins. But even with reds, the contact should normally be in small amounts for brief intervals. This is primarily accomplished by keeping free sulfite levels lower (around 30 ppm) during racking and storage.

Enzymatic Browning
Most of us have witnessed the rapid enzymatic browning of fresh sliced apples soon after being exposed to air. Some of our hybrid grape varieties, most notably Kay Gray, Zilga and E.S. 5-3-89 are subject to rampant enzymatic browning of a similar nature. This form of oxidation will thwart most conventional winemaking precautions to protect juice and must from oxygen. Some varieties seem to have less zealous enzymes than others. We know of some cases where susceptible wines were scrupulously kept from oxygen and never went through the browning process. We know of other cases where the browned and oxidized fruit pulp dropped out of the juice leaving an unoxidized wine. But don't count on either of these things happening.

The safest way of dealing with varieties known for extreme enzymatic browning is to disable the enzymes as soon as possible. In especially susceptible varieties such as Kay Gray we add a solution of Polyclar and water directly into the crushing vessel or press basket. Bentonite removes proteins, including enzymes, so it too can work. Use it only when it does not interfere with desired enzymatic activity.

Hydrogen Sulfide
This is almost exclusively a red wine problem. When hydrogen sulfide is first evident, it has a pronounced, sulfurous rotten egg smell. After a few weeks, hydrogen sulfide can combine with other chemicals and become mercaptans, which are less volatile, with a nose best described as "skunky." Finally, after a few more months, the mercaptans are oxidized and become disulfides, with a smell described as "sewer gas."

All of these horrible smells are desperate cries for treatment or disposal. Hydrogen sulfide can be treated readily by aeration and racking off of the fruit solids that form the gross lees. It is good practice to get wine off fruit solids relatively soon after primary fermentation is done and to rack when fine lees buildup begins to approach one half inch (one centimeter) in the bottom of the carboy.

Untreated hydrogen sulfide converts to mercaptans, a more stable chemical form. Mercaptan treatment requires exposure to copper, usually by racking through an unoxidized copper tube or over an unoxidized copper plate.

Disulfides, resulting from untreated mercaptans, are the most stable of all, and are very difficult to treat successfully. An ascorbic acid addition can convert disulfides back into mercaptans, which then can be racked over copper. Another treatment described in *Modern Winemaking* involves the addition of one ounce of mineral oil per gallon of wine (15 ml/l) to absorb the disulfides. Twice daily, vigorously stir the oil that rises to the surface. Repeat this for four days. Remove the oil by drawing it off the surface with a wine thief or a turkey baster and discard it. Finally, fill your carboy to the brim and mop up the remaining oil film. Expect the disulfide-salvaged wine to be of reduced quality.

Hydrogen sulfide needs some source of sulfur in order to form. One source is the amino acids present in grapes, two of which are sulfur compounds. When the yeast runs out of the tiny amount of oxygen it needs to multiply, it will scavenge oxygen from the amino acids and release sulfur. Some yeasts, such as Montrachet, are more prone to hydrogen sulfide production. This process is reversible, which is why aeration works to eliminate hydrogen sulfide. Hydrogen sulfide also can be produced from sulfur spray compounds remaining on grapes. Often, hydrogen sulfide will be apparent during active fermentation, so use your nose to keep your must out of trouble. The only other time you are likely to encounter hydrogen sulfide forming is over gross lees, when settled fruit pulp begins to decompose and release sulfur.

Fruit Quality Problems Present at Harvest

Unripe fruit can sometimes produce herbaceous or vegetal flavors. More typically though, unripe fruit will show as an absence of flavor, aroma, mouthfeel, or finish. While aging and exposure to oak can mask the problem, the wine will never possess the highlights of one made with perfectly ripe fruit. Over-ripe fruit can produce off flavors and aromas that are fruity but alien to wine, particularly in some of the hybrids with table grapes in their parentage. Fruit damaged by hail, birds, or wasps, often has high populations of spoilage organisms that can doom a wine to failure. Minimally damaged fruit should be treated with 50 ppm of dissolved metabisulfite at crush, which will suppress most spoilage organisms. Badly damaged fruit should be discarded. If not treated, you can expect problems from acetobacter and wild yeasts.

Fermentation-related Problems

Inoculation with a very slow starting or non-starting yeast invites microbial spoilage problems. One value of starting a yeast properly is that you are certain it is actively fermenting when you add it to the primary fermenter. If there are no visible signs of fermentation after thirty-six hours, then it is time to add another starter, possibly a more vigorous yeast strain such as *K1*.

Delayed Racking off Lees

Gross lees with lots of fruit pulp invite spoilage. Once induced malolactic fermentation has started and gross lees have obviously settled, it is time to rack. The same is true for additives such as Bentonite and Sparkolloid™. While not a spoilage medium, Bentonite and Sparkolloid™ settlings will in time impart an undesired clay-like character. Salts resulting from acid reduction with calcium carbonate quickly impart a bitter chemical flavor, so it is best to rack just as soon as frothy bubbling ceases and the salt has fallen out, usually within an hour.

Poor Clarification of White Wines

Most white wines will quickly clear of most particulate matter but will have a slight, uniform haze. Unless there are pectins remaining in the wine (the pectic enzyme may not have worked against all types of pectins), Sparkolloid™ should readily clear the haze. Ideally this is done shortly before cold stabilization. Chilling to near freezing can expedite the clarification process. If pectins are not the problem, then the next most likely suspect would be other proteins. Add one-half teaspoonful of grape tannin per five gallons of wine (1.4 g/18.9 l) and wait a few weeks. If nothing happens, try Sparkolloid™ again.

Preventing and Minimizing Problems

Instructions and checklists can only go so far in helping you avoid problems. An experienced winemaker knows what healthy wines look, smell, and taste like as the wines develop. Watch for typical patterns of progression specific to each yeast and each grape variety. Someone who has made several good wines from the variety can be of great help. While you will find that most white wines follow much the same pattern, as do many reds, the exceptions are worth noting. Once you know what is normal, you will be attuned to potential problems.

Chapter 13

Aging

The living, changing nature of wine is a big part of its mystique and appeal. Usually though, we do not speak of wine as changing but rather aging. The sensory progression of the aging process is well known to experienced wine tasters, and especially to tasters of fine (expensive) classical *vinifera* wines. The actual processes that comprise aging are not well known because they are complicated almost beyond belief! Most wine tasters probably do not want explanations based on organic chemistry, with its reversible transformations and enzymatic alchemy. Winemakers do not need to be Ph.D. chemists, but we do need to understand how to anticipate and make use of the aging process. So let's start with a summary of the sensory changes that accompany aging and follow with a look at the ways a winemaker can use, and sometimes influence, the changes to improve wine quality.

Sensory Changes in Wine Influenced by Aging

Well made wines tend to age slowly, gracefully, and predictably. There are major variations between grape varieties in the rate at which they age and how they show age. However, the direction of the changes in color, aromatics, taste, complexity and softness are relatively predictable.

Color
Red wines shift from purple to red to brown. Many of our hybrids begin with much more of a purplish cast than would a typical vinifera. Color saturation decreases. White wines shift from pale greenish overtones toward amber. Not many wines have a greenish cast.

Aroma
Fresh fruitiness gradually gives way to more wine-like aromas that become less like grapes over time. As esters develop and lend the wine increasing complexity, you may struggle to label the aromas. Young white wines often may have a citrus smell that dissipates within a year. Yeasty smells will typically be gone within months.

Taste

Sharp acids will soften. Flavors will begin to marry and become harmonious. Prominent, up front, fresh fruit flavors subside and become more like preserved fruit that is more apparent in the middle mouth and finish. Flavors and aromas can become layered to provide different subtle, multiple fruit sensations.

Mouthfeel

Tannins will soften, sometimes to the point where they can be described as "supple." Roughness gives way to smoothness.

What Winemakers Need to Know About The Aging Process

Consider the chemistry of aging as your winemaking partner. If you have applied the practices covered in the last chapter, then you can have the confidence and patience to let the wine develop into what it wants to become. Any blending, adjusting, or fine-tuning we do early in the aging process must anticipate the changes brought on by aging. The desirability and degree of aging is dependent on winemaking style, which should be determined by grape variety and harvest parameters (Chapter 11). Let's look at how aging and style interrelate.

Germanic Style Whites and Rose's

Because aromatic fruitiness, crispness, and varietal character are the highlights, we want only limited effects of aging. Once yeasty and citrus aromatics have subsided and the rough edges are off this wine, in four to twelve months, it is ready to drink. Fruity esters will be prominent. Acids should have lost their harshness but still lend a crispness. Likewise, the small amount of tannins in the rose' should soften a bit.

Neutral Whites

When made as a varietal, neutral whites emphasize a mellow, supple complexity that usually requires time to develop. Absence of residual sugar, malolactic fermentation, oak tannins, and alcohol levels up to 13% all contribute to a wine needing less free sulfite than Germanic style whites. This allows a gentle aging in the bottle, as aldehydes and esters slowly develop to soften the rough edges. Neutral whites will lack the pronounced varietal aroma of the fruity whites but have more complexity and structural balance. Malolactic fermentation, resting the wine on its lees, and exposure to oak are all practices that contribute to complexity but downplay varietal fruit, thereby both simulating and enhancing the aging process. The goal is to make the fruit quality more wine-like rather than disappear. No fruit equals no character. Neutral whites could normally be expected to improve with one to two years of aging, enough time for flavors and aromas to come together harmoniously.

Full-bodied Whites

Like neutral whites, complexity is emphasized. However, here, varietal character should be an added dimension. These wines could be ready to drink in 18 months, but some will have the potential to peak at four years.

Exposure to oak and resting on fine lees contribute to body and add to the graceful aging process. The challenge of making a full-bodied white wine is to gain complexity and body without losing the influence of fruit. Rather than being lost, the fresh, up-front fruit will mellow into a more wine-like character.

White Dessert Wines

The intense aromatics and concentrated fruit that typify this style lend themselves to the benefits of aging for two or more years. Sometimes though, the fruit does not hold up and, as a result, the wine loses the intense character that makes it special. This is more likely with wines made from juice concentrated by ice crystal removal, than with naturally ripened fruit.

Fruity Reds

Carbonic maceration style wines typically have the least aging potential of any wine. They emphasize simple fresh fruit character and can be ready to drink in a few months. They resemble fruity whites in many ways but are inherently more complex. These wines also have lower sulfite requirements and more tannin than whites, so they mature a bit differently. But when the fruit begins to fade, roughness hiding behind the fruitiness may become apparent, and the wine will have lost its youthful charm.

Medium-bodied Reds

Unlike all of the styles above, tannin plays an important role in aging these medium-bodied red wines. After a year, acids and tannins are still likely to be a bit rough, with complexity only beginning to develop. Fruit character changes from simple, fresh fruit to harder-to-define, complex, multilayered flavors and aromas suggestive of many fruits. Cold climate winemakers may find many of their medium-bodied reds ready to drink within a year because they do not have quite enough tannin or ripe fruit to fit into to this style. If the grapes are not fully ripe or don't produce enough tannin (many of our varieties don't), they are going to need some blending help. Medium-bodied reds should sit in a carboy for a year before bottling decisions are made. Most can comfortably age in the carboy for another year if you need to wait for a suitable blending component. Medium-bodied reds normally have acids that require the softening of malolactic fermentation plus some help from oak tannins. The sharpness of the grape tannins is the main determinant of how long these wines need to age. Ideally, you want the tannin to soften before the fruit disappears. Typically these wines require a year of aging and may benefit from a year or two more, depending on tannin level.

Full-bodied Reds

Full-bodied reds, with the most tannin and alcohol usually can stand the most aging. The indicators of being ready to drink are the same as with medium-bodied reds. Full-bodied reds, loaded with middle tannins, are rarely made with cold climate grapes. If you manage to make one, the tannins could take years to soften. Remember that we are looking for the astringent, dry tannins, and not the bitter ones. Even though bitter tannins can polymerize to form longer chains of astringent tannin, extreme bitterness will not be resolved by aging. Astringent tannins mask bitter tannins to some extent, so bitterness can become more apparent as middle tannins subside. Oak tannins are absolutely essential in full- bodied reds. They augment the aging process by adding, among other things, vanillin, which a desirable aldehyde (a partially oxidized alcohol). Barrel aging is particularly appropriate for this style because it not only adds tannins, it also condenses the wine by up to 10% due to evaporation.

One caution. After a few months, a full-bodied red can present a very distorted picture of what it will eventually become. Expect it to be quite rough. Attempts to soften and balance it when young could rob it of highlights and potential for balance. Let it age for a year or two and assess it then.

Late Harvest Reds

High alcohol, concentrated fruit, tannin, and moderate to high acidity should work together to make late harvest reds age well for many years. Make sure there is adequate tannin and enough sulfite to prevent brettanomyces. Seal it with a good cork and let it develop. Not all varieties or harvests are created equal though, so you should open a bottle periodically to make sure the fruit is not starting to fade. If the fruit is fading, but the wine is otherwise free of defects, add it to a younger late harvest red.

Variables That Affect Aging

Oxidation

If oxidation is not controlled, it can quickly spoil a wine. The goal for controlling oxygen in white wines is simple. Keep it out! Yeast needs only a tiny amount of oxygen to multiply cells. Even if you take precautions such as racking into containers sparged with inert gas, maintaining adequate free sulfite levels, and minimizing wine handling, the wine still will absorb some oxygen. Controlling oxygen in red wines is a balancing act, because they may produce hydrogen sulfide when starved for oxygen during or shortly after fermentation. Also, they require small amounts of oxygen over time to soften tannins. Excessive oxygen contact for both whites and reds can cause a wine to age prematurely. A wine that should take a year or more for acids and tannins to soften may seem ready to drink in three months. Prematurely aged wines will not have the highlights of a gracefully aged wine, nor will they last.

Sulfite

In both its free and bound forms, sulfite has a significant effect on aging. Insufficient free sulfite invites uncontrolled oxidation and the growth of spoilage organisms. These problems are accentuated when pH levels are high or alcohol levels are low. Conversely, wines with exceedingly high sulfite levels will have a retarded and distorted aging process. A red wine may retain the purplish color of youth well beyond its time. But over-sulfited wines not only age slowly, they age unevenly. Fixed sulfites can impair the subtle chemical interactions of normal aging, resulting in a wine that never becomes supple and harmonious.

Tannins

These substances are like good friends in two ways. The good tannins get better with age, and it pays to seek out the mellow tannins in favor of those that are bitter. Beware of bitter tannins, usually extracted from seeds and sometimes from stems. Tannins change in structure as they age. Some may combine with pigments and fall out as sediment, acting in the process as antioxidants. The larger effect comes from tannins physically combining with other tannin molecules to form longer chains (polymerization). Short tannins taste bitter, and middle tannins have a dry, astringent character, as polymerization provides a softening and mellowing effect. If you can detect a pronounced bitterness in the finish of a wine shortly after fermentation, then it should probably be stripped out with Polyclar. Some forms of bitterness manage to elude this process, however, and remain apparent as a clear and disturbing aftertaste.

Storage Temperature

High temperatures will speed all chemical processes, including aging. Slow and gentle is better, which is why wine seems most content when stored at about 55 °F (12 °C).

Light Exposure

Light speeds the negative effects of aging. Wines affected by extended light exposure are likely to lack flavor highlights. Sunlight and fluorescent light have a more pronounced effect than incandescent light. Keep wine out of the light, whether in carboys or bottles. Colored bottles reduce but do not eliminate the degradation.

Fruit Quality

Aging sometimes unmasks problems, rather than causing them. The shortcomings associated with poor quality or unripe fruit are a prime example. Poor quality grapes rarely produce the underlying complexity and depth of character needed for aging. If used at all, poor quality fruit is best used to produce a fruity young wine, albeit not a very good one

One final caution: Some interspecific hybrid varieties have quirky chemistry, which results in atypical aging patterns. Red wines made from hybrid varieties that you might expect to age well may not take up oxygen in quite the same way as red wines produced from *vinifera* varieties. As a result, these hybrid grape wines may not benefit from aging for as long as wines from *vinifera* grapes.

Ideal Aging Environment

A fully topped-off five-gallon (18.9 l) glass carboy, racked off any sediment, shielded from light, and kept at a cool and stable temperature provides, for the patient winemaker, a nearly ideal aging environment. A well maintained 20 to 60 gallon (75 to 225 l) oak barrel is even better for most reds, but this is likely to be beyond the scope of most readers. Aging occurs more slowly and gently in carboys than it does in wine bottles. Likewise it is slower in larger bottles than in smaller ones. So unless you are in a hurry to drink your wine, or have very limited storage space, be patient. A delay in bottling has the further advantage of helping you more accurately blend and fine-tune your wines.

Chapter 14

Tasting and Evaluation Skills

Just as making a sound wine rests on mastering the mundane, the artistic part of winemaking rests on development of analytical tasting skills. You can make sound wines by following the rules of basic winemaking and avoiding mistakes. But rarely will this be enough to bring out all of the highlights the wine has to offer. This requires artistry.

Some people might think that tasting is totally subjective, comes naturally, and does not need to be learned, but it in fact does. Analytical tasting is a highly structured process with intense focus on key sensory elements that tell us about a wine in great detail. Our senses give us some very precise information once we know what to look for and once they are calibrated by experience. While specific gravity, temperature, free SO_2 level, and pH are better measured by instruments, our senses can be trained to detect and evaluate smells and tastes better than any instrument available to home winemakers.

Books written about wine tasting are generally aimed at the consumer, not the winemaker. All of what they have to say is relevant to us, plus as winemakers (once we learn a few interim steps) we can use the information to adjust, balance, and improve our wines. The ability to analyze wine by appearance, smell, and taste will allow you to shape your wines artistically, according to your winemaking plan.

Learning How to Taste and Evaluate Wine

Wine tasting cannot be learned solely from a book, but a book is a good place to start. We recommend two books and will summarize some of the ideas put forth in them to get you started on the right track. While many good books are available about evaluating wine in an objective and structured way, our favorite is *Making Sense of Wine, a Study in Sensory Perception* by Alan Young. Young tells us exactly how the human senses work as detectors of wine quality, what can deceive them, and how they can be trained to help us more precisely evaluate a wine. He connects wine chemistry and sensory cues in sufficient detail to be of great help to the amateur winemaker. We consider Young's book required reading.

Marian Baldy's *The University Wine Course* is also a valuable reference that contains much information on commercial wine tasting as well as helpful exercises to become familiar with key flavors and aromas.

Three themes emerge from these books:

1. You must learn to make the best use of your senses, be aware of what can confuse them, and train yourself to focus on what each sense is telling you.

2. You should be able to distinguish flavors and aromas that give wines their character.

3. You need words (descriptors) to pinpoint and communicate to others what you are experiencing. This is especially true with our sense of smell.

Both Young and Baldy cover wine tasting and evaluation in detail that is beyond the scope of this book, but none of the detail will be wasted on a winemaker striving for quality. No matter how hard you try, you cannot learn too much about evaluative wine tasting.

The Sensory Evaluation of Wine

One way or another, winemakers need to learn how to evaluate the following characteristics in a finished wine

1. Appearance

Color, clarity, and the look of the wine's surface all forecast a lot about the wine's condition. Color can tell us how gracefully the wine has aged. Very young red wines often start as purplish, changing to carmine, to brick, to amber or tawny, and finally, brown. Color plays a greater part in the appeal of wine than many amateur winemakers might guess (see Chapter 17). It helps to know the typical color and intensity of the variety you are evaluating, given its age. Noting how far out to the edge of the glass the color extends suggests how much life the wine has left. The farther out the better. White wines range from nearly colorless to pale straw, to yellow, to amber, to a lifeless pale brown.

Clarity ranges from turbidity to a jewel-like brilliance that seems to amplify light. Brilliance forecasts an outstanding wine, while turbidity or cloudiness forecasts a problem wine on its way to the dump bucket. Winemakers may initially be more tolerant of cloudiness because they have seen it in young wines before fining. Cloudiness in a bottled wine however, signals spoilage. Similarly, any dullness on the wine's surface suggests you are viewing a very small mushroom farm, and these are not good mushrooms. Analyzing the appearance of a wine gives us valuable information about its condition and quality, which is likely to be confirmed by our sense of smell.

2. Smell

Smell tells us more about good wines than any other sense. Identifying and naming smells is the part of wine tasting that takes the most practice and reveals the most about quality. The Aroma Wheel, developed by Dr. Ann Noble of University of California, Davis, is an excellent tool to standardize the naming and grouping of aromas in wine. Become familiar with it and use it. It will improve your ability to place a description on what you smell in your wines, to compare wines produced from different grapes, in different styles, and in different years, and to diagnose wine problems.

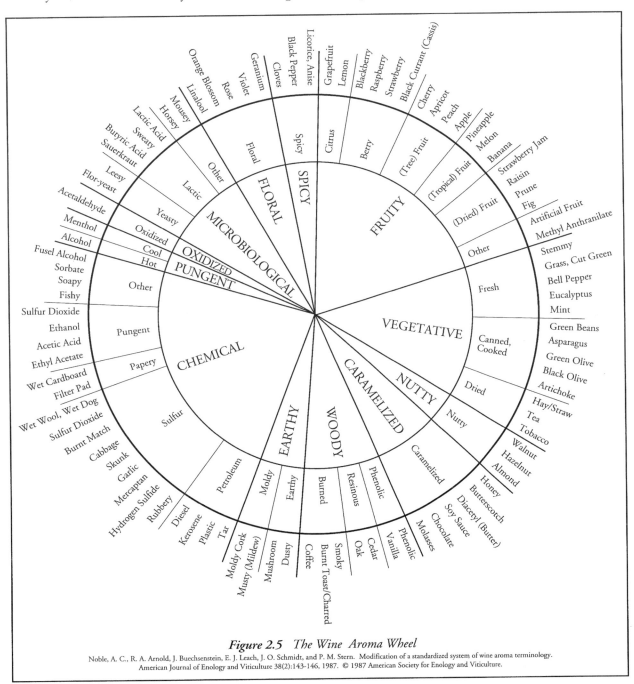

Figure 2.5 The Wine Aroma Wheel

Noble, A. C., R. A. Arnold, J. Buechsenstein, E. J. Leach, J. O. Schmidt, and P. M. Stern. Modification of a standardized system of wine aroma terminology. American Journal of Enology and Viticulture 38(2):143-146, 1987. © 1987 American Society for Enology and Viticulture.

Many people assume that taste is the most important element of wine. After all, we refer to "wine tasting," not "wine smelling"! However, if you are "tasting" something other than sweet, sour, bitter, or salty, what you are really experiencing is retro-olfaction or smelling while exhaling. This is not a matter of semantics but of human physiology. Most wine drinkers are familiar with the "swirl and sniff" technique for evaluating wine aromatics. This gives them a fair impression of the up-front qualities of a wine. Smelling by retro-olfaction (also called retro-nasal) yields a different set of impressions more attuned to a wine's middle mouth and finish. This can be confusing because middle mouth impressions are a combination of smell, taste, and feel. Finish, or aftertaste (mostly "after smell"), likewise includes impressions from other senses, such as a bitter aftertaste or a burning sensation in the throat from alcohol.

There's one more complication. Many older, complex wines change as they are exposed to oxygen while in the glass. Within minutes, the aroma profile can reveal new layers (usually good ones) or give up what little life was left in the old wine and go dead. Younger wines may have a "closed nose" and not show much aroma or flavor. "Closed nose" implies that this is a temporary condition that will change for the better with warming, letting the wine "breathe," or with further maturation in the carboy or bottle. Wines with a closed nose may simply be those that fall in the age gap between a typical young wine that is losing its fresh fruity character and a more mature wine that is just beginning to develop more complex aromatics.

Smell is of particular interest to the winemaker because of what it indicates about the chemistry of a developing wine. The most abundant volatile smells come from aldehydes, alcohols, and esters, and all contribute to the bouquet we associate with an aged wine. Aldehydes are oxidized derivatives of alcohol and, in small amounts, add positive notes to a finished wine. Vanillin, an aldehyde resulting from the contact of oak and wine, is an example. But aldehydes can be precursors of acetic acid, which in more than small amounts will be perceived as spoilage. In most red wines, controlled oxidation is a requirement to developing a complex and balanced wine. The aldehydes, being products of oxidation, give us measures of how well or how badly this has gone. When aldehyde problems are detected early enough, corrective action can be taken by treating with Polyclar and, one week later, adding 50 ppm of metabisulfite.

Alcohol is a family of related compounds that include volatile oils found in fruit that we identify as "apricot" or "blackberry" or many other distinctive aromas.

Esters comprise a chemical family in which some of the children turned out well, while some of the others went wrong. The good ones produce fruity notes not evident in unfermented juice. The bad ones begin as vinegar (acetic acid) and end up smelling like nail polish remover (acetone). Fruity esters may have been lurking in the grapes, or produced by yeasts during cool fermentation or by a slow interaction between acid and alcohol. Winemakers need to be alert to the first signs of off odors in their wines and recognize them for what they are. Fermentation problems and microbial infections often can be corrected with little or no lasting reduction of wine quality if action is taken soon enough (see Chapter 12). Herbaceous or vegetative odors are frequent problems with fruit that is not fully ripe, a predictable problem for cold climate grapes harvested during a shortened growing season. Once you detect the herbaceous or vegetative odors, you are left with four possibilities. First, it may go away with age. Second, oaking may cover it. Third, blending may hide it, although this is unlikely if the compound has a low sensory threshold. Fourth, you may be able to convince unsuspecting souls that the smell is part of the varietal nose and is a wine that just needs to be paired with the right kind of food.

3. Taste

Our taste buds are limited to sensing sweet, sour, bitter, and salty, all of which may be present in a wine. Typically wines have a balance of the first three tastes, with detectable saltiness found only in wines with unusual chemistry, or grown in salty soils.

Sweetness. Sweetness comes from residual sugar, alcohol, glycerin, and other wine components. Residual sugar is present in all wine, because some grape sugars are unfermentable. Alan Young notes in *Making Sense of Wine* that people vary considerably in their ability to detect sugar, but a threshold of about 0.4 % for whites and 1.5 % for reds is common. Sweetness is among the least of alcohol's sensory effects on wine, but it contributes the suggestion of sweetness to full-bodied reds. Similarly, glycerin, which is sort of a halfway step between a sugar and an alcohol, lends fullness and sweetness to the finish. Finally, many people mistake fruitiness in a wine for sweetness. Fruitiness applies to the "mouth filling" sensation without a syrupy aftertaste. This is a good sensation to remember when trying to balance sugar and acid in a fruity white. It is why the style is called "fruity white," not "sweet white" wine.

Sourness. Sourness in wine comes mainly from tartaric, malic, and to a lesser degree, lactic and citric acid. While each acid has its own character, their combined presence is perceived as the wine's Total Acidity.

With a few exceptions, tartaric acid is found only in grapes. Fully ripened grapes, particularly grapes grown in warm climates, typically have a high proportion of tartaric acid relative to malic acid. It's no surprise then, that the taste of tartaric is associated with ripeness.

Malic acid is present in a wide variety of fruits. Many associate its taste with green apples, but that's a bit of a distortion. Malic acid can add crispness to a fruity white or rose´ wine as long as there is some tartaric acid for complexity and balance. Malic acid has a hardness and aggressiveness that can make tasting anything else in the wine a challenge. A red wine with a lot of malic acid, a lot of young tannin, and high alcohol, for example, would be quite a harsh assault on the senses. This is why many reds are put through malolactic fermentation. Lactic acid has only half the strength of malic acid and has the soft, some would say buttery, quality of a wine that has moved from young and fruity to aged and vinous (or, if you prefer, winey).

Fresh grapes have small amounts of citric acid, which is most apparent in whites during and shortly after fermentation, hence the grapefruit nose. Usually this nose fades within a year. While citric acid is rather sharp in the mouth, a small amount, added after all fermentation is complete, can add a pleasing freshness to whites.

Adjusting the amount and kind of acid is a powerful tool for shaping the final taste and balance of a wine. It is addressed in Chapter 15.

Acetic, carbonic, and tannic acid affect the taste of wine in ways different from the preceding four acids. Volatile acidity includes acetic acid (vinegar) and ethyl acetate. Acetic acid is good in very small amounts because it adds liveliness to the nose without smelling like vinegar. Carbonic acid (dissolved CO_2) is felt as spritziness and stops being an acid when the CO_2 has dissipated. Tannic acid is tasted as bitterness, or is felt as astringency, and not counted as part of total acidity. It is, in fact, an acid. The additive quality of tannin and acid partly explains why tannic reds are not palatable at acid levels as high as typical whites.

Bitterness. Bitterness is extracted from grape skins, seeds, and stems in the form of tannins. Some of these tannins later polymerize (form longer molecular chains), lose most of their apparent bitterness, and are experienced instead as astringent. Bitterness is a prominent feature of some beverages and foods such as coffee, tea, beer, chocolate, and red wine. Too much bitterness quickly becomes a fault. Usually a winemaker will want to reduce bitterness in a red to a just perceptible level, expecting it to soften in time. Pronounced bitterness will most likely not soften before the fruit fades and the astringency begins to decline. Astringency and, to a lesser degree, fruitiness tend to mask bitterness. Ideally, fruit character should still be apparent when the tannins have become soft and supple.

Some bitter salts (not to be confused with saltiness) are sometimes found in a wine, most often as a result of neutralizing acids. Reducing acid with calcium carbonate yields a bitter salt that is slow to precipitate completely. Minimize this by racking the wine off of the precipitate twice: first, within an hour of adding calcium carbonate, and again, when the rest of the bitter salt drops out. Bitter salts are always perceived as a fault.

4. Touch

It may seem odd at first to associate tactile sensation with wine tasting, yet this is how we evaluate astringency, alcohol level, mouth feel, viscosity, and carbonation.

Astringency.   Astringency is felt as dryness in the mouth, or as a fuzziness on the teeth. Full and medium-bodied reds absolutely require a noticeable astringency to have "backbone." The winemaker must make a guess about the aging potential of the wine's fruit and adjust astringency accordingly. Ideally, the astringency softens to a point of suppleness, and complexity is at its maximum before the fruit fades. This is less of an issue with cold climate grapes, because few of our reds have the astringency to make extended aging necessary or desirable.

Irritation.   Irritation, in the form of a burning sensation, comes from alcohol. The threshold for this sensation in most people is above 12%. High levels of acid and tannin heighten the burning sensation. Faint irritation is generally perceived as good, but too much is judged as a fault.

Apply Your Tasting and Evaluation Skills

Now that you have waded through a detailed description of wine tasting (actually only the minimum you need to know), we must tell you that reading about it is not enough. You need to acquire a broad spectrum of taste experience, and probably the best way to do this is with good quality wines produced from *vinifera* grapes. Tasting *vinifera* wines may seem like a digression to cold climate winemakers who are most likely working with hybrid grapes. However, there are a number of good reasons to digress.

1. Well made commercial *vinifera* wines are readily available and are often evaluated in print by wine experts.

2. *Vinifera* wines can be found in all the styles you wish to explore.

3. *Vinifera* wines are likely to be inherently more balanced than wines from hybrid grape varieties.

4. Wines made from *vinifera* grapes grown in the coolest of climates often are made in styles similar to those used in wines made from hybrid grapes.

5. Centuries of experience have gone into making wines from most *vinifera* grapes. By now, the winemakers should have it right!

You may ask, "If tasting commercial *vinifera* wines teaches me so much, why not try making wine from them?" Why not, indeed! We know many hybrid grape winemakers who also work with *vinifera* grapes, and their experience often shows in the quality of their hybrid grape wines. If you can get frozen or fresh premium *vinifera* grapes shipped to you, then give them a try. Try for the best quality grapes you can get. Peter Brehm frozen grapes and juice, while not cheap, are the best we have found. All you can learn from improperly ripened or marginal quality grapes is humility. Our experience with grape concentrates is limited by intention. Concentrates are convenient and relatively cheap, but there is not much a winemaker can learn from them.

If you discover *vinifera*-like qualities in your wine, you will probably want to highlight them. Wines made from the St. Pepin grape often are made in a fruity Germanic style. Knowing the wide range of what Riesling and Gewurtztraminer can taste like should help you make a better St. Pepin wine. Reading wine reviews can help you find good examples and suggest what is considered desirable or undesirable in that style of wine. Try to label what you are tasting and smelling with descriptive words. Your ability to make critical sensory evaluations of wine can and should become your most important testing device. Your sensory evaluations can be calibrated by:

1. Reading about how to objectively judge commercial wine.

2. Comparing your evaluation with experienced wine judges, preferably over all of the winemaking styles.

3. Applying the sensory evaluation skills you have learned to the wines you are in the process of making.

Get Feedback From Knowledgeable Tasters

We recommend that you submit your wines for formal evaluations at competitions to see how judges' evaluations differ from yours. Ideally, you should get feedback both from judges who make wine and from those who do not. We are convinced that those who make wine are better at assessing the future of young wines that are not yet ready to drink. Experienced tasters may never taste a wine before it is bottled. Yet winemakers must make key blending and fine-tuning adjustments based on what they expect it to taste like in its prime. A winemaker's taste may become biased by repeatedly having to make these early decisions. As a result, the winemaker may acquire a taste for younger, harsher, more acidic wines. To counter this bias, we need feedback from non-winemaking judges, who are usually better at judging a wine that is closer to its prime, or beyond its prime. The final test of a wine, and the quality of winemaking, is what it is like in its prime.

Know Your Own Wine Tasting Biases and Shortcomings

What wines do you like best? You could be in trouble if you prefer wines from grapes grown exclusively in a hot climate, because cool climate grapes are normally not going to taste like they came from Morocco. If you like more acidic wines or sweeter wines than other tasters, know that your wines may seem out of balance to them. A second opinion from a judge with a bias different from yours can help. Bob does not bottle a wine until he gets his wife's opinion on acid level (she usually prefers less acid). If you know someone with a better nose than yours, get his or her help.

Many winemakers have struggled with trying to fine-tune and blend wines without the necessary tasting and evaluation skills. Our fine-tuning and blending results showed a lot of improvement after we got better at tasting. Save yourself some time and aggravation by refining your tasting and evaluation skills. Meanwhile, get help from more experienced tasters, particularly when you are making blending decisions.

Chapter 15

Fine-Tuning and Balancing

So far you have been reading mainly about how to prevent bad things from happening to your wine and waiting for it to mature. Now it is time to get rid of the minor flaws and make some adjustments that can quickly improve wine drinkability. Although most of the wines we fine-tune and balance will not be quite ready to drink, they will give us some clear indications of what they are likely to become. Fine-tuning and balancing depends on your ability to assess a wine's strong and weak points. It also requires that you know how to act on your assessment. Here are some things you can accomplish by fine-tuning and balancing:

1. Hazes can be cleared with fining agents.

2. Acid levels can be increased, decreased, or counterbalanced by sugar.

3. Tannins can be reduced by fining or increased by adding grape tannin.

4. Bitter aftertastes can be minimized with Polyclar or masked with glycerine or grape tannin.

5. Aromatics can be enhanced by using the glucolytic enzyme AR2000™.

6. Absence of body, middle mouth, or finish can be corrected with additives or by blending.

7. The pH level can be corrected to a level for safe aging by acid adjustments.

Adjusting White Wines

Let's start with whites because they are ready sooner and are comparatively easy to assess.

White wines usually can be assessed soon after they have cleared and the pronounced yeasty nose subsides. We do an initial evaluation of fruity whites after three to four months and all other styles after six months. Evaluating them later is fine if you are willing to wait. Consider the following questions as you evaluate a white wine.

Is the Color Appropriate for This Varietal?

Browning, a sign of oxidation, is the most common problem in whites. However, if it is confined to particulate matter, it usually can be removed with Polyclar. If your wine is orange (not gold or amber, but orange), do something about it. Strip out the orange or change it to a rose with a bit of red wine of the right hue.

Is the Wine Perfectly Clear?

You may have remaining pectins, a protein haze or, least likely, an iron haze. Try adding a bit more pectic enzyme and let the wine sit at room temperature for a week. If there is no improvement, add 1/4 teaspoonful of powdered grape tannin per 5 gallons (0.6g per18.9 l) and wait for another week. Finally, you can try treating once more with Sparkolloid™, but avoid this step until you are sure other measures will not work. Do not bottle a hazy wine unless flaws do not matter in your usage.

Have the Aromatics Developed Enough to Express a Clear Varietal Character?

While the aromatics are likely to be distorted in a very young wine, they should not be faint or absent. Aromatics are often enhanced by the addition of the glucolytic enzymes in AR2000™ from Gist-Brocades, sold by Presque Isle Wine Cellars.

How Would You Describe the Acid?

Is the acid too high? Too high in malic acids? Too rough? Too soft? Acid gives the impression of softening as it ages, so allow for it in your evaluation. Acid can still be lowered with potassium bicarbonate at this late stage, but don't overdo it. It will neutralize the tartaric acid preferentially, so the malic acid component will be relatively more prominent. Residual sugar can effectively balance relatively high acid, but should not be used with a wine that has gone through malolactic fermentation. While it is wise to reduce very high acid now, rather than later, delay balancing acid and sugar in wines you plan to blend.

Does the Wine Make a Good First, "Up-Front" Impression?

The first impression, "up front" fruit, is more important with fruity young wines than with other styles. If it does not have good "up-front" fruit, then it is not going to be a good fruity young wine. You can either blend it with something that will give it some fruitiness, or you need to detect something positive about it to make it a useful blending component. Neutral and full-bodied whites depend less on fruit but rely more on character in the middle mouth and finish.

Does the Wine Have a Pleasing Middle Mouth and Finish?

Even young whites should have flavors carried into the middle mouth and finish. The middle mouth and finish normally take time to fully develop, but if they are absent in an early assessment, they are likely to be no more than faint when fully developed. If a wine is light-bodied, it will stay that way unless you make additions or blend. A half-teaspoon of powdered grape tannin per five gallons (1.2g/18.9 l) can sometimes perk up the body and finish. Tannin will accentuate the sharpness of a wine, so be cautious when adding it to a high acid wine. The middle mouth and finish often make the difference between a pleasant, drinkable wine and one that is outstanding.

Does the Wine Have a Bitter Aftertaste?

Pronounced bitterness in the finish is a definite fault that requires corrective action. Try removing it from a small sample with Polyclar. At the very least, this should reduce bitterness. Astringency can effectively mask bitterness, so try adding 1/2 teaspoon of grape tannin per 5 gallons (1.2g /18.9l). If what remains is still objectionable, add a small amount of glycerin, 2 ounces per 5 gallons (60ml per 18.9 l), to mask it further. Blending is another option. First, try blending with a small sample and let it marry for a few weeks before deciding if the blend is successful.

Does the Wine Fit the Style for Which it was Intended?

Remember that the idea of style depends on anticipation of a wine's highlights and strong points, while downplaying its weak points. Sometimes though, wines do not develop as expected and are poor examples of the intended style. Decide if the wine is caught between styles and needs a slight push in one direction or another. This usually can be accomplished by blending. Occasionally, we have successfully changed the style of a wine by adding oak. For example, a wine made in Germanic style that, in the end, did not have much fruit, can sometimes be pushed toward a more neutral-style white wine by oak addition. It is worthwhile to go back to your winemaking records and try to find clues that suggest why your style choice was not realized.

Does it Need Blending?

Can some of the shortcomings you noted in earlier questions be resolved by adding the right blending component? Typical components will have such strengths as fruity aromatics, crisp acidity, body, or good fruit in the finish. Look for the necessary characteristics in your wine inventory. Often you may find what you need in an older wine that already has been bottled. If not, you may want to store your wine and wait until you have the needed blending component.

Does it Contribute Something Special as a Blending Component?

Sometimes a wine is more valuable for what it can add to other wines than if it were bottled as a varietal. It is likely to have one or more of the four characteristics mentioned above.

Is this a Wine I Will Want to Drink?

If not, do not bottle it. If you can identify the problem (oxidation, extreme volatile acidity, brettanomyces) and know aging will not help, get rid of the wine. If you are unsure of the problem, store it for at least three months and see how aging affects it.

Note About Cold Climate White Hybrid Grape Varieties

While wines from some white *vinifera* varieties can age gracefully for a decade or more, do not expect this from wines produced from white interspecific hybrid grapes. We would be surprised to find a wine made from a white hybrid that is still improving after four years.

Adjusting Red Wines

Red wines made with the carbonic maceration process can be evaluated soon after the byproducts of malolactic fermentation have dissipated, usually two months. Conventionally fermented fruity red wines often can be assessed after four months and medium- and full-bodied reds in one year.

Ask all of the same questions in evaluating red wines as you did for white wines, while keeping in mind three key differences. Red wines go through a somewhat different aging chemistry than do whites. Unlike white wines, controlled oxidation helps reds mellow and mature. Second, tannins in red wines have a major effect on aging, while we can all but ignore them as a factor in white wines. Finally, red wines are inherently more complex, so what most of us want from a red wine is clear evidence of graceful aging.

Medium-bodied and full-bodied red wines almost always should undergo malolactic fermentation and exposure to oak, which soften and add complexity in ways similar to aging. These are two of the three ways to expedite the results of aging without losing quality. The third is through fining to reduce excess tannin. We almost never have excessive tannin in cold climate red wines and, if we did, it probably could be balanced better by blending.

What we are after with medium-bodied and full-bodied red wines is a harmonious wine that has lost its rough edges but still retains vivid suggestions of lush, ripe fruit. If your wine fits this description after six months, drink it soon, for it will not last. Your wine is showing signs of premature aging, most likely caused by a very high pH, excessive exposure to oxygen, early absence of free sulfite, or very overripe fruit.

Two Additional Rewards

The process of balancing and fine-tuning your wine offers two incidental bonuses. First of all, you now know your adjusted wine is progressing in a healthy and predictable manner. Secondly, it cannot help but improve your analytical tasting skills.

Chapter 16

Blending

Finally, we have reached the winemaking subject closest to our hearts! Blending is the winemaker's first real chance to work magic. Flawed wines can sometimes be turned into good ones! Good wines can be transformed into exceptional ones, and spoiled wines can be manipulated endlessly to become slightly less bad. Not everything goes as expected with blending, but the nasty surprises become less common with experience. At its best, blending can fill in the gaps of a wine, adding aromatic and flavor characteristics that give it a balance it would otherwise not have. Our cold climate grapes often have such gaps.

This chapter tells how to evaluate a wine's shortcomings and then blend to improve it. Once you have developed the skills to assess what can be improved in a wine, then the actual blending is a matter of experience with a bit of trial and error. Judging the result calls for the same skills used when balancing and fine-tuning wines.

What Can Blending Improve?

Color
Winemakers must pay close attention to color, because it makes a huge first impression on wine drinkers. Color sets expectations for taste.

Red wines can range from just slightly darker than a rose´, to inky dark red. With their *Vitis riparia* genetic background, most cold hardy grape varieties for red wine give you all of the inkiness you will ever want. Hues can range from purple to brick red, to an oxidized brown, normally reflecting the age, condition and, to some extent, the pH of the wine. Avoid orange hues. Copper or salmon might work, but not orange. When feasible, use blending to transform it into a red. White wines can be almost colorless, or range from greenish-yellow to amber. Rose´ wines can vary from a slight pinkish cast to an intense rosy red, almost as dark as a Beaujolais.

Normally, with cold climate red wines, the color adjustments will be subtle. If your color extraction was inadequate, blend for more intensity. While you want the color true to type, high color intensity forecasts intense taste, and faint color suggests poor flavor extraction. Color results can usually be judged immediately after blending.

Acidity

Blending for acid content or complexity seldom works without some preliminary acid adjustments, because you rarely have high and low acid wines that perfectly complement one another. Most cold hardy grapes tend to have high acidity, so having a low acid component is uncommon. Sometimes low acid fruits like elderberry can be added to a higher acid red grape wine with positive results, provided the flavors and aromas do not clash. We have had better luck with augmenting low acid fruit wines with small amounts of high acid grape wines. You can immediately judge the taste of the blend fairly well if you allow the acids and tannins to soften somewhat. Check the resulting Titratable Acidity (TA) and make sure the pH level is still in the safe range (under 3.6).

Tannins

Each of the three tannin groups requires a different blending strategy, so begin by tasting for bitter, middle, and long tannins. Bitter tannins are mainly from seeds and stems. They are most noticeable as a lingering aftertaste that sugar will not mask. If you have ever tasted wild plums or chokecherries, the back of your tongue still has vivid memories of bitter tannin. Treat the bitterness as described in the previous chapter.

Middle tannins, also called sweet tannins, are astringent, not bitter. They leave a dry, chalky feeling (not taste) in the mouth. Middle tannins also tend to mask bitterness. Cold climate red wines almost never have enough middle tannins, so any red wine high in middle tannins will be a valuable blending component. Young and delicate reds, not intended for aging, do not and should not have much middle tannin.

Long tannins are typically gained with oak aging and complement middle tannins.

Judging your blend for proper tannin balance will be complicated by three factors. First, because tannin and acid augment one another, a properly tannic wine might now taste too acidic. Be careful not to misjudge this as too tannic. Second, if your tasting session with tannic wines goes on for a while, you may become desensitized to the tannin and not notice subtle differences. Finally, middle tannins in particular tend to soften with time.

Flavor

The taste of wine is routinely classified in three phases: beginning, middle mouth, and finish. Evaluating each phase independently allows for a more analytical tasting. The beginning can be described as your first impression. Fruit usually dominates it. Middle mouth impressions are dominated by feel. How the wine fills the mouth is experienced as body, sharpness of the acid, and astringency. Finish relates to lingering tastes, which can be fruit, astringency, bitterness, or sweetness.

Nose

The term "nose" includes the aroma from the grapes and the bouquet from the yeast and other fermentation products. Sparkling wines and carbonic maceration wines have a very pronounced bouquet component and, to a lesser degree, so do most young wines. Change the nose of these wines only with great reluctance. It is extremely important to make sure that the nose is right. Most of the nuances that differentiate one wine from another are either here, or are forecasted here. Blending to improve the nose usually involves adding pleasant notes to a wine lacking in nose. Many off odors have extremely low thresholds of human perception, so diluting them sufficiently by blending is often hopeless. Sometimes it seems that an off odor has been covered up, only to have it emerge a month later. Let samples of apparently successful blends rest for a month to see how they hold up. When aromatics clash in trial blends, however, it is usually apparent within minutes.

The Blending Mentality

It might be tempting to think of blending as a way of constructing or fabricating a wine from ingredients, much as you might make soup from ingredients. But such thinking greatly exaggerates the amount of influence the blender has on the finished product. More often, the blender will be trying to nudge the wine in the right direction by unveiling the lurking good qualities and by masking the bad ones. We can begin by categorizing wines based on their role in blending.

Varietals

These are wines with pronounced, recognizable character that should be showcased in the final wine. When making a varietal wine, think, "Let the wine become what it wants to be." Try to bring out what is there, and be cautious about anything that changes its character. Any blending additions must be done cautiously with white varietal wines, because they are very delicate. Usually the goal with white varietal wines is to only extend the finish or fill in the middle mouth. With varietal reds, we may simply want to add a nuance to the complexity of the nose or slightly enhance the tannins in the middle mouth.

Neutral White Wines

Neutral whites often have complexity and body but do not have a pronounced varietal character. Neutral whites are often kept on fine lees, undergo malolactic fermentation, and even oak treatment to enhance body and complexity. Typically, these wines are better when served with food than when they stand on their own. Blending with several other neutral wines can further add to complexity. Food wines are, by their nature, not as showy as varietals, which is why they are complementary with food. Blending decisions must take into account that it takes a while for the flavors to marry. Note that, without body and complexity, this component is not a true neutral white but probably should be classified merely as an "extender."

Exaggerated Components

Out of balance wines, with an excess of one or more desirable properties, can be considered exaggerated components. Useful properties may be high or low acid level, aromatics, or tannins. These components comprise the heart of blending strategy and allow us to fill in the holes of a varietal, add complexity to a food wine, or construct a Rhone-style red wine. Having components available with many different positive attributes allows the blender many more ways to improve a wine. Exaggerated white wine components are usually limited to adding fruit, aromatics, and body. Reds inherently have more flavors and complexity than whites and, as such, offer a much broader range of blending possibilities.

Rhone-style Red Wines

While good varietal red wines have been made from cold climate grapes, we would expect the best full-bodied red wines in the North to be produced by Rhone-style blending. Rhone-style reds require two or more reds that combine to produce a character different from any of the individual varieties. Think of it as inventing a well-balanced new varietal wine. "Complexity," "layers," and "balance" are all good descriptors of what to expect. Sometimes the aroma of one grape variety may dominate, but there will be other aroma and flavor notes apparent from other grapes. Try to have a clear idea of what each grape variety is expected to contribute to the blend. Rhone-style wines are likely to be very confusing for beginning blenders. Varietal and exaggerated components will comprise most of the blend, but the balance will distinguish it from other wines.

Generic Red Wines

These are more humble versions of the Rhone-style blends. The goal here is to produce a balanced, drinkable wine to be served with regular meals. You draw from the red wines on hand and put them together in such a way that the blend is better than any of the components. There will be a strong temptation to blend so that there is nothing left over. Resist the temptation. Think of making a good house red as preparation for becoming a Rhone-style blender.

Extenders

Wines that contribute no additional good qualities but can be added without noticeably reducing quality of the blend can be considered extenders Don't push it to the outer limit. If you are working on an exceptional wine, use an extender cautiously, if at all. Neutral wines often can be used as extenders.

Problem Wines

Wines having excessive volatile acidity, that are slightly oxidized, or that will never be good on their own are problem wines. Try them only in small test batches of blends. If the blending experiment fails, you can simply pour it out. This is worth trying only if the problem wine has some very good qualities to contribute. Even then, blending with a problem wine is a highly questionable practice. Problem wines that are devoid of good qualities should be discarded. Do not fret over what you have lost as you pour this wine down the drain. Rather, think of the waste of time and effort you are avoiding. Bob confesses to working harder on his problem wines than his good ones and has very little to show for it.

Creating Components

An important part of wine blending is having a "palette" of blending components available. Some ideas for producing components are discussed below.

Grow Grape Varieties With Different Characteristics

It is tempting to plant a whole vineyard of one or two varieties that excel in your area. But we can almost guarantee that your wines will be simple and mediocre. Remember, in most cold climate grapegrowing regions, single hybrid grape varieties often do not produce complete, balanced wines. Planting complimentary varieties will minimize the problem. For white wines, most of your vines can be varieties that produce a neutral wine. There are many grape varieties that can serve as a neutral blending base wine. You should also plant at least one aromatic white variety and one variety that will contribute *vinifera*-like acidity and body to your blend. For red wines, plant a range of varieties that bring different characteristics to your wines including interesting aromatics, tannins, or color. The last section of this chapter and the Varieties Appendix offer some ideas about the special wine characteristics of selected northern grape varieties.

Vary the Amount of Skin Contact in Your Wines

Sometimes optimal skin contact time becomes apparent long after you have had to make the decision to take the must off the skins. If you have enough grapes, you can make separate batches of wine, one on the high and one on the low end of skin contact time. The extreme form of this tactic is to draw off a fraction (15 to 30%) at crush for a rose´ and leave the remainder with concentrated skin contact. This approach is commonly used with Pinot Noir and would probably work well with Foch. The minimal skin contact fraction will be less tannic and slightly more acidic.

Keep Press Run Fractions Separate

Free-run juice is lower in tannin and is fruitier than press run juice, which in turn is lighter than the final press run. Keeping the fractions separate is very simple if you have enough juice. Commercial wineries use this strategy and blend the fractions back together by taste. Sometimes, they may not use the final pressing in a premium wine if it is too harsh. You should probably try this at least once with every red to see how the components differ. You could follow the same proportional blend the following year, but remember that harvest conditions are different every year.

Use a Different Yeast Selection in Each Batch

Yeast strains can differ greatly in their production of aromatics and flavors and in their extraction capabilities. Be sure to use strains with characteristics that are distinct from one another because differences can be subtle. Inoculating one batch simultaneously with two strains usually does not work well because one strain will tend to strongly dominate. A variation on this strategy is to initially inoculate with a strain like Cotes de Blanc that does not finish well and, when fermentation is about half complete, inoculate with a strong finisher like Premier Couvee.

Produce Some Fruit Wines

Experimentation with fruit wines rich in middle tannins and fruity aromatics can be rewarding to the adventurous winemaker. However, fruit wines and grape wines are not usually blended together for several good reasons. Fruit wines typically have pronounced flavor and aroma characteristics that can overwhelm the complexity and balance of a grape wine. Secondly, their chemistry can differ enough from grape wine to make the blend unstable, so color density, aroma, and flavor could change months after bottling. Finally, commercial winemakers in some countries will confront legal barriers to the practice. Now that we have done our duty and warned you about the unpopularity of fruit / grape wine blends, here are two successful blending examples using small (less than 5%) fruit wine additions.

Black Currant (*Ribes nigra*) wine can contribute middle tannins and some rich fruity aromatics. The best varieties impart a pronounced cassis aroma. *Aronia melanocarpa* (Black Chokeberry) wine, produced from steam-extracted juice, adds dense red color, concentrated middle tannins, and berry-like flavors. Tom uses 2% of Aronia wine in his Minnesota port wine blend with noticeable improvement of tannin and complexity. These minor additions of fruit wines can result in greatly improved red wines in regions where extremely cool summers produce red wines that are thin and light in color.

Produce Some *vinifera* Wines

We do not recommend trying to grow *vinifera* varieties in most northern grape growing regions. However, we would certainly not argue against producing some *vinifera* wines to use in blending. Flash-frozen, crushed red wine grapes and pressed white wine grape juice from premium California wine grapes are readily available in small quantities (5-gallon or 18.9 l containers) at reasonable prices. Wines produced from these frozen materials are usually excellent and can be extremely useful blending components. Even as very small blending additions, they can improve many hybrid wines.

Trade Wines With Friends

Short on blending components? Simply trade some wines with your winemaking friends. Single bottles will do for initial blending experiments. If you hit on a really great blend, you can always bargain for more!

Blending Practice

Reading about blending can take you only so far. If you are able to assess the strong and weak points of your wine, then you are ready to practice the basic blending concepts described above. You may find, however, that you lack a wide range of blending components. This can be resolved if you can collaborate with a few winemaking friends and share blending components. Try to include at least one experienced wine taster in your group. Initially, confine your efforts to wines that are ready or almost ready to drink. For comparison to your blends, use commercial wines made in the same style.

Prepare the Right Setting
Find a comfortable, informal, well-lit setting, free from alien smells and distractions. Avoid anything that will numb your sense of taste or smell. Even though you are not in solitary confinement, you should be on a temporary diet of bread (preferably French) and water. Set out three tulip shaped wine glasses. These are specially designed to concentrate the nose of wines. Also set out a spit bucket, graduated syringes, or some other tool for adding small, measured amounts of sugar syrup solution, tartaric acid, vodka, and glycerin. You may want to devise a standard form for tasting notes, a judging sheet, or simply a blank sheet of paper.

Establish a Tasting Order
Like a formal wine tasting, you will want to start with dry and more neutral whites first, moving to increasingly stronger flavors and aromas and to sweeter wines. If you taste reds in the same sitting, take a short break after the whites, then go from the least tannic and alcoholic red wines to the heaviest and most tannic. Limit yourself to putting together a maximum of five finished blends unless you are an experienced and confident taster.

Practice Formal Evaluation Skills
A blending evaluation begins just like a wine judging, except you get to try and correct what you don't like. Bear in mind that some of your corrections may be misleading. Some flavors and aromas take a while to marry. Your blending may actually create some chemical instabilities.

For practice, start with some good commercial varietal wines and evaluate them for having too much or too little of something. Try some blends in your glass with wines that you think might improve these commercial varietal wines. Measure the proportions of wines that make the best blend and note it down. Next, try the same thing with your own wines.

Be sure to keep detailed notes if you plan to scale up your in-the-glass blending experiments and blend larger quantities. Good notes also will help you recognize changes when you reevaluate months later. Almost certainly the later evaluation will not be the same as the initial one, conducted only minutes after blending in the glass.

Field Blends

So far, we have discussed only blending with wines that have achieved a degree of stability. Now it is time to see how blending concepts can be helpful beginning at harvest. First of all, we will be thinking of our white wines as varietals, neutrals, or exaggerated components. Our red wines will be divided into varietals, carbonic maceration candidates, and components. All should be vinified separately so that you can blend components by choice, not convenience. It is tempting to do field blends in which the grapes are blended even before crushing. If you field blend, you are making a blending decision far earlier than you should. Make wine from each grape variety separately and then blend the finished wines. There is one exception to this rule. If you have only a small amount of a grape variety that you know will complement a much larger amount of another, then you can safely add it.

Compatible Blending Partners

Once you have made wine from your chosen varieties a few times, you will know what blends are likely to work well together. Until then, here are the characteristics of some likely blending partners. But first, please note that many special varietal characteristics are highly dependent on ripeness. Many white varieties show their ripeness by the amount of fruit character, while some reds can change character with ripeness, showing distinctly different aspects of the variety. In any case, each harvest year is different enough to require you to test your blending decisions. When harvested before full ripeness, a grape variety may lack enough varietal character to stand on its own. Conversely, some neutral grapes develop distinctive varietal character in some years when there is enough heat for them to fully ripen. If you have an exaggerated component that can impart a ripe fruitiness, you may be able to add it to a marginal varietal wine, nudging that varietal wine into something better. St. Pepin, for example, is a fruity grape variety that, when ripe, will stand adequately on its own as a varietal wine. But it is improved in mouthfeel by blending with a more neutral wine like Prairie Star or Bianca.

Blending Characteristics of White Grape Varieties

St. Pepin
St. Pepin often is made without any blending or in a blend with its sister, LaCrosse. However, only 10% of Prairie Star or 15% of Bianca improves the body and finish of a St. Pepin wine. Not fully ripe, St. Pepin may lack its characteristic fruity *vinifera*-like nose, which may require trial additions of fruity aromatic components.

LaCrosse
This grape ripens later than St. Pepin, has higher acid, and is less aromatic. When fully ripe, it should be tried as a varietal that some prefer to St. Pepin. Try blending a small amount of St. Pepin with your LaCrosse for complexity and added aromatics.

LaCrescent

This is a new variety with a pronounced apricot nose when fully ripe. It offers great potential as a blending component to add fruity aromatics to white wines that require help. Neutral wines could be added to LaCrescent without loss of character.

E.S. 5-3-89

E.S. 5-3-89 produces a fine true muscat wine without any blending. Late harvest wines from this selection have been outstanding. E.S. 5-3-89 also can be used in small amounts to add muscat aromatics to more neutral whites.

Ravat 6

This French Hybrid grape variety produces a wine that very much resembles a Chablis or White Burgundy in character, alcohol, and aromatics. However, it tends to be rather high in acid and is best blended with a white wine of lower acidity.

Seyval Blanc

Seyval does not ripen well in northern climates, so it is often without much fruit character. Adding LaCrescent or E.S. 5-3-89 could add an apricot aroma similar to that which Seyval develops on its own when fully ripe.

Prairie Star

This new variety is most useful in adding body to many of northern whites that need it. In good years, it has a nice floral nose and can be made as a varietal.

Bianca

Bianca is a very neutral wine that has good body. We have used it exclusively as a blending component.

E.S. 10-18-30

This selection from Elmer Swenson has an appealing *vinifera*-like acidity and a faint cotton candy nose, typical of many hybrid grapes. All of our experimental blends with Louise Swenson (from 90/10 to 50/50) have worked, although the best blends have been near an 80/20 proportion.

Louise Swenson

"Louise" has a light, delicate floral nose that could easily be overpowered by blending with a strongly aromatic component. We prefer it blended with a small amount of E.S. 10-18-30 or Prairie Star, which improves the quality of its acidity and mouthfeel.

Kay Gray

This grape has a perplexing winemaking history because of two faults in its chemistry that must be countered in order to produce a palatable wine. It is extremely susceptible to enzymatic browning. The early addition of Polyclar removes the problem. Also, it produces pronounced off flavors and aromas when overripe. Removing overripe berries and clusters in an otherwise properly ripened harvest is essential. When the two faults are avoided, Kay Gray can produce a clean, relatively stark food wine. Try blending with 10 to 25% Louise Swenson.

E.S. 6-16-30

This Swenson selection produces a light white wine with crisp acidity and a delicate floral nose. By itself, E.S. 6-16-30 is a good food wine, reminiscent of a French Muscadet. It can be improved by blending to enhance its body and nose.

Swenson White

This new variety from Elmer Swenson makes a light-bodied wine with a pronounced flowery nose. It can be improved with a small addition of a wine from Prairie Star or Bianca for better body.

Blending Characteristics of Red Grape Varieties

Foch

Marechal Foch is easily the most versatile variety on our list. Depending on harvest parameters, it can be made into any of five classic styles. Four of the styles can be improved by blending, with rose´ usually being the exception. Leon Millot and Joffre, sisters of Foch, all blend readily together. Many prefer Millot to dominate the blend. A 10 to 20% addition of Frontenac to a Foch wine adds dark cherry notes and increases complexity. Foch can have a strong herbaceous quality that will overpower most blending subtleties. Try to minimize the herbaceousness with oak before attempting to blend. Foch made with the carbonic maceration method is unlikely to be herbaceous, so blending some with a medium-bodied Foch can help cover subdued herbaceousness.

Joffre and Leon Millot

These varieties are so similar to their sister Foch that, even though they will be distinct with any given harvest, any blending generalization will not be of help. All three sisters vary more depending on ripeness and geography. Dramatic differences have been noted between wines from Foch grown in Oregon and Minnesota.

St. Croix

St. Croix usually has a herbaceous quality remindful of tobacco, which some find appealing. As with Foch, herbaceousness is best subdued prior to blending. Again, carbonic maceration and oak addition greatly reduce herbaceousness. Our blending experience with St. Croix is very limited, but its low acidity and relatively neutral character should give it versatility.

Frontenac

This new variety from the University of Minnesota has been available to the winemaking community for only a few years and we are still looking for the best ways to make it as a varietal. We struggle with it because of its high acidity, and because its pronounced cherry nose and flavor is sometimes too extreme as a varietal. Frontenac's exaggerated character, of course, makes it a very useful blending component. Blending with Foch almost always works. It should help almost any red that needs a fruity note but should be particularly good in a port-style red.

Troubador

Troubador has been used primarily to contribute color, alcohol, and density to red dessert wines. In Minnesota, allowing the fruit to hang until late in the season increases the intensity of these useful traits. Troubador lacks the aromatic complexity to stand alone as a red wine. Blending with a small amount of MN 1094, for example, produces a very interesting and rather intense heavy-bodied red table wine.

DM 8521-1

This selection from Minnesota breeder, David Macgregor, has produced some fine, well-balanced, intense red varietal wines in Minnesota. It can be used in blends to add tannins and aromatic complexity to other northern reds lacking these traits.

Castel 19.637

Wines from this old French Hybrid selection have a complex spicy, black pepper-celery aroma that is a useful component to add aromatic complexity to more simple wines. Castel tends to have these aromatic characteristics even when less than fully ripe, making it an appealing variety to grow for red wine blending in extremely cool, short-season climates.

Analyzing Blending Results

One season of blending experience can teach you a lot about the grape varieties you have chosen. The blending problems you faced can reveal, in great detail, the strengths and weaknesses of each grape variety. This is particularly true if the blending components were well ripened and well vinified. When the wines have aged enough to show their true character, you will be able to sort out the successful blends from those that have fallen short. Analyzing success is fairly easy. Look at the harvest parameters, vinification methods, and blending formula. Could anything have been better? Do others also find the wine to be pleasing? Maybe you are on the edge of making an exceptional wine. Disappointments are more difficult to analyze because the poor results may or may not be the result of blending decisions. Start by asking why you are dissatisfied with the wine.

Were There Flaws That Remained or Required Drastic Measures to Remove?

If you can prevent or reduce the flaws next year you can avoid highlight-reducing drastic measures. Remember that blending is more effective at coping with an absence of something good, than it is at covering up something bad.

Were you disappointed by the absence of fruit?

If the fruit was not fully ripe, you cannot expect the best fruit quality to be present in your wine. While fruit quality can sometimes be added with a blending component, there are limits to how much ripe fruit character a component can add to a wine made with unripe grapes.

Was the Wine Unbalanced?

Sometimes balance achieved by blending is hard to judge. When blending is done too early, the lush, young fruitiness can overwhelm your nose and taste buds. This is an asset if you plan to drink the wine when it is very young. Otherwise, let your wine age longer before trying to blend.

Were the Aromatics Faint, Unpleasant, or Mismatched to the Taste of the Wine?

Aromatics are the most difficult aspect for a blender to anticipate. Test blends should marry for one month to three months if you are trying to make a radical change. Harvest parameters often have a huge impact on wine aromatics, so expect blending for aroma to be an annual balancing act.

Does the Wine Lack Harmony?

Any aspect that clashes with varietal character almost certainly will disrupt harmony. Blending two wines made in very different styles can produce inharmonious sensory confusion. Your blending imagination has gone too far when a sensory impression of a wine does not fit with the one preceding it. *The University Wine Course* by Marion Baldy covers the subject of harmony well.

We can learn more from what has gone wrong than from blending successes, so analyze carefully, apply what you have learned, and keep good notes.

Chapter 17

Making a Good Impression: Appearance, Bottling, and Labeling

First impressions, particularly visual ones, count far more than you might expect and will have the most influence on subjective judgments, such as winetasting. Even trained wine judges must work hard to keep their scoring of visual factors from biasing other judging elements. There is, however, good reason why visual impressions have such strong influence on our subsequent judgment. Appearance is a fairly good forecaster of how the wine will smell and taste. Hazy wines forecast spoilage or lack of refinement, while brilliantly clear wines forecast brilliant flavors.

Wine Appearance

What can be done to make the visual impression of a wine work in your favor? Let's start with appearance of the wine itself. Make sure the color is true to varietal type and shows no sign of oxidation. Good clarity also is an absolute requirement.

The highest level of clarity is obtained by filtration, a step that we stubbornly try to avoid. We prefer patience to filters because filters can strip out desirable aromas and flavors. Patience also will keep you from bottling wines that appear clear, only to drop sediment after bottling. Sediment in the bottle often will leave a bad visual impression, even though it might mean only the wine was bottled too soon. Many white wines cleared by Sparkolloid™ will drop a small amount of sediment three months after the initial clearing. Blended wines and those to which sweet reserve additions have been made are most likely to throw sediment. Wines not thoroughly cold stabilized can drop tartrate crystals, which many people consider a flaw, but this is never a clarity issue. Make a point of decanting and rebottling any wine with sediment before using it in settings where unopened bottle impressions matter. Otherwise, decant immediately before serving.

Commercial wineries often are concerned with heat stabilization because their wines may be subjected to conditions far warmer than would ever occur in a wine cellar. Proteins remaining in the wine can turn a wine cloudy when exposed to enough heat. If your wines are stored in a cool place, this should not become a problem.

Sediment is more acceptable in older reds (more than three years) where sediment is considered a normal part of aging. Tannins, pigments, and even tartrates drop out of red wines. Wines that drop sediment were traditionally put into bottles with raised bottoms (punts) to simplify decanting. This brings us to the subject of bottle style.

Bottle Style Selection

Bottle type should forecast wine style. You can use this stereotyping to your advantage. Browsing the shelves of a wine store will give you a good sense of what kinds of wines and bottles go together. Let's look at common bottle styles and what they suggest.

Brown Hock

This tall, slender, and gradually tapering bottle is now used for either Germanic or Alsatian style wines. It has partially replaced the green hock, which still may be used for Alsatian and Moselle wines.

Flint

These are clear bottles, usually in the shouldered Bordeaux shape and used to display color. Flint bottles usually are for wines intended for early consumption. Roses´ and light, fruity reds look good in them, as do whites with good color. Do not use them for medium reds or for wines that belong in hocks.

Burgundy

Burgundy bottles offer a wide range of possibilities. They can be used for full-bodied whites, which is why Chardonnay producers use the light amber version of it. It is also used for some reds, such as Rhone-style wines and, of course, Burgundy. Bottle color ranges from golden to brown to green. With red wines, you have latitude on bottle color, but we would be reluctant to use gold for a red wine meant for aging. Avoid emerald green bottles for red wines, because they suggests freshness, crispness, and even unripeness, none of which you want to come to mind when drinking medium-bodied and full-bodied reds.

Bordeaux

Bordeaux bottles are for the medium- and full-bodied reds. The colored ones range from pale green (fine for a young, fruity red) to tan to the most common greenish brown. This is a very practical shape because it stacks well horizontally and has plenty of room for tall labels.

Half-size

Sometimes known as splits, these bottles can be used for any wine but are particularly useful for dessert wines. Not only are dessert wines served in smaller quantities, but also the bottle size hints at its concentrated flavor and aroma.

Port-style
These are usually decorative, stocky, shouldered heavy-duty bottles often in a dense brown color. It is probably pretentious to put any cold climate wine in a classic port bottle, but it definitely gets attention.

Champagne
These bottles should only be used for sparkling wines.

Everything Else
Everything else, including bottles with odd shapes and colors, will stand out, but they will not have the advantage of the positive associations of the classic-style bottles.

Labels

The label is your final chance to take advantage of positive stereotypes. Bob's first fruit wine was labeled "Rhubob." Bob has since decided that humor is not the first impression he wants to make, although Bonny Doon Winery has shown that it can work. The impression he wants to give now is simple and direct. His label now simply has his winery name, the varietal name, the vintage year, and some line artwork, as shown below. You may prefer to have your own name followed by "cellars," "winery," or "vineyards." Choose "vineyards" if you actually have one and maybe even add "Estate Bottled" under the varietal name. Artwork is a nice addition if it does not result in clutter that takes attention away from the the important thing: your wine!

Designed by Caroline Portoghese

Appendix A

Recommended Grape Varieties

Our list of recommended grape varieties would be very short, indeed, if we were unwilling to include less than perfect varieties. Most of the varieties described in this appendix either require some special attention in the vineyard or some special winemaking adjustments to bring their unusual hybrid grape chemistry into balance. Some require both. Simply put, most of these varieties are less forgiving in the winery than traditional wine grapes, but they can produce very satisfying results for knowledgeable growers and winemakers.

This appendix describes thirty grape varieties that meet various climatic needs of the most northern regions of grapegrowing. Photographs of these varieties appear in Color Plate 2 at the end of this appendix. Some of these varieties, such as Foch, Millot, Seyval, St. Croix, Kay Gray, St. Pepin, and Vandal-Cliché are readily available from commercial nurseries in North America. Rondo, Reform, Bianca, Zilga, and Castel can be obtained from certain Baltic and Scandinavian nurseries (see the Resources Appendix for details). Other varieties described here are more difficult to obtain. With their recently discovered potential, these varieties are only beginning to become available in their native regions. Growers should consider obtaining cuttings of these and propagating their own plants. In the Resources Appendix to this book, we have provided some grower association resources that can help you find the more obscure varieties. Please observe restrictions on the import of material from other countries, as well as plant patents.

Grape growing and winemaking in extreme northern climates are pioneering efforts with both risks and rewards. Most of the interspecific hybrid varieties and selections we recommend are very new and, as a result, have not been widely planted. Our descriptions of these varieties are as conclusive as possible at the present time. However, we still have a lot to learn about many of these grape varieties. As a grower and winemaker, you can contribute to that knowledge by testing and evaluating the lesser known of the varieties described here and sharing your findings with the cold climate grape growing community.

Super Hardy

D.M. 8521-1

David Macgregor has been breeding grapes in Minnesota for 25 years and has some excellent selections for red wine. This is one of them. D.M. 8521-1 has tightly-formed, winged clusters averaging 90 g (range 70-120 g). Berries are small (1 g). It ripens midseason in Minnesota to high sugar content. Wines produced from well-ripened fruit of this selection have had dense color, some tannins, and good fruit in the nose and mouth. The vine is extremely disease resistant and has outstanding winter hardiness. It has never injured in Tom's vineyard, even in the coldest winters. It is not very vigorous, but vigor and productivity can be enhanced by grafting on a rootstock such as E.S. 15-53. For commercial plantings, grafting would be essential to ensure adequate production. D.M. 8521-1 should be more widely propagated and tested in the coldest regions of northern viticulture. Macgregor developed D.M. 8521-1 from a cross of [E.S. 283 x (*Riparia* x Merlot)] with *Riparia* 37 x Chambourcin (pretty good grandparents for wine!). Perfect flowers.

Troubador

A selection by David Macgregor from a cross of *V. riparia* x St. Croix. Troubador has rather small (40-50 g), semi-loose, clusters of small (1 g) berries, so it is not for commercial production. But cold climate amateur growers should be interested in this one. In central Minnesota, this selection develops high sugar content by midseason. Acidity is somewhat high but quite workable. The juice is very dense and deep red in color. Troubador is an excellent dessert wine ingredient and also makes a good red table wine. It is quite resistant to diseases and extremely winter hardy. Troubador has never been winter injured at Tom's vineyard site in Minnesota. This variety has extremely high vigor. This needs to be controlled by pruning to a high bud count for good fruit production (120 buds in a mature vine) and by giving it a lot of trellis space. A divided trellis with double cordons accommodates its vigor and allows a high number of buds be left for fruiting. Perfect flowers.

E.S. 10-18-30

E.S. 10-18-30 is a promising white selection for the extreme winter hardiness it has shown so far in Minnesota, surpassing Kay Gray and approaching even wild *riparia* in both field and controlled freezing tests. Berries are small (1.5 g) and produced in tight Millot-sized clusters (ave. = 90 g, range 80-150 g). In some years, E.S. 10-18-30 can have some problems with shot or green berries. It ripens early north of St. Paul, by the first week in September, to high sugar level of 22 °Brix or higher. E.S. 10-18-30 will probably find its place as a blending wine. Wines from E.S.10-18-30 have shown excellent body or fullness in the mouth, good acidity, and long finish, much like a good Chardonnay. These characteristics are often lacking in northern white wines produced from hybrids. E.S. 10-18-30 can be used to add these desirable characteristics to weaker wines. It is non-foxy but has a hybrid candy-like nose, which is more pronounced in extremely ripe fruit. For optimal quality, harvest it 5-7 days before full ripeness.   E.S. 10-18-30 was selected by Elmer Swenson from some 200 seedlings that resulted from this cross. It is the best culturally of all these seedlings. The vine is slightly susceptible to Black Rot and Anthracnose, but remains healthy under moderate spray programs. Its vigor is low to moderate. Shoots tend to grow upright, so a low or middle cordon style is training is called for. It is much more productive when it is grafted to a vigorous rootstock such as E.S. 15-53. For commercial use, we recommend that E.S.10-18-30 be grown only as a grafted vine. E.S.10-18-30 has outstanding genes for wine, its grandparents being Chardonnay and Cabernet Sauvignon. Perfect-flowers.

Hardy (to approximately –31 ºF or –35 ºC)

Varajane Sinine

The name means Early Blue in Estonian. It is the best grape variety in Estonia. Jaan Kivistik, at the Rapina Agricultural College, discovered this variety and has evaluated it for many years. Varajane Sinine has some unique traits that are of interest to northern growers. Most significantly, it is one of the very earliest blue grapes to ripen, maturing along with Jubileinaja Novgoroda in 110 to 120 days and 650 to 750 DDC (1170 to 1350 DDF) of heat. For example, on 9/9/98 in Rapina, the sugar content of berries from Varajane Sinine ranged from 17.0 to 20.5 ºBrix, with moderate acidity. Berries were rather soft to pressure, the seeds were reddish turning brown, close to ripe for winemaking. Varajane Sinine was ripe in Estonia when the Minnesota varieties, St. Croix and Beta, growing right next to it, were still green. Berries are small to medium (ave. = 1.1 g; range 1.3-1.9 g), blue with a gray blush. Clusters are small (95 g), cylindrical, and a bit loose. The wine is light red, rather Beaujolais-like, with hints of cherry fruit. Malolactic fermentation is an essential part of winemaking with Varajane Sinine to reduce sharp malic acid. Crops are moderate, on the order of 4.5 kg per plant. Good winter survival has been observed in Estonia in a recent winter with a mid-winter low of -27 ºF (-33 ºC). Covering is recommended for the first two years of growth. After that, the vine can be cultivated without winter protection throughout Estonia. Its origin unknown. Perfect flowers.

Hasansky Sladky (Kazan Early)

This variety was named after Kazan, a Russian city located about 400 miles east of Moscow near the Ural Mountains.   However, it was developed nearly fifty years ago by the Ukrainian breeding program in Magarach. This extraordinary blue grape has the ability to ripen in the extremely cool climates of Latvia and Estonia. Hasansky Sladky has long, slightly loose clusters that weigh an average of 90 g (range 70-120 g) and with small-medium (2 g) berries. The juice is clear, not red. Hasansky is best suited to light red "café" wines in the "Spatburgunder" style of the Ahr Valley in Germany. Processed with a yeast that encourages fruitiness, such as D-47 or 71-B and skin contact limited to only 4-5 days, the wines are quite fruity, with some nice tannins in the mouth and with no hint of foxiness. The wine is remindful of a Beaujolais nouveau. In cool climates, the acidity tends to be high and has to be reduced by malolactic fermentation. In the vineyard, Hasansky Sladky is quite disease resistant, except for a moderate susceptibility to Powdery Mildew. It has shown good winter hardiness, down to at least -31 °F (-35 °C) mid-winter cold. Hasansky results from a cross of Dalnyvostochyni #60 with *Vitis amurensis*. Perfect flowers.

Zilga (Dvietes 4-2-108)

The name Zilga in Latvian is poetic, loosely translating to "deep dark-blue waters." Typically, by mid-September in Latvia, Zilga will have a sugar content of about 18 °Brix, with the fruit very ripe to the taste, having a characteristic flavor of blueberries or lingonberries. The acidity is moderate. The berries are medium-large (3 g), blue with sky-blue shading. The clusters are medium, tightly formed and with a wing. The average weight of the cluster is 161 g (range 92-270 g). Zilga is a very vigorous and productive vine. It is capable of producing 20 kg of berries from a single vine, even in the cool wet Latvian summer. To date, attempts at winemaking from Zilga have been less than satisfying. We include it here because of its productivity and great cultural adaptability to cool, wet, frost-prone climates. Learning to make decent wine from Zilga will take some time, if indeed we ever learn how to work with it. The juice is prone to oxidation and needs careful measures, such as Polyclar treatment, to prevent this. Zilga wines produced by semi-carbonic maceration are typically purple-red, with a nose described as "cranberry" with "mineral" overtones. These also have a hint of foxiness. Rose´-style wines from Zilga are remindful of fruit wines, with strawberry being the predominant aroma. Zilga wines are improved in mouthfeel and aromatics by an addition of dense aromatic red wines from either Holubok or Foch. Zilga is very disease resistant. Among all Sukatnieks' selections, Zilga is the most hardy, having survived winters of -40 °F (-40 °C) in Belarus. Currently, Zilga is in quarantine by the USDA at Geneva, New York. If it passes virus testing, it should be available to American growers by 2002-2003. Zilga results from a 1964 cross by Latvian breeder, Pauls Sukatnieks of (Smuglyanka x Dvietes Zilas) x Jubileinaja Novgoroda. Perfect flowers.

St. Croix

Many award-winning red wines in Minnesota have been produced from St. Croix. It is also the main red wine variety at many wineries in Quebec. Clusters of St. Croix are medium and slightly loose, with the berries resembling those of Beta in size and color. St. Croix ripens in midseason in the St. Paul area of Minnesota. The acidity is moderate, but the grape struggles to make 20 °Brix in sugar. This is true even in hot summer climates, such as in Missouri. The juice is a pale rose and the wines can be quite dark in color. The lack of tannins in St. Croix wines is fairly common and needs to be corrected by blending. The wines often suffer from a tobacco-like nose. However, fruitier wines have been made from St. Croix grapes fermented with semi-carbonic maceration techniques. The press run fraction can produce some very special wines. St. Croix tends to be vegetatively vigorous, but not terribly productive of fruit, so care must be taken in pruning to leave a sufficient number of buds to balance the vegetative vigor. Typically, St. Croix vines will survive mid-winter cold down to -25 to -27 °F (-32 to -33 °C) without injury. The roots are a bit less hardy and need snow cover in really cold winters. Grafting on a superhardy rootstock may slightly enhance its hardiness and productivity. St. Croix was developed by Elmer Swenson in Osceola, Wisconsin from a cross of E.S. 283 x E.S. 193. Perfect flowers.

Sabrevois (E.S. 2-1-9)

This selection from Elmer Swenson is the lesser known sister of St. Croix. Nearly 50,000 vines of Sabrevois are grown commercially in Quebec. It derives it's name from the village of Sabrevois near the Richelieu River south of Montreal. The cluster is small to medium in size (ave. = 80 g, range 60-100 g) and somewhat loose. The black berries are small to medium in size (ave. = 1.5 g). The fruit ripens in mid-season, about a week after St. Croix. The acidity of Sabrevois tends to be higher than St. Croix but very workable. Like St. Croix, sugar content rarely exceeds 20 °Brix even in very ripe fruit. Wines from Sabrevois can have a pleasant berry-like fruitiness in the nose and mouth but tend to lack body and tannin, and are very dark in color. They are pleasant wines, but can be improved by blending. Vines of Sabrevois are vigorous, yet they sometimes struggle to set a sufficient crop to balance their vegetative vigor. Good production and balanced growth has been achieved using a divided trellis system. Sabrevois has been injured in Minnesota only in the most severe winters. It is considerably hardier and more reliable than its sister, St. Croix. Like St. Croix, Sabrevois is a seedling from a cross of E.S. 283 x E.S. 193. Perfect flowers.

Frontenac (Minnesota 1047)

Frontenac is a village on Lake Pepin, a wide place in the Mississippi River, just southeast of St. Paul. It also is the name of the French governor who lost Quebec to the British. The variety is very productive of moderately-loose medium to large clusters of medium-sized blue-black berries. The vine can overproduce, so it needs to be cluster-thinned for the best quality fruit. The fruit matures rather late, the last half of September in Minnesota. Grown in insufficient heat or picked prematurely, it will be herbaceous and very high in acid. Frontenac wine will develop a characteristic cherry nose when produced from properly-ripened grapes. With a long season, the fruit can build high sugar levels. Acidity drops precipitously at the very end of the season, long after sufficient sugar is developed. You must be patient with it and avoid the urge to harvest it based on sugar content alone. Frontenac wines must go through malolactic fermentation to reduce this excess acidity to a workable level. This vine has excellent resistance to mildew except for black rot to which it is moderately prone. Its hardiness is significantly better than St. Croix, being injured in central Minnesota only in the most severe winters. Selected by Peter Hemstad at the University of Minnesota from a cross of *Riparia* 89 x Landot 4511. Perfect flowers.

Skujins 675 (Moskovskij Ustoicivij)

Kaspars Skujins was a Latvian grape breeder who worked at the Tymiryazev Academy of Agriculture (TCXA) in Moscow. In Russia, this selection has been named Moskovskij Ustoiciivij. The Latvians prefer to call it Skujins

675. This variety is one of the earliest ripening and most promising of the varieties we evaluated for white wine potential in the Baltic region. On September 13th, 1998 in Riga, Latvia, Skujins 675 measured 20 °Brix, with a pH of 3.3. These numbers reflect nearly perfect ripening for white wine production. The wines from Skujins 675 are still highly experimental. Wines with the best aromatics have been produced from grapes grown in cool summer areas and harvested before full ripeness around 18 °Brix. Aroma of the wines ranges from "pineapple"and "lychee" in the best samples to "bubblegum" in wines produced from overripe grapes. The juice is prone to oxidation, so careful measures are required to prevent this during processing. The berries of Skujins 675 are small-medium in size (1.5 g) and the moderately loose clusters range from 90 to 120 g. The vines are productive and set fruit well in poor weather. Skujins 675 buds out relatively late in the spring and, if shoots are damaged by late spring frost, has the ability to produce a substantial crop on secondary bud growth. Skujins 675 also blooms late. For all these reasons, this variety has commercial potential for Baltic countries, as well as for certain cool season areas of the U.S., such as Maine, the Lake Superior Shore, and Puget Sound. Currently, Skujins 675 is in quarantine by the USDA at Geneva, New York. If it passes virus testing, it should be available to American growers by 2002-2003. The vines of Skujins 675 are quite winter hardy and are grown without winter protection throughout the Baltics and Belarus. Skujins 675 resulted from a cross of Pearl of Csaba x Amurskij with the old Minnesota variety, Alpha. It contains genes from four grape species, *Vitis vinifera*, *Vitis amurensis*, *Vitis Labrusca*, and *Vitis riparia*. Perfect flowers.

Kay Gray

This variety was named by its developer, Elmer Swenson, after the wife of his friend, Dick Gray, former director of the Minnesota Freshwater Biological Institute. Through many years of testing in Minnesota, this variety has proven to be one of the most culturally reliable white grape varieties available. It usually suffers little injury with mid-winter temperatures down to -35 °F (-37 °C) or even colder. At extremes, such as -40 °F (-40 °C), this variety has been injured at some sites and uninjured at others. Kay Gray also is extremely resistant to diseases. The berries on Kay Gray are medium to large (3.5 g) and are produced in small to medium clusters (ave. = 96 g, range 70-120 g) that are tightly formed. By early September in the St. Paul, MN area, the fruit is fully mature at 20 to 22 °Brix and rather low acidity (0.7-0.8 %). However, if allowed to ripen fully, it develops some objectionable aromatics for winemaking. Harvest Kay Gray prior to full maturity, at 15 to18 °Brix. Great care must be taken to avoid oxidation while processing the fruit into wine. This includes one or more of the following techniques: cold processing the fruit and juice, addition of anti-oxidants such as Polyclar during processing, cool fermentation of the wine, minimal racking, and careful use of CO_2 during racking operations. Interesting results also have been obtained with *sur lies* processing and malolactic fermentation. A neutral wine for table use or for blending can be produced from Kay Gray. In exceptional years, a well-made Kay Gray wine can have a flowery nose and stand on its own as a varietal wine. This variety is a mainstay in white wine production at several wineries in Quebec, Canada. Kay Gray is an open-pollinated seedling of Golden Muscat selected by Elmer Swenson. Perfect flowers.

E.S. 6-16-30

This white wine selection from Elmer Swenson ripens its fruit in early September in the St. Paul area, with nice parameters for winemaking, sugar around 20 to 21 °Brix and acidity around 1.0%. Clusters are medium in size (ave. = 126 g, range 60-160 g). The berries also are medium sized (ave. berry = 3 g), and are a deep golden color when fully ripe. The wine has been described as a bit austere, with a delicate, flowery nose in most years, and some astringency in the mouth and finish, remindful of a French muscadet. In the vineyard, E.S. 6-16-30 is very resistant to diseases and grows with moderate vigor in an orderly, slightly trailing manner. Controlled freeze testing and years of experience in the vineyard have shown that E.S. 6-16-30 is hardier than St. Pepin and is a reliable producer following winters in the -31 °F (-35 °C) range. Its secondary and tertiary buds seem to have a knack for surviving even colder temperatures and producing some fruit. It is susceptible to cold following late winter warm spells. This selection should be more widely tested in Minnesota and Quebec. E.S. 6-16-30 was selected by Elmer Swenson from a cross of E.S. 2-3-17 x E.S. 35. It has perfect flowers.

St. Pepin

In recent years, some of the best white wines in Minnesota have been produced from St. Pepin. This variety has medium-sized berries and clusters that are loosely formed. It ripens in mid-September near St. Paul, Minnesota, with sugar content typically around 20 °Brix and acidity around 1.0%. Clusters of St. Pepin can sometimes ripen to 26 °Brix, which may produce some off flavors and aromas. Production can be a problem in this pistillate variety, particularly in years with poor conditions for pollination. Prune St. Pepin to a generous bud count to ensure decent production. On their own roots, vines of St. Pepin can be expected to suffer bud injury if the temperature drops much below -25.6 °F (-32 °C). It does not quite make it into our -31 °F (-35 °C) hardiness category. Recent studies at the University of Minnesota have shown that St. Pepin's hardiness can be improved significantly by grafting it onto superhardy rootstocks. St. Pepin was developed by Elmer Swenson of Osceola, Wisconsin. It is from an early Swenson cross of E.S. 114 x Seyval. Pistillate.

LaCrosse

LaCrosse was developed by Elmer Swenson of Osceola, Wisconsin and named in 1985 after the city on the Mississippi River. It is a mainstay of the new commercial wine industry in Nebraska. LaCrosse has a medium, slightly loose to compact cluster around 100 grams and medium berry. It ripens two weeks after St. Pepin, late season in the southern half of Minnesota. In warm summer areas such as Nebraska and southern Minnesota, sugar will typically reach 19-21 °Brix in well-ripened LaCrosse grapes, with workable acidity. In both Minnesota and Nebraska, the best wines from LaCrosse have been dry whites fermented in oak and with the acidity softened by malolactic fermentation. Some excellent fruity semi-dry wines also have been made. Depending on wine style, descriptions of aromatics in LaCrosse wines range from pear, apricot, and slightly muscat to citrus and floral. LaCrosse wines have proven to be good varietal food wines and also have been valuable as blending components with lighter wines such as Louise Swenson to which it adds body and finish. LaCrosse is reliably hardy to around –25 ºF (-31 ºC), but suffers bud injury at temperatures much colder than this. In Minnesota, LaCrosse vines usually are protected over the winter. In Nebraska, where winters are slightly less severe than in Minnesota, LaCrosse succeeds without winter protection. Vigor and productivity of LaCrosse vines are moderate, and can be somewhat improved by grafting on a vigorous superhardy rootstock. It is moderately susceptible to Black Rot. LaCrosse is a sister of St. Pepin. Both resulted from an early Swenson cross of E.S. 114 x Seyval blanc. Perfect flowers.

LaCrescent (MN 1166)

This is one of the best new white wine selections from Peter Hemstad at the University of Minnesota. It has long slightly loose clusters with a small wing and turns a beautiful golden-brown color when fully ripe. The clusters average 120 g (range 80-200 g) with smallish (1.5 g) berries. Ripe fruit of LaCrescent typically produces a wine with a pronounced and delicious apricot-like flavor. It is an excellent blending component to add good aromatics to more neutral white wines. By midseason, the selection can develop high sugar in hot climates such as Minnesota, but acidity also remains rather high and needs to be reduced during winemaking. The wine can be very good, balanced and with good body. In the vineyard, LaCrescent is moderately susceptible to Powdery Mildew and Downy Mildew, so it needs a careful spray program. MN 1166 has proven to be much hardier than St. Pepin, but has suffered injury in the coldest winters. It has proven to be susceptible to cold damage following early spring warm spells. Developed from a cross of St. Pepin x E.S. 6-8-25. The latter is Riparia 89 x Muscat Hamburg. Perfect flowers.

Swenson White (E.S. 6-1-43)

Another relative newcomer from Elmer Swenson, Swenson White is a challenger to St. Pepin in terms of vineyard performance and wine quality. The clusters of Swenson White are medium to large (ave. = 152 g, range 90-230 g) and rather loose. The berries are large (4 g) and yellowish. They are thick-skinned, allowing them to hang on the vine, unmolested by insects, late into the fall season. This selection ripens rather late, struggling to make 22 ºBrix by the first of October in the St. Paul area. The acidity is moderate. White wines produced from Swenson White have a pronounced flowery nose remindful of St. Pepin and a long fruity finish. There also is a slight *labrusca* flavor in wines made from very ripe fruit. With its ability to hang on the vine and its good aromatics, this selection also should be a good candidate for late harvest wine or ice wine.

It is very disease resistant. Swenson White is about as hardy as St. Pepin, so it barely makes it into the -31 °F (-35 °C) category. It is a seedling of Edelweiss x E.S. 442. Perfect flowers.

E.S. 5-3-89

Want some muscat flavor in your wine? Grow some E.S. 5-3-89 and use it as an aromatic addition to a more neutral white wine. This white grape has fairly compact, medium-sized clusters (80-140 g, ave. =105 g) and medium (2.5 g) berries. These ripen rather late in the season north of St. Paul, with a pronounced true muscat aroma. The berries have tough skins and can hang on the vine late into the fall. They are suitable for a late harvest wine, making 25 °Brix or higher in a good ripening year. The wine is quite *vinifera*-like and rich in aromatics. The vine is one of the most disease-resistant selections developed by Elmer Swenson, being virtually immune to Downy and Powdery Mildew and Black Rot. It has rather low vigor. Vines of E.S. 5-3-89 have more acceptable growth and production when grafted on a hardy, vigorous rootstock, such as E.S. 15-53. The vines are about as hardy as St. Pepin or slightly hardier. This selection is from a cross of E.S. 2-4-13 x E.S. 2-5-5. It has partially reflexed stamens, but usually sets fruit rather well.

Prairie Star (E.S. 3-24-7)

This is a mid-season white wine grape from Elmer Swenson. It is usually harvested at 20 to 22 °Brix during the third week in September in the St. Paul area. Prairie Star has long, slightly loose clusters that, on heavy soils or on grafted vines, can average 177 g (range 120-240 g). On lighter or less fertile soils, cluster size will be closer to the lower end of this range and production will be less. Berries are small-medium, averaging 2.5 g. The fruit matures to excellent sugar and acidity for white winemaking. The typical wine from Prairie Star is neutral, but not foxy. It has a fullness in the mouth and finish that is uncommon among our hybrid grape varieties. In some years, wines from Prairie Star develop a delicate floral nose that allow them to stand as single variety wines. In most years, however, Prairie Star is best used as a blending component to add body and finish to thinner white wines. The vine is one of the hardiest white wine varieties, suffering little damage in all but the harshest, -40 °F (-40 °C) winters. At some Minnesota vineyards, it has survived even these conditions with little injury. Prairie Star also is rather resistant to mildew diseases, with the exception of Black Rot and Anthracnose, to which it is moderately susceptible. Poor fruit set has been observed in some seasons at a few sites. This variety has a tendency for its shoots to break off in strong winds early in the season. Low cordon training systems, using catch wires to secure the shoots, should be explored to prevent this problem. High cordon training systems should be avoided. It was developed from a cross of E.S. 2-7-13 x E.S. 2-8-1. Perfect flowers.

Louise Swenson (E.S. 4-8-33)

This selection was bred from a cross of E.S. 2-3-17 x Kay Gray. However, as a wine grape, it will never be confused with Kay Gray. Berries average around 3 g and clusters are small to medium, conical, somewhat compact, and average 105 g (range 70-130 g). In five years of trials, the wine from Louise Swenson has been outstanding for its quality and consistency from year to year. The wine is without any negative hybrid characteristics, and has a typical delicate aroma of flowers and honey. This wine's only significant fault is that it is rather light in body. Blending with a variety such as Prairie Star makes it a more complete wine. Louise Swenson rarely exceeds 20 °Brix, even if left to hang past midseason. Acidity is moderate and needs no reduction. Observed at many sites around south-central Minnesota, this variety has shown little or no winter injury even in the most severe (-40 °F) winters. It has an orderly growth habit, with moderate vigor on most sites. It buds out relatively late in the spring compared to other interspecific hybrid grape varieties. Unlike its father, Kay Gray, the clusters hang free of the tendrils. Disease resistance is generally very good, with some susceptibility to Anthracnose. Observations on very sandy sites suggest that Louise Swenson may be sensitive to droughty conditions. On sites of this type, irrigation may be required in dry years. This grape should be grown much more widely in the North for its consistent wine quality, outstanding winter hardiness, and good cultural behavior. Perfect flowers.

Vandal-Cliche

This new grape variety for white wine was developed in Quebec and recently named for its two developers, Mario Cliché and Joseph Vandal. It is being planted widely in the areas around Quebec City and Ottawa, where it has made winegrowing possible on a commercial scale. One vineyard alone has 15,000 vines planted. Vandal-Cliche usually needs about 1100 Degree Days DDC (2000 DDF) of heat to ripen to a sugar content of around 20 °Brix. However, years of experience in Quebec have proven that the best Vandal-Cliche wines have come from fruit harvested just before full maturity, at a sugar content of around 18 °Brix. Even at full ripeness, the acidity tends to be somewhat high in this variety, with a large proportion of the acids in the form of malic acid. A malolactic fermentation is essential to eliminate the malic acid and balance the wine. The result is a crisp, neutral wine that is good with food or can be blended with more aromatic components. Vandal-Cliche is extremely vigorous and productive, often setting four clusters per shoot. Cluster thinning to two clusters per shoot is mandatory. Experiments with various training methods in Quebec have shown that a divided trellis system is best suited to the vigor and productivity of this vigorous variety. Vandal-Cliche is generally a healthy vine but if left unsprayed can contract Powdery Mildew and Anthracnose. It has proven to be fully winter hardy in the area around Quebec City and is grown there on a commercial scale without winter protection. Vandal and Cliché developed this grape from a cross of Prince of Wales x [V. riparia x (Aurore x Chancellor)]. Perfect flowers.

Tender (Require winter protection in cold winter areas)

Jubileinaja Novgoroda

This extraordinarily early ripening white grape variety was developed by Kuzmin at the Central Genetic Laboratory in Michurinsk, Russia. It was named to celebrate the 1000th Anniversary of the ancient city of Novgorod in western Russia, near the present-day border between Russia and Estonia. Jubileinaja Novgoroda requires a growing season of only 110 to 120 days. In early September of 1998, we traveled around the Baltic region on a grape exploration trip for the United States Department of Agriculture. This is one grape variety that really got our attention. In Minsk and Pinsk, Belarus and in Rapina, Estonia, sugar content of Jubileinaja Novgoroda consistently ranged from 18.5 to 22 °Brix, with well-developed flavors that can be described as similar to pineapple or tropical fruit. The fruit was delicious. It was one of the few varieties that showed full maturity under Baltic and Belarusian conditions in 1998. Jubileinaja Novgoroda produces an attractive, slightly loose cluster of 80 to 120 g. Berries are round and medium in size (2.3 g). It has good fruit set under cool wet conditions and good *botrytis* resistance. It is very susceptible to Downy Mildew and needs careful fungicide sprays for this disease. It is hardy to about -22 °F (-30 °C) without protection. Some reports indicate that it is bothered by basic soils. This super early ripening variety resulted from a cross of Blanc Precoce de Malingre x Russki Konkord (Concord x Vitis amurensis). Perfect flowers.

Veldze

In 1959, Latvian grape breeder, Pauls Sukatnieks selected Veldze for its earliness from a planting of 3,000 seedlings. Berries are white, medium to large in size (average 2.9 g) and are partially seedless. The clusters are long and somewhat loose, ranging from 100 to 130 g. Veldze has the ability to develop acceptable sugar content for white winemaking even under extraordinarily cool summer and fall conditions. Sukatnieks recorded a sugar content of 18.4 °Brix in Veldze even in 1980, a year of record cool summer temperatures in Latvia, with a total heat accumulation of only 1367 Degree Days C (2460 Degree Days F). When well-ripened to 18 to 20 °Brix, Veldze has rich and pronounced flavors of ripe, tropical fruit (bananas, papayas), with no foxiness. The flowers are reported to be extremely frost resistant. Veldze suffers winter injury at temperatures around -4 °F (-20 °C), so it requires heavy winter protection in most northern areas. Developed by Sukatnieks from a cross of the *vinifera* variety, Madeline Angevine with the local Latvian variety, Dvietes Zila. It is the most *vinifera*-like of Sukatnieks' selections in both leaf and fruit. Perfect flowers.

Sukribe

This is Sukatnieks' most impressive-looking white grape, with medium to large golden berries packed into a long, medium-large cluster averaging about 130 g. In early September, 1998 sugar content was consistently around 18.5 °Brix wherever we sampled it in the Baltics. Winemaking from Sukribe is still highly experimental. To date, wines have been pretty neutral in flavor and nose, but with some hints of tropical fruit. The wines are not foxy. Sukribe has good potential for use as a blending base wine or as a crisp, neutral food wine. The Sukribe vine is productive. It is grown without winter protection in most of the Baltic region. Sukribe is hardy to around -22 °F (-30 °C). It was developed by Sukatnieks from a cross of the *vinifera* variety, Madeline Angevine with the local Latvian variety, Dvietes Zila. Perfect flowers.

Reform

Developed in Hungary, Reform has been quite reliable in setting and ripening fruit in the Copenhagen area, including the cold wet year of 1998. Typically, it is dead ripe in Hungary by mid-August and in the Rheinpfalz by late August. Clusters are medium in size and slightly loose, with small to medium berries. The flavor and aroma of fully ripe Reform grapes are that of ripe oranges. Reform rarely develops this aroma in very cool areas, such as Copenhagen, yet it still produces a fine white wine in these cooler regions. It is not foxy. Reform would be tender in Minnesota, with hardiness about like Seyval. From a cross of Perle Csaba x Aurore. Perfect flowers.

Bianca

This is one of the new varieties that has aroused great interest in Hungary during recent years. Bianca produces longish clusters, medium in size, with medium-sized berries that ripen to a yellow-green color. Ripening is quite early, suitable even for climates such as Denmark, where it typically develops a sugar content of around 18 °Brix with workable acidity. The sugar content is higher in areas such as Minnesota, with warmer summer and autumn conditions. Wines from Bianca in Minnesota have been notable for their excellent body and mouth feel, a seemingly rare trait in hybrid white wine varieties. It has been used with success in blends, adding body and substance to lighter white wines such as St. Pepin. It is very disease resistant. It breaks buds in mid-season. Bianca ripens its wood well but is still very tender in cold winter areas, where it needs to be protected. It was developed by Csizmazia and Bereznai in Hungary from a cross of Eger 2 x Bouvier. Eger 2 is a seedling of Seyve-Villard 12-375. Perfect flowers.

Seyval (Seyve-Villard 5-276)

For many years, Seyval was the leading white wine variety in Minnesota and Wisconsin. Due to its tenderness in winter and rather late ripening, it has lost popularity in recent years. However, Seyval is still a mainstay in the commercial wine industry in Quebec, where over half the acreage is planted with this variety and protected by soil over the winters. Seyval has large clusters and can be very productive. Cluster thinning to one cluster per shoot is mandatory to avoid overcropping and to advance ripening. The wine from Seyval is neutral, tart, and lacking in body when produced from grapes that are not fully ripe. That said, the wine is still quite good. In cooler climates such as Quebec, Seyval can produce outstanding sparkling wines. In climates with more heat, such as southern Wisconsin, Iowa, Illinois, and Missouri, Seyval ripens more fully, producing a fine white wine with good body, beautiful straw yellow color, and aroma that is remindful of Chardonnay. Seyval has a strong upright growth habit. Training systems must be selected that fit this habit of growth, particularly if the vines are to be protected over the winter. Seyval is French-American hybrid developed from a cross of Seibel 5656 x Seibel 4986. Perfect flowers.

Ravat blanc (Ravat 6)
When well-ripened, Ravat blanc is capable of producing a very fine white wine, with acidity, mouth feel, long finish and aromatics that are reminiscent of fine White Burgundy. It is perhaps the classiest of the French-American hybrids for white wine production. Ravat blanc produces long, compact medium-sized clusters that average 170 g (120-240 g) with berry size around 2.5 g. The fruit turns a deep golden color when fully ripe. The sugar content can range up to 24 °Brix under good conditions for ripening, but the acidity tends to remain somewhat high, often 1.3 to 1.4 g/l. Ravat blanc grows with moderate vigor and is only moderately productive. Growth is semi-upright and it is adaptable to the low training systems for protected vines. The vine is somewhat susceptible to Black Rot and Powdery Mildew. It is quite tender to winter cold and needs to be carefully protected in most northern regions. Ravat blanc was developed from a cross of Seibel 8724 x Chardonnay. Do not confuse this with Ravat 51, also called Vignoles. Perfect flowers.

Castel 19.637
This red wine variety with large clusters of smallish berries has performed well in several cool climate locations, including Nova Scotia, Denmark, and the Ottawa, Ontario area. Data from all three of these areas indicates that Castel has the ability to continue to ripen, to accumulate sugars and reduce acids, even in very cool autumn weather. Castel has the potential to ripen to very high sugar levels, up to 24 °Brix, uniformly surpassing Foch and Millot in direct cool-climate comparisons. It may not reach those levels of ripeness in cooler regions or very cool seasons, but it will ripen to a very workable sugar-acid balance for red winemaking. Acidity tends to be rather high, on average, slightly higher than Foch. This can be reduced by malolactic fermentation. Wine produced from Castel by conventional red wine techniques is intensely colored and tannic. The wine is complex and interesting. Varietal flavors will vary depending upon the degree of ripeness, ranging from "cedary" in less ripe fruit to "spicy" in fully mature fruit. Semi-carbonic maceration (10% crushed fruit; 90% whole clusters) also has been used successfully with Castel to bring out some blackberry-like fruitiness. Even in these wines, however, there tends to remain some spicy-herbaceous element. Its deep color and tannin content make Castel especially useful as a blending component with weaker red wines. It has outstanding disease resistance and high vigor. Vines of Castel are quite tender and require careful winter protection in cold winter areas. This old French-American hybrid grape came from a cross of *vinifera* variety Cincaut with *Vitis rupestris*. Perfect flowers.

Rondo (Geisenheim 6494-5)

This red wine grape, developed in the Rheingau region of Germany, has been one of the standouts on trial in Denmark. Rondo has medium-sized berries and clusters, about twice the size of the variety Leon Millot. The leaves and growth resemble *Vitis amurensis*. Growth is a bit trailing and fairly vigorous. Rondo ripens to workable winemaking parameters in the cool (750-850 DDC or 1350-1530 DDF) climate of Denmark, making 18 °Brix and acidity around 1.0 to 1.1% in an average year. Rondo seems to develop good varietal character for winemaking even when less than fully ripe. Danish growers describe the aroma as intense fruit, "raspberry," and very *vinifera*-like, with no hybrid overtones. A bit one-dimensional, the wine benefits from oak or blending to improve its complexity. Fermented conventionally, the wine has a deep ruby-red color with none of the bluish hues common in hybrids. The most successful Rondo wines in Denmark, however, have been fruity, lighter colored reds produced with carbonic maceration techniques. Rondo buds out early in the spring, with Millot. It sets fruit well even in the worst of seasons for cold and rain. It is reported to have a tendency to lose dormancy during periods of freezing and thawing, making it susceptible to winter injury during these periods. Considering this tendency, and its general lack of winter hardiness, Rondo should be carefully protected in cold winter areas. The variety is more mildew-resistant than *vinifera*, but moderately susceptible to Powdery Mildew. Rondo was selected from a cross of Saperavi Severnyi x St. Laurent. Saperavi Severnyi is Fruher Malingre x *Vitis amurensis*. St. Laurent is the premier red wine grape of the Rheinphalz. Perfect flowers.

Marechal Foch

Marechal Foch is the mainstay of the wine industry in Minnesota and Wisconsin. It is extremely versatile for winemaking. Award-winning winemaker, Philippe Coquard, working at Wollersheim Winery in Wisconsin, produces three very different wines from Foch, depending on ripeness. Coquard harvests Foch before full ripeness, at a sugar content of 19 °Brix, pH of 2.9, and total acidity of 1.5%, to produce an outstanding rose wine, with appealing cherry-like aroma and flavor. With slightly more ripe fruit, sugar content of 21 °Brix, pH of 3.1, and total acidity of 1.3%, he uses a semi-carbonic fermentation to produce a nouveau-style wine, with good acidity and fruitiness. Red table wines, suitable for aging, can be produced from fully ripe Foch grapes, with sugar content of 23 °Brix, pH of 3.3, and total acidity of 1.0%. These can be excellent, with deep color, good middle tannins, and rich ripe fruit aromas. The best of these have competed well against the best American *vinifera* wines. Foch produces medium-sized clusters of small-medium berries. A significant amount of heat is required to fully mature Foch fruit. Central Minnesota, for example, is on the fringes of this area, with full ripening possible only in best years. Foch tolerates mid-winter temperatures down to about -25.6 °F (-32 °C), or even a bit colder without injury. Some growers in Minnesota accept the risk of potential injury and leave it up on the trellis. Others protect their Foch vines in the winter. Foch is very resistant to Downy Mildew, but somewhat susceptible to Powdery Mildew. It was developed by Kuhlmann working at Colmar in

Alsace, from a cross of 101-14 Mgt x Goldriesling. The latter is Riesling x Courtiller musque. Perfect flowers.

Leon Millot

Leon Millot is an earlier ripening sister of Marechal Foch. Millot has produced some of the very best red wines in Minnesota. It also has been grown for wine quite widely in Denmark. Using semi-carbonic maceration, some excellent Millot wines have been produced in Denmark. However, Millot does not ripen fully there and the wines lack the body and depth that can be achieved with fully ripened Millot fruit. The fruit can achieve an excellent balance of sugar and acidity for wine production. Leon Millot is fairly tender and needs winter protection in areas where temperatures are much colder than -15 °F (-26 °C). Millot is from the same cross as Foch. Perfect flowers.

Marechal Joffre

Joffre is the earliest of the three Kuhlmann hybrids described here. It can ripen fairly well in a climate such as southern Quebec but does not ripen well in the cooler Baltic region. Joffre's cluster and berries are very similar to Millot, but slightly smaller. Sugar and acidity are very good for winemaking, with the acidity less a problem than in Foch. The wine from Joffre can be good, either as a rose′ or red wine. The color is deep red, and it has a cherry-like aroma similar to, but not as pronounced as Foch. Joffre grows as a trailing, vigorous vine, with excellent disease resistance. Long cane pruning is required in order to leave sufficient buds for balanced crop. Joffre is tender and requires winter protection in most northern areas. It is from the same cross as Foch and Millot. Perfect flowers.

Color Plate 2

Photo by Tom Plocher

D.M. 8521-1

Photo by Tom Plocher

Troubador

Photo by Tom Plocher

E.S. 10-18-30

Photo by Tom Plocher

Varajane Sinine

Photo by Tom Plocher

Hasansky Sladky

Photo by Tom Plocher

Zilga

Photo by Charles Knox

St. Croix

Photo by Tom Plocher

Sabrevois

Photo by Mark Hart

Frontenac

Photo by Tom Plocher

Skujins 675

Photo by Tom Plocher

Kay Gray

Photo by Charles Knox

St. Pepin

LaCrosse

LaCrescent

Swenson White

E.S. 5-3-89

Prairie Star

Louise Swenson

Jubileinaja Novgoroda

Veldze

Sukribe

Reform

Bianca

Seyval

Ravat Blanc (Ravat 6)

Castel 19.637

Rondo

Marechal Foch

Leon Millot

Marechal Joffre

Appendix 2

Resources

Sources of Vines and Cuttings

Lake Sylvia Nurseries
13835 51ˢᵗ Ave
South Haven, MN 55382
USA
(Hardy Minnesota selections, including Troubador)

Windwater Vineyard & Nursery
13100 Halstad Ave.
Lonsdale, MN 55046
USA
Tel. 507-744-2467
gmogren@means.net
www.windwatervineyard.com
(Hardy Minnesota varieties, including Prairie Star and Louise Swenson)

Northwind Nursery & Orchards
7910 335ᵗʰ Ave NW
Princeton, MN 55371-4915
USA
Tel. 612-389-4920
(Hardy Minnesota varieties)

Edible Forest Nursery
Kevin Bradley
Edforest55@hotmail.com
(Hardy Minnesota varieties)

Great River Vineyard
35680 Highway 61 Blvd.
Lake City, MN 55041
USA
Tel. 651-345-3531
grapes@rconnect.com
www.greatrivervineyard.com
(Frontenac, St. Pepin, other Minnesota varieties)

St. Lawrence Nurseries
325 State Highway 345
Potsdam, NY 13676
USA
Tel. 315-265-6739
(Hardy Swenson varieties)

Ed Daugherty
St. Francois Vineyard
1669 Pine Rdige Trail
Park Hills, MO 63601
USA
Tel. 573-431-4294
winevine@il.net
www.stfrancoisvineyard.com
(Vines of hardy Swenson selections)

Lon J. Rombough Enterprises
P.O. Box 365
Aurora, OR 97002
USA
Tel. 503-678-1410
www.hevanet.com/lonrom
(Hybrids, some Swenson selections;
Cuttings in quantity; also plant finding services)

Grafted Grapevine Nurseries
Herman Amberg
2399 Wheat Rd.
Clifton Springs, NY 14432
USA
Tel. 315-462-3288 or 716-526-6742
(*Vinifera*, French-American Hybrids; Custom grafting services)

Foster Concord Nurseries
10175 Mileblock Road
North Collins, NY 14111
USA
Tel. 716-337-2485 or 800-223-2211
(American and French-American Hybrid wine grapes in all quantities)

USDA Clonal Germplasm Repository-Geneva
Plant Genetic Resources Unit
Cornell University
Geneva, NY 14456-0462
USA
www.ars-grin.gov/ars/NoAtlantic/Geneva/
(Cold hardy grape collection-1800 accessions; cuttings on special request for research purposes)

Alain Breault
313 Begin Street
Brigham, Quebec J2K 4Y5
CANADA
Tel. 450 263-7127
Coquine@enDirect.qc.ca
(Swenson selections in Canada; Vandal-Cliché)

Bert Dunn
RR 4
Tottenheim, Ontario
CANADA LOG 1W0
Helbert@idirect.com
www.hardygrapes.tottenheim.on.ca
(cuttings of hardy Minnesota and Quebec varieties)

Swedish University of Agricultural Sciences
Balsgard Experiment Station
Kimmo Rumpunen
Department of Horticultural Plant Breeding
S-291 94 KRISTIANSTAD
SWEDEN
Tel. 46 44 755 33
Fax. 46 44 755 30
(Baltic grape varieties from heat-treated material)

Latvian Growers Club
Dr, Andris Dishlers
Madonas iela 27 dz. 104
RIGA LV-1035
LATVIA
Tel. 371 2 588 340
dishlers@biomed.lu.lv
(Baltic grape varieties)

Ole Bonsdorff Nursery
Ejbyvej 98
DK-4632 Bjaverskov
DENMARK
Tel. (45) 5682 1094
(Reform, Rondo, Castel, Don Muscat, and other early ripening varieties)

Regional Sources of Information:
Associations and Organizations

Minnesota Grape Growers Association
35680 Hwy 61 Blvd.
Lake City, MN 55041
USA
www.mngrapes.com
(Publish annual report and *Notes from the North* quarterly; sponsor annual symposium and other events)

Purple Foot Wine Club
Nancy Wood
2820 Wind Cave Ct.
Burnsville, MN 55337
USA
(Publish monthly newsletter and tasting events)

University of Minnesota
Horticulture Research Center
Mr. Peter Hemstad/Dr. Jim Luby
600 Arboretum Rd.
Excelsior, MN 55331
USA

Nebraska Winery &Grapegrowers Association
C.J. Schweitzer, Secretary-Treasurer
Emerald Hills Garden
P.O. Box 39B
Valparaiso, NE 68065
USA
(Quarterly newsletter)

University of Nebraska-Lincoln
Dr. Paul Read, Viticulturlist
P.O. Box 830724
Lincoln, NE 68583-0724
USA
pread@unlnotes.unl.edu

Southwest Missouri State University
Department of Fruit Science
State Fruit Experiment Station
Dr. Murli Dharmadhikari, Enology
Dr. Sanliang Gu, Viticulture
Mountain Grove, MO 65711
USA
(Sponsor Annual Midwestern Grape and Wine Conference; publish bimonthly *Vineyard and Vintage View*)

Horticulture Research Institute of Ontario
Dr. K. Helen Fisher
P.O. Box 7000
Vineland Station, Ontario
CANADA LOR 2EO
Hfisher@uoguelph.ca
Tel. 905 562-4141 ext. 142
Fax. 905 562-3413

Club de Recherche et de Developpement en Viticulture
Robert Le Royer
182 Route 221
Napierville, Quebec JOJ 1L0
CANADA
Tel. 450 245-0208
Fax. 450 245-0388
leroyer-st-pierre@sympatico.ca

Association Des Viticulteurs de l 'est Ontarien
Carole Lavigne/Raymond Huneault
1818 St-Felix
Bourget KOA 1EO
Ontario
CANADA
Tel. 819 827-2103
Raymond.Huneault@videotron.ca

GROWWINE
www.littlefatwino.com
(Central Ontario-based clearing house for information of interest to cold
climate winegrowers)

Central Ontario Grapegrowers Association
Dr. Bryan Pell, President
Peregrine North Vineyards
Contact via www.littlefatwino.com/coga.html

Agriculture Canada
Dr. Andrew Jamieson
Atlantic Food & Horticulture Research Center
32 Main St.
Kentville B4N1J5
Nova Scotia
CANADA
Tel. 902-679-5705

Cool Climate Enology and Viticulture Institute
Brock University
500 Glendridge Ave.
St. Catharines,
Ontario L2S 3A1
CANADA
www.brocku.ca/ccovi/

University of Wyoming
Research and Extension Center
Dr. Roger Hybner
663 Wyarno Rd.
Sheridan, WY 82801-9619
Roger-Hybner@agmail.uwyo.edu

Foreningen af Danske Vinavlere (Association of Danish Grape Growers)
Mr. Peter Lorenzen, President
Slettensvej 210
DK-5270 Odense N
DENMARK
Tel. 45 66 18 67 28
peterlorenzen@mail.tele.dk
www.vinavl.dk
(Publish annual report and quarterly *Vinpressen*)

Latvijas Vinogu Audzeta Klubs (Latvian Grape Growers Club)
Dr, Andris Dishlers, Director of International Relations
Madonas iela 27 dz. 104
RIGA LV-1035
LATVIA
Tel. 371 2 588 340
dishlers@biomed.lu.lv

Swedish University of Agricultural Sciences
Balsgard Experiment Station
Kimmo Rumpunen, Grape Curator
Department of Horticultural Plant Breeding
S-291 94 Kristianstad
SWEDEN
Tel. 46 44 755 33
Fax. 46 44 755 30

University of Helsinki
Meeri Saario
Faculty of Agriculture and Forestry
Dept. of Plant Production
LATOKART.KB
PL 27
Helsinki 00014
FINLAND
Meeri.saario@helsinki.fi
Tel. 358 9 191 58333

Dobele Horticultural Plant Breeding Experiment Station
Dr. Silvia Ruisa, Grape Curator
Graudu 1
Dobele LV-3701
LATVIA
Tel. 371 372294
ruisa@ddsis.lu.lv

Rapina Agricultural College
Jaan Kivistik, Grape Curator
Rapina,
ESTONIA
Tel. 372 279 61608
Jaan@aed.rapina.ee
http://www.rapina.ee/aed/

Botanical Garden
Vilnius University
Darius Ryliskis, Curator
Kairenu 43
LT-2040 Vilnius
LITHUANIA
Tel. 370 2 317944
Fax. 370 2 317 429
Darius.ryliskis@gf.vu.ltwww.gf.vu.lt/depts/garden/botgarden.htm

German Federal Research Institute for Grape Breeding
76833 Siebeldingen,
GERMANY
www.dainet.de/genres/idb/vitis/vitis.htm
(Maintains the International *Vitis* Database)

Belarusian Research Institute for Fruit Growing
Dr, Romuald Loiko, Grape Curator
2 Kovaleva St.
Samokhvalovitchy
Minsk Region 223013
BELARUS

Agrocompany Named by Lenin
(Agrofirma im. V.I. Lenina)
Breznoje, Stolinskij District
Brest Region, 225532
BELARUS

Winemaking Supplies

Presque Isle Wine Cellars
9440 W Main Rd
North East PA 16428
USA
Tel. 800 488-7492
info@piwine.com
(Best supply and equipment source for home and small commercial wineries in the U.S.; Peter Brehm frozen juice; catalog contains lots of useful technical information)

Scott Laboratories
2220 Pine View Way
PO Box 4559
Petaluma CA 94955-4559
USA
Tel. 707 765-6666
www.scottlab.com
(Hard-to-find yeasts and enzymes; informative catalog)

Scott Laboratories
1845 Sandstone Manor, Unit 14
Pickering Ontario LIW3X9
Canada
Tel. 905 839-9463
www.scottlab.com
(Hard-to-find yeasts and enzymes)

Vinquiry
7795 Bell Road
Windsor CA 95492
USA
Tel. 707 838-6312
info@vinquiry.com
(Hard to find yeasts and lab equipment)

Joseph Palla Cellars
30586 Moonlight Bay
Lindstrom, MN 55045
USA
Tel. 651 459-8313
(Broker for Peter Brehm frozen premium grape juice in Minnesota-Wisconsin area)

Row Covers and Frost Protection

Peaceful Valley Farm Supply
P.O. Box 2209
Grass Valley, CA 95945
USA
Tel. 888 784-1722
(Agribon, Tuffbell, SRM Red self-reflective mulch, Frost Shield)
www.groworganic.com

Harmony Farm Supply
PO Box 460
Graton, CA 95444
USA
Tel. 707 823-9125
(Tuffbell)

Polymer Ag Inc.
P.O. Box 9665
Fresno, CA 93793
Tel. 559 495-0234
(Anti-Stress 2000)

Texel
485, Des Erables
St-Elzear, Beauce Nord
Quebec Canada GOS 2JO
Tel. 418 387-5910
Fax. 418 387-4326
www.texel.qc.ca
(Arbotex and other geotextiles)

General and Introductory Books on Grapegrowing

Cox, J. From Vines to Wines: The Complete Guide to Growing Grapes and Making Your Own Wine. Storey Books, 3rd editio*n, 256 pages, 1999.*

Growing Grapes in Minnesota. Produced and sold by the Minnesota Grape Growers Association, 1993. (see address under organizations above*)*

Phillip Wagner. A Winegrower's Guide. Wine Appreciation Guild, 240 pages, 1998 (this is the original 1965 version recently reprinted in paper-bac*k).*

Weaver, R.J. Grape Growing. John Wiley and Sons, 384 pages, 1976.

Winkler, A.J., Lider, L.A., *and Kliewer, W.M.*   General Viticulture. University of California Press, 2nd edition, 710 pages, 1975.

Grapevine Disease Information

There are many university websites that present excellent information on recognizing, preventing, and controlling grapevine diseases. Two that we especially like for the Midwestern and Northeastern United States are:

Kovachs, Laszlo. *Diseases of Grapevines in Missouri.*
http://mtngrv.smsu.edu/GrapeDiseases.htm
(Kovachs' web site also contains many links to other web sites on grapevine diseases)

Weigle, T. and Kovachs, J. *Grape IPM in the Northeastern United States.*
http://www.nysaes.cornell.edu/ipmnet/ny/fruits/grapes/grmanfs/index.html